CHANGE AND CONTINUITY IN EASTERN EUROPE

Change and Continuity in Eastern Europe

Edited by

Timo Piirainen

The University of Helsinki

Dartmouth

Aldershot • Brookfield USA • Singapore • Sydney

Published by
Dartmouth Publishing Company Limited
Gower House
Croft Road
Aldershot
Hants GU11 3HR
England

Dartmouth Publishing Company
Old Post Road
Brookfield
Vermont 05036
USA

British Library Cataloguing in Publication Data
Change and Continuity in Eastern Europe
  I. Piirainen, Timo
  947.086

Library of Congress Cataloging-in-Publication Data
Change and continuity in Eastern Europe / edited by Timo Piirainen.
    p.   cm.
  Includes bibliographical references.
  ISBN 1-85521-499-7 : $57.95 (U.S. : est.)
  1. Europe, Eastern–Economic policy–1989- 2. Europe Eastern-
-Economic conditions–1989- 3. Europe, Eastern–Social conditions.
4. Mixed economy–Europe, Eastern. 5. Post-communism–Europe,
Eastern. I. Piirainen, Timo.
  HC244.C435   1994
  338.947–dc20   94-11911
                                                         CIP

ISBN 1 85521 499 7

Contents

List of Tables and Figures

Tables

Figures

Contributors

Elina Haavio-Mannila is Professor of Sociology and Head of the Department of Sociology at the University of Helsinki, Finland.

Jyrki Iivonen is an executive research analyst at the Finnish Institute of International Affairs, Helsinki, Finland.

Kaisa Kauppinen is a senior scientist at the Institute of Occupational Health in Helsinki, Finland.

Markku Kivinen is a senior researcher at the Finnish Academy of Sciences, Helsinki, Finland.

Jyrki Käkönen is Head of Tampere Peace Research Institute, Tampere, Finland.

Timo Piirainen is a senior researcher at the Department of Social Policy at the University of Helsinki, Finland.

Jussi Simpura is a senior researcher at the Social Research Institute for Alcohol Studies, Helsinki, Finland.

Pekka Sutela is a senior research analyst at the Unit of Eastern Economies at the Bank of Finland, Helsinki.

Igor Travin is Head of the Department of Urban Research at the St. Petersburg Institute of Sociology, Russian Academy of Sciences.

Timo Vihavainen is Docent of Russian and East European Studies at Renvall Institute at the University of Helsinki, Finland.

1 Introduction

Timo Piirainen

During the last four years Europe has experienced events that are among the most important in its entire history. The political map of Europe looks today completely different from what it was in the year 1989. The Soviet empire has dispersed and a great number of nation states have emerged in its place. The multinational states Yugoslavia and Czechoslovakia have also drifted to smaller pieces. Germany has been reunited as the bipolar ideological and political antagonism has come to an end in Europe.

The twentieth century has witnessed three major ruptures during which the political reality has rapidly and radically been transformed. Changes comparable to these experienced during the past four years took place earlier during the years 1914-18, when the Habsburg empire, imperial Russia and Germany collapsed, and again during the years 1939-45, when first Hitler and Stalin and later the Allied powers re-arranged the national borders in Europe. During the first of these two periods the rearrangement of the political map of Europe happened as a consequence of a world war, whereas during the years 1989-93 the environment changed without a catastrophe on a global scale. The old power seems just to have melted away, leaving behind a vacuum — and the violence, as in Yugoslavia, Georgia and Moldova, has burst out only after this great change, as the local powers compete to fill the political vacuum.

Europe now faces an entirely different geopolitical and economic reality. The division of Europe and the antagonism between two competing political orders and military blocs have ended, and the member nations of the dissolved eastern system are now striving to integrate more closely into the structures of the west. In this new environment the new Eastern European societies are searching for new identities and new coordinates.

The old and the new reality

The stability in the world during the Cold War relied on the presence of two antagonistic military blocs. In making decisions nation states always had to take into account the security interests of the two blocs and of the two opposed global superpowers, and this was especially true for small Eastern European nations. Military threat was an inherent extension of politics, as von Clausewitz put it. In that Clausewitzian world military aggression between nation states was considered a rational and expedient means of achieving the goals that might not have been attained by solely diplomatic means.

The disappearance of the split between the east and the west has, however, created a qualitatively entirely new environment in Europe. Military threats no longer function adequately as an extension of politics; the exercise of organized violence in the relations between modern and highly industrialized nations can no longer be regarded as rational. After the collapse of Soviet socialism and the disappearance of the division between the east and the west the formation of a new system of relations is taking place in Europe. In the most fortunate case, this new environment could be characterized as a 'post-Clausewitzian' reality.

At first glance, this notion seems to be overly optimistic: aggression has not disappeared from Europe with the end of the Cold War, but, on the contrary, we have witnessed violence and bloodshed that would have been quite unimaginable during the *pax sovietica* of the past decades. What are then the grounds on which we may talk about the Clausewitzian reality as being past history in Europe?

In a feudal, or agrarian, society the principal means of production was arable land. In order to gain wealth and hegemony, as large as possible fertile territory was needed, and kings and emperors thus strived to conquer each other's land. In the capitalist society, or in the industrial society of the old type, the ruling means of production was mass industry. Hegemony in relation to neighbouring nations was attained by possessing the resources needed for industrial production — natural resources and labour force — as well as markets for the products. It was possible for a nation state to take these resources and market areas into its possession by military force.

Global hegemony today, however, is not based on flourishing agriculture or on the ability to produce as much cement and iron rail as possible. The most advanced industrial, or post-industrial, nations are creating prosperity by producing something far more intangible. While economic growth in the old industrial society was based on the expansion of the volume of the production, growth in a post-industrial society is not, in the first place, quantitative, but is based rather on the fact that the products are better, more intelligent and technically more advanced than before. The ability to create innovation and intelligence is the basis of economic growth and hegemony. The most advanced industrial countries have shifted from extensive economic growth to intensive growth.

If the source of hegemony is the possession of as many fields and vineyards as possible, it is rational to try to annex more fields and vineyards from neighbours. If the basis of hegemony is a mighty merchant fleet, it is rational to try to sink the fleet of competitors. If the basis of the hegemony is a voluminous industrial production, it is rational for a nation to try to acquire as much labour force and raw materials as possible — and if no other means are available, then by taking these resources from neighbouring nations by force.

But if the basis of the hegemony is the capacity to produce innovation and intelligence, the situation is different. Japan is a country without a large military force, and natural resources in its territory are scarce; but nevertheless it undoubtedly is one of the most important powers in the world today. The reason for Japan's hegemony is its ability to load its products with intelligence — and this hegemony is neither acquired by military power nor can it be captured by a competitor using military force.

Intelligence and innovation are things that are difficult to create by coercion. It is the ever-increasing significance of intelligence and innovation for production that most crucially contributes to the coming of the post-Clausewitzian world. The tiny silicon chip on which the microprocessors are engraved caused the collapse of the Soviet socialism, as the popular remark expresses it. The Soviet socialist economies could not achieve similar progress in the field of computer and information technology as the advanced capitalist countries. The system based on coercion was able to increase the volume of production, it could generate extensive growth, often by unscrupulously exploiting the natural environment, but it nevertheless continued to lag farther and farther behind in the competition with the industrialized countries of the west.

Even though the threat of the outbreak of a large-scale military conflict between two opposed treaty organizations in Europe has disappeared, this does not, however, necessarily mean that Europe has automatically become a far safer continent than it used to be in the Cold War era. As the old threats have vanished, new ones have emerged instead. Table 1.1 illustrates in ideal-typical manner the options and threats related to the change in the environment.

Table 1.1. The Clausewitzian and the post-Clausewitzian world.

	CLAUSEWITZIAN WORLD	POST-CLAUSEWITZIAN WORLD
Basis of prosperity and hegemony	Mass production, military power	Intelligent production
Basic unit	Territorial domain, nation state	Region, network, supranational agency
Nature of conflicts	Between nation states, global	Local
Risks	War, world war	Terrorism, environmental catastrophes
Complexity of the system	Relatively small	Great
State of the system	Often relatively stable	Dynamic, chaotic
Degree of predictability	Relatively high	Low

It was suggested above that while in the old environment mass production and military power were the basis of prosperity and hegemony, in the new environment intelligent production striving toward intensive growth is the determining factor. A large military force has become a handicap in the new environment and the countries freest to pursue this new technological superiority are those without this handicap, most notably Japan and Germany (cf. Kennedy, 1988).

In the post-Clausewitzian environment nation states can no longer be regarded as the most principal actors or basic units. Territorial boundaries are losing their importance; increasingly often either individual regions, often crossing the boundaries of nation states, or supranational agencies and networks, such as the European Union or multinational corporations, are the main frameworks of decision making. The movement of labour and capital obey national borders to an ever decreasing extent. Decision-making power is either shifted upwards, from the nation state to the supranational level, or decentralized from the national central administration to the regional level.

Due to the decreased significance of the nation state the violent confrontations in the post-Clausewitzian environment usually have the nature of local conflicts, e.g. terrorism and ethnic clashes, instead of large-scale conflicts or wars between nations. Whereas the risks connected to armed conflicts in the old environment were global, i.e. the ultimate threat was that of a massive nuclear confrontation, in the new environment the risks are more local. Environmental crises are also a major threat; these risks do not conform to the territorial boundaries of the nation states, either.

Compared to the new environment the old Clausewitzian reality was a relatively stable and transparent one, and orientation in it was easier than in the post-Clausewitzian reality. The state of the old system was more stationary and making predictions was easier. The new environment seems more ambiguous, incalculable and difficult to explain.

Change and continuity

The ideal-typical scheme presented above of the transition from a Clausewitzian to a post-Clausewitzian world is based on the idea of modernization. It is assumed that the changing logic of production in the industrialized world produces changes also in the social structure, political system and mentality of the people — i.e. a new rationality of post-industrial, 'thoroughly modern' societies is emerging which, in its turn, contributes to the formation of a new system of international relations. As is the case with so many other conceptualizations created in sociology to describe social change, the simple pair of concepts developed above contains also a utopian element. Appearing to be a true disciple of the enlightenment, its author presupposes that the changing logic of production will bring about a more civilized social reality. If the world is transformed to a single complex network, a kind of supranational 'organic solidarity', the nodes of this network cannot use such crude methods as military aggression in settling their disputes.

This book deals with the transformation of Eastern Europe, particularly of Russia, the principal heir of the Soviet empire. Presenting the conceptual scheme of the transition from a Clausewitzian to a post-Clausewitzian Europe in this context suggests that the Soviet Union and its socialist allies in Eastern and Central Europe were in many essential respects not modern societies and it was the increasing pressure towards modernization, from inside these societies as well as from abroad, that most crucially contributed to the collapse of Soviet socialism. Many characteristic features of Soviet society — the command economy, the centralized, authoritarian rule and the cult of personality connected to it, the disproportionately large share of the military in the national product, the virtually non-existent political mobilization outside the official state apparatus or the lacking public spirit among the people subject to paternalistic rule — can by no means be considered as much 'socialist' as traditionally Russian (cf. e.g. Pipes, 1974; Srubar, 1991; Parland, 1993). In the light of statistics describing the level of industrialization, urbanization, the distribution of public services or literacy and education, the Soviet socialist societies seemed to be approximately as modern as Britain, Belgium or Sweden; but when the internal logic of these societies is examined the picture becomes entirely different. The notion of Marx about the fateful contradiction embedded in the very foundations of the capitalist society seemed to be especially true in the case of Soviet socialism.

If we accept as the point of departure this meta-explanation pointing out the pressures toward modernization as the prime mover of the transition in Eastern Europe, may we then simply assume that what is to be expected in Europe is a more or less straightforward development toward a post-Clausewitzian world of decreasing aggression between nations? Not necessarily, as the example of Yugoslavia shows us.

If we for a moment continue to think about the course of European history in terms of modernization, we can interpret the greatest tragedies of modern history, most notably the rise of National Socialism in Germany, as anachronistic lapses from the trajectory of modernization. To use a metaphor from psychology, the catastrophes were caused by regression, i.e. by temporary relapses to earlier stages of development, usually during crises of some kind. According to this 'pro-enlightenment' view, the question in the Germany of the 1930's was not about some kind of metaphysical 'dialectic of enlightenment' turning inevitably reason to its antithesis (see Adorno & Horkheimer, 1969; cf. Bauman, 1989), but about the temporary abandonment of the patterns of social activity and orientation characteristic to the modern world and re-adoption of earlier, more archaic objects of self-identification, such as race, religion, ethnicity or the nation.

We are currently witnessing this kind of regressive lapse in Yugoslavia. When Moses descended from the mountain he saw to his grief and disappointment that his dismayed people had in the wilderness resorted to worshipping a golden image; it is upsetting for us to see today that in the turmoil in Yugoslavia people are abandoning the organic solidarity of a modern society for the more archaic patterns of identification, for religion and for ethnicity, with tragic consequences.

Anachronisms are characteristic to Eastern Europe in transition from Soviet socialism towards a market economy. The first impression of these societies is that of flux and rapid change, 'of all that is solid melting into air', but along with the change and transformation there exist also persistent continuities, traditional patterns of social activity and orientation. If the future of the East European societies is formed by an interplay of change and continuity, of traditional and modern elements, we are, first of all, anxious to know whether this anachronistic co-existence of old and new may produce more of destructive outcomes than we have already witnessed. Are such devastating lapses from the trajectory of modernization as in Yugoslavia still likely in future? Of the most crucial importance is, of course, the development of Russia, a military power with the largest arsenal of nuclear weapons in the world.

About the book and its authors

This book has certain futurologist aspirations — in the weak sense of
the word. The authors accept the fact that forecasts and predictions
cannot be made about the future of societies inhabited by human beings
with free will. Especially many degrees of freedom prevail, furthermore, in the Eastern Europe of today. The futurologist ambitions have
therefore been limited to the creation of such *Gestalten* or possible
worlds which might have a heuristical function and which might help
us to better see the inherent opportunities and threats in the present
situation. In spite of this emphasis on the future, many of the articles
in this book appear, however, to concentrate on the study of the past
history of Soviet society. This approach can be regarded as justified, as
the future of Eastern Europe is built on the legacy of Soviet socialism
and understanding the current transition requires the analysis of that
society.

The authors of this book are among the most prominent Finnish and
Russian social scientists, and most of them have a long research experience with questions related to Eastern European societies. In Chapter
2, Jyrki Käkönen analyzes the changes in the international relations in
Europe; the transformation processes that are taking place in Northeas-
tern Europe are examined as an exemplary case of the overall transformation of the international environment. In the following chapter, Jyrki
Iivonen examines the reasons for the disintegration of the Soviet Union
and the political legacy passed on from the Soviet Union to its successors, particularly to Russia. What are the alternatives of political development that may emerge on the basis of this heritage?

In Chapter 4, Pekka Sutela presents a discussion of the problems
related to the economic transition in Eastern Europe and of the prospects of Russia on its way from a command economy towards market
relations. Timo Vihavainen examines in Chapter 5 the moral and ideological dimension of the upheaval in Russia and offers some sugges-
tions as to the new ideologies that are filling the vacuum left by the
sudden disintegration of the Soviet state.

In the Germany of the 1930's the impoverished middle class voted
Adolf Hitler and his National Socialist Party to power. A continuous
decline of living conditions could persuade the Russians, too, to

demand a strong authority in the place of experiments with democracy that do not seem to improve the lot of the ordinary citizens. Timo Piirainen examines in Chapter 6 the development of living conditions and social inequalities in present-day Russia. In Chapter 7, Markku Kivinen presents a careful analysis of the class structure in the Soviet society, anticipating simultaneously future tendencies of social differentation.

The transition to market economy requires, sooner or later, the adoption of a social policy similar to the policy models employed in the industrial countries of the west. Jussi Simpura examines in Chapter 8 social problems in Russia and the Baltic countries and the social policy measures that could be designed to alleviate these emerging problems. The picture of daily life and social problems in conditions of economic upheaval and transformation, as presented in some of these earlier chapters, is supplemented in Chapter 9 by Elina Haavio-Mannila and Kaisa Kauppinen in their elaborate study of the status of women and the relation of genders in Russia and Estonia. In Chapter 10, Igor Travin presents the view of an urban researcher on the transition, describing the changes in St. Petersburg. In the final Chapter 11 the views and conclusions of the authors are knit together and scenarios of a very general nature are presented concerning the future of Eastern Europe.

References

Adorno, Theodor & Horkheimer, Max (1969), *Dialektik der Aufklärung*, S. Fischer Verlag, Frankfurt am Main (first published in 1944).

Bauman, Zygmunt (1989), *Modernity and the Holocaust*, Polity Press, Cambridge.

Kennedy, Paul (1988), *The Rise and Fall of Great Powers. Economic Change and Military Conflict from 1500 to 2000*, Unwin Hyman, London.

Parland, Thomas (1993), *The Rejection in Russia of Totalitarian Socialism and Liberal Democracy. A Study of the Russian New Right*, Societas Scientiarum Fennica, Helsinki.

Pipes, Richard (1974), *Russia under the Old Regime*, Penguin Books, Harmondsworth.

Srubar, Ilja (1991), 'War der reale Sozialismus modern? Versuch einer strukturellen Bestimmung', *Kölner Zeitschrift für Soziologie und Sozialpsychologie*, vol. 43, no. 3/1991.

2 Russia, the Baltic States and the Nordic Countries: International Relations in Transition

Jyrki Käkönen

Introduction

With the collapse of socialist regimes and the end of the Cold War, new options have started to present themselves to the countries of Northern Europe in terms of foreign policy orientations and regional connections. These options, however, are determined in the context of wider international structures. In contrast to the expectations of the CSCE in Berlin and Paris (UM, 1991 and UM, 1992), the end of the Cold War did not create a united Europe or uniform economic and political structures. It also seems that the Hegelian idea of the end of history, as presented by Fukuyama, remains a rather distant scenario (Fukuyama, 1992, pp. 173-183, pp. 341-350, pp. 400-413).

Instead of split into two, Europe today is in fact divided into three parts. The Iron Curtain has now been replaced by a poverty gap. During the Cold War the difference between the socialist countries of the East and the capitalist countries of the West in terms of wealth and affluence remained more or less unchanged. In this sense it may be argued that socialism succeeded as a social and economic system

(Arrighi, 1991). It was only with the changes in the economic and political structures in Eastern Europe that the gap in social wealth began to grow.

In many former socialist countries the recent reforms of economic and political structures have served to intensify internal contradictions. The most dramatic case of course is Yugoslavia, where the decentralization of power to the local level caused the unified territorial state to disintegrate. Economic recovery has been slowed down by the struggle for power to fill in the vacuum created by the collapse of socialism. This obviously means that the poverty gap will be there for quite some while.

However, this poverty gap or 'Hunger Curtain' does not neatly divide Europe into two: between the poor Slavic Orthodox countries of Eastern Europe and the expanding European community, there is a grey zone consisting of Slovenia, Croatia, Hungary, the Czech Republic, Slovakia, Poland and the Baltic states. In this intermediate zone, economic and political recovery will be faster than in the Slavic Orthodox zone: these countries will move faster to establish contacts with the EC and in this way create a secure buffer zone between the EC and the heirs of the Soviet Union. This is a strategy of NATO's, whose idea it is to integrate the former socialist Catholic Europe into Western Europe via NATO (Helsingin Sanomat, 15 September 1993).

Western European integration, which is unlikely to lead to the new European superstate envisaged in the Maastricht Treaty, is a completely different framework. Any remaining hopes and expectations of a real superstate were effectively thwarted at the EC Summit in Edinburgh on December 4-6, 1992. At the same time as the process of integration is moving ahead, there is also continuing disintegration. The regional policy adopted by the EC (McDonnell and Ganier-Raymond, 1990; Meyers, 1990) provides the basis for the development of regions both within states and across state borders. As far as citizen decision making is concerned, these regions will assume increasing importance over and above states (Kirkinen, 1991; Mennola, 1992), which are bound to lose some of their power to EC agencies. Several regions have been outlined in Europe, most notably Mediterranean Europe mainly around France, Central Europe mainly around Germany, and Baltic Europe under strong German influence. In addition, scholars have referred to the North Sea region, the Barents region, and the Arctic region (Linzie and

Boman 1991, pp. 223-226). The Barents Region Council for Cooperation was established in January 1993 by Norway, Sweden, Finland and Russia. The EC is a founding member in the Council.

Discussions of new regional communities have also emphasized ethnic, national and linguistic features. In August 1992 political geographers from the United States estimated that during the next 20 years Europe will see the founding of a dozen new states, including Scotland, Basque, Catalonia, Sami and Brittany. Furthermore, Italy and Belgium would both split into two parts (Los Angeles Times, 25 August 1992). In fact, Belgium has already been divided into two under an umbrella of a federation. This kind of development not only opens up new opportunities for international relations, but also forces these relations in a new direction.

Russia

Up until the Second World War the Soviet Union was very much a European superpower — even though the heir of Czarist Russia had a territory extending all the way to the Pacific Ocean, and even though the Comintern provided the Soviet Union with at least some influence over the Communist parties that had grown up around the European colonies. It was only through its military role in World War II that the country grew into a military superpower. Then, during the Cold War, the Soviet Union emerged as the chief adversary of the United States in the field of international politics. The emergence of the Soviet Union as a global power occurred even later, i.e. with the introduction of Soviet intercontinental ballistic missiles (ICBMs) and the founding of its global navy. When the Cold War ended and the Soviet Union disintegrated, the major part of the Soviet military apparatus, and especially its global reach, was left in Russian hands. However, owing to economic and political factors, Russia is no longer considered a global power. Rather, Russia has returned to its traditional role as a European power (Thee, 1992, pp. 18-20).

In fact there are good reasons to question the status of Russia even as a European superpower. The role of Russia can be evaluated in different ways depending on the time perspective adopted and on how the internal development in Russia is assessed. The situation today is that Russia is in need of foreign (Western) aid; at the same time, Russia is a country with enormous natural resources and huge reserves of cheap labour to attract Western capital. The EC is interested in Russia's oil and gas resources, which could help to strengthen the Community in relation to Japan and the US. Recently a number of Western companies have been showing increasing interest in Russian forest resources. Agreement on the wide-scale utilization of these resources will constitute a serious threat to the Scandinavian forest industry and most particularly to the entire Finnish economy, which remains heavily dependent on this one single sector. The price of standing timber in Russia is lower than in Scandinavia, and production costs in joint ventures in Russia will also be lower. This means that in the near future, 'traditional' Scandinavian products may be losing a large part of their share of the West European markets for timber, pulp and paper products.

If the unification of Germany is anything to go by, it seems reasonably safe to assume that Russia will remain outside the process of European integration. The German Democratic Republic was a relatively small economic power compared with the Federal Republic of Germany — at least if the relationship between the two countries is compared to that between the European Community and the successors of the Soviet Union, or even Russia alone. The German economy has run into a number of unexpected problems since unification. Western Europe will hardly be willing to accept a similar, or even heavier burden that would follow with integration. On this basis it is very unlikely that Russia will be admitted as a member of the European Community. On the other hand, Russian membership would also undermine the benefits from economic inequality to Western capital.

Poverty-stricken Eastern Europe has brought the development problem to Europe, complete with its North-South dilemma and all its advantages and drawbacks. This is clearly seen in the way that West European countries are allocating funds of development aid to former socialist countries.

On the basis of the German example it is also a fairly safe assumption that it will take Russia perhaps 15-20 years to resolve all its economic problems. After World War II, the Federal Republic of Germany recovered within about ten years. However, Germany had the benefit of Marshall aid, and with its entire infrastructure in ruins it had to rebuild its production machinery from scratch, which meant that it could take full advantage of new technology. It also had an extensive experience of both market economy and democracy to fall back on. None of these conditions apply to Russia, which furthermore needs much more Western aid. Besides, the old market economy countries are currently struggling with their own economic problems, and apart from having to help Russia they must also try to support the other former socialist countries. In short, it seems clear that the economic recovery of Russia will take a very long time, at least if the country is determined to follow the course advocated by Yeltsin's regime.

There are several reasons why Russia will remain plagued by numerous instability factors for a very long time. The chief factor is the continuing struggle for power over the state apparatus among different political groups in the country. If we look at the situation from an 'old-Russian' or nationalist point of view, Russia appears to be a defeated state in which true Russianism has been betrayed. Together with economic insecurity, this may help to bring the so-called conservative or anti-reformist forces to power. At the same time, we would see a profound change in Russian foreign policy: at the very least Russia would try to isolate itself from Europe, but it might also try to restore the borders of the Czarist Russian Empire.[1]

Russia's problems are very much exacerbated by the difficulties of keeping the state in one piece. In Siberia there are increasing calls for autonomy and even independence by some of the small peoples there who are sitting on top of vast natural resources, including oil and diamonds. Similar political goals are also in evidence in the Republic of Karelia, another area that according to US political geographers will be achieving independence in the near future. The Kola region, for its part, is expected to join forces with a Sami state to form the Arctic Confederation (Los Angeles Times, 25 August 1992). All of these speculations are based on the strengthening aspirations of regional actors to shift the locus of power downwards from the central level and in this way to benefit from the natural resources that in a centralized world economy have mostly benefited the centre.

Russia's complete disintegration would serve to strengthen the position of the conservative forces in the country. One of their arguments is that the West actually wants this to happen and that it is supporting disintegrative tendencies in order to consolidate the position of both Western Europe and the United States in the international system. The reformists in Russia need Western support; the conservatives, on the other hand, rely on traditional Russian values. If the conservative forces were to gain power in Russia, that would represent a serious threat to the West and effectively restore the order of the Cold War.

From the point of view of Russia's neighbours the recent developments in Russia may seem rather disquieting. Of the Nordic Countries Finland shares a long border with Russia, and it has long been feared that the mounting problems of hunger and unemployment in Russia may cause a massive influx of people across that border into Finland. In the northern parts of the country, the most dramatic estimates of the size of the potential refugee population have equalled the number of people living in the whole Kola area. The risk of a serious refugee problem is heightened by domestic conflicts in Russia as well as several environmental catastrophes that have been revealed in different parts of the country. However, the historical evidence indicates that Russian people are not very likely to move out of their home country even in the face of famine and unemployment. Furthermore, from the Finnish point of view it is important to bear in mind that there are already 200,000 Russian refugees from other areas in the St. Petersburg region. These people lack both proper shelter and food. Another factor that is thought might well cause an inflow of refugees into Finland, especially from the St. Petersburg region, is a nuclear accident in any of the nuclear power stations in that area.

All of these scenarios must be taken seriously in official Finnish security policy. The same threat factors are also pushing the Finnish authorities towards various Western alliances. In Finland there can be sensed a deep fear today of being left alone with the threat caused by the developments in Russia. This is quite understandable in view of the Finnish collective memory — to say nothing about the statements by such Russian politicians as Zhirinovsky, who has repeatedly reminded that Finland is traditionally a part of Russia.

The Baltic republics

In 1991 the Nordic countries had different and even conflicting views on the independence of the Baltic republics. The last member of the Nordic Council to recognize their independence was Finland, who even after the attempted *coup d'etat* in Moscow in August 1991 continued to issue careful statements in consonance with its 1948 friendship treaty with Russia. Therefore, on 22 August President Koivisto issued a press release in which he said that the Estonian people have to reach agreement with the Soviet authorities before Finland can recognize their independence. However, just three days later the Finnish Council for Foreign Affairs announced that the Baltic states had advanced so far with the process of independence that Finland would be able to start negotiations in order to establish regular diplomatic relations (Ulko-politiikka, 1:1992, p. 90). On 29 August Finland referred to the historical reorganization of the Baltic states in the 1920's, saying that it was valid again.

Although the independence of the Baltic republics achieved wide recognition in the international community, the newly independent states have had considerable difficulty in finding their place within that community. As they are all former members of the Western European community, that is where they have turned now. Both the Lutheran and the Catholic religion occupy a strong position in the Baltic republics, providing a strong link with Western culture. The ethnic and cultural frontier between East and West runs along the eastern borders of Finland, Estonia, Latvia and Lithuania, tying all these countries together. On the other hand, the level of economic development clearly separates the latter three from Finland, and this distinction will un-doubtedly be strengthened by Finland's membership in the European Union. The Baltic republics will have to remain outside for quite some time.

To a certain extent the Baltic republics share the same national inter-ests as Finland and Sweden. All of them are concerned about the prevailing conditions of political and economic instability in Russia. But whereas all five countries are interested in the prospect of joining NATO, the Nordic countries are not willing to guarantee the security of the Baltic republics. In any event the NATO factor separates the two former neutrals from the three former Soviet republics: in a recent report NATO has made it clear that while it is interested in the prospect of Finnish and Swedish membership, the Baltic republics should only be granted NACC status in the same way as the Russian Federation.

After 50 years of Soviet rule that started with a military invasion, the Baltic republics are understandably concerned about the security threat represented by Russia. The border between Russia and the Baltic republics separates countries that are suspicious of each other. For Baltic sovereignty, efficient border control is a matter of crucial importance, and therefore a priority concern in the Baltic republics today is to strengthen their national armies as quickly as possible. This does not, however, imply an increase in military power in the Baltic region, since the Russians are at the same time withdrawing their forces from the Baltic republics. As their military capacity compared with Russia's is very limited, the Baltic republics would like to have Western security guarantees for their future independence. However, this is a policy which contributes to widening the gap between the new East and the West rather than bridging that gap. While the policy adopted by the newly independent Baltic republics is fully understandable, it is certainly not conducive to wider cooperation or to a more peaceful Europe. In this respect the interests of Western Europe are in conflict with the interests of the Baltic republics. There is a dilemma here which may easily spill over into a serious conflict in that the Russian population living in the Baltic republics do not enjoy equal economic and political rights with the native people: the Russians there today remain largely without political citizenship, and they are widely regarded as representatives of a hostile occupation power. In this sense the Russians represent a serious threat to the internal security of the Baltic republics.

The civil rights of the Baltic Russians is a critical issue as far as the stability of Northern Europe is concerned. Representatives of the Russian government as well as conservative circles in Russia have pointed out that Russian interests are closely bound up with the interests of the Russian people in the newly independent neighbouring countries. This means that the rights of the Russian population in the Baltic republics have a direct bearing on the state of international relations in Northern Europe. At the same time, they are also reflected in the internal development of Russia. The support enjoyed by conservative circles in Russia will increase in direct proportion to the number of Russian refugees from former Soviet republics (Bezberezhev, 1992).

On the issue of Russian civil rights in the Baltic republics, the European Council, the EC and the CSCE have all adopted a low profile. They have not wanted to encourage the Balts to step up their nationalistic policies. At the same time, however, Western Europe has insisted that all remaining troops of the Red Army must get out of the Baltic republics as soon as possible. There is no room for negotiation on this question: the principle of national sovereignty requires that no foreign troops can be present in an independent country without the express acceptance of the host country. However, these two Russian problems seem to be interrelated. On several occasions Russia has made it clear that the withdrawal of its troops from the Baltic republics depends on the future civil rights of the Russian minorities there. Quite obviously then, the withdrawal of Russian forces is a political question. This was clearly seen in Lithuania, from where Russian troops have already been withdrawn.

In the present situation the low profile assumed by external powers on the civil rights question is quite apparently in conflict with the strict position they have adopted on Russian military presence in the countries concerned. This is an important point, for beyond this conflict there also looms the risk of an open armed conflict not only internally but also regionally. All Baltic states should now work to avoid this conflict, or at least to avoid the growth of chauvinistic attitudes. However, in the European Council Finland has observed that Soviet laws can no longer be valid in the independent Baltic republics; therefore Russian settlers who have moved in during the Soviet reign do not have the right of citizenship. This is an adventurous opinion: it means that Russians are regarded as illegal settlers in the Baltic republics, and according to international practice illegal settlers and immigrants can be expelled. If this were to happen, there would very probably follow an open conflict in the region.

In addition to the problem of nationhood there are other factors in the Baltic republics and elsewhere in the former socialist countries that are bound to cause instability. One of these factors is the changing system of political practice, which has served to create a political power vacuum — even though the former power elite continues to hold a fairly strong position in many former socialist countries. With the disintegration of the party state, opportunities were created for new political elites to occupy leading positions at the top of the power pyramid. However, as the top of the pyramid is still very narrow, the struggle for power may easily assume violent forms. In some cases this has led to the creation of new states instead of the former unified state, making it possible for several political and economic elites to find a place at the top. This has been the case in the former Czechoslovakia, and it was also the case in the former Yugoslavia.

As yet the struggle for power in the Baltic republics has not led to a Balkanization of the political entities there. However, rival political forces are currently fighting for leadership in their respective societies, which are still in the process of reshaping their social and political systems. This has made it difficult to form stable political coalitions, which in turn may easily cause inconsistency in the internal and foreign policies pursued. In some of the Baltic republics the situation tends to be more complex than in others. In Estonia, for example, there are still several different armies with different positions vis-à-vis the state and government; some of them are clearly not under close state control but are associated with certain political parties (Raid, 1992). Political struggle does not mix very well with military activities; the risk of civil war is real, as was acutely obvious in Estonia in the summer of 1993. In the prevailing situation of uncertainty it is very difficult for foreign powers to give aid to the Baltic states for purposes of building up their national armed security, as it is not always clear what kind of forces they will be supporting. On the other hand, there are already clear indications that the situation is beginning to settle down. In Estonia, for example, the state is gradually beginning to gain control over the relationship between different armies.

The international orientation of the Baltic republics is also problematic as far as the Northern European community is concerned. Following the disintegration of the Soviet Union and their declarations of independence, the Baltic states had high hopes and expectations of close cooperation with the Nordic group. These hopes were strengthened by the founding of the council of the Baltic Sea region in Copenhagen in 1991. However, the Nordic countries have understandably been less willing to accept the Baltic republics as equal partners in the Nordic Council. One problem that certainly complicates any efforts at wider Baltic cooperation is the lack of any collective goals in the Baltic republics' international orientation.

From a Nordic point of view there are at least two major problems. First, in a situation of equal cooperation the Nordic countries would have to carry the main burden for the economic development of the Baltic republics. With the ongoing economic recession, the Nordic countries simply do not have the resources to do this, especially if they want to maintain their traditional global orientations. In this respect the reconstruction of the economy in the Gaza strip competes with the reconstruction of the Baltic economies. On the other hand, it is not at all self-evident that the Nordic countries really want to see rapid economic growth in the Baltic republics. The development gap is a definite advantage for the Nordic economies as far as Baltic cooperation is concerned and indeed in terms of their own trade interests, for in their own production strategies they can easily take advantage of the lower labour costs in the Baltic states.

Another problem occurs in the field of national security policies. Given the limited military capacity of the Baltic republics to guarantee their national security interests vis-à-vis Russia, they would be very interested in stepping up security cooperation in the Baltic Sea area. Defence cooperation would certainly strengthen the credibility of the national defences of the small Baltic states, and therefore they have turned to the Nordic countries to obtain at least some sort of security guarantees. However, the latter have not been willing to bind themselves to a potential situation where the internal development in the Baltic republics might lead to a conflict with Russia.

The obvious conclusion that flows from the arguments above is that the Baltic republics and the Nordic countries have somewhat contradictory interests, which makes it hard to coordinate any cooperation between these two groups. At the same time it is important to note that the Baltic republics have themselves made only little progress in developing their mutual cooperation. They have different goals and different outward orientations: Estonia is interested in cooperation with Finland and Sweden, Lithuania is more interested in cooperation with Central Europe and with Belorussia and Ukraine, and Latvia has its eyes both on Sweden and on the United States.

Having said that, there are also important similarities in the foreign policies of the Baltic rim states. This is particularly true of the Baltic republics and Finland, who all want to join the Western European community and who for historical reasons regard Russia as a major threat to their future existence. During the Cold War the Baltic republics were part of the Soviet Union, so understandably they now want to take critical distance. However, this is a very costly policy in terms of their national economies and security policies. Russia is a suspicious actor who will continue to analyse its own position vis-à-vis the Baltic states carefully. In this process the Baltic Russians are an important parameter. For the Baltic states it is going to be very hard indeed to compensate for the loss of Russian markets. After trade with the other heirs of the Soviet Union collapsed, they have also had increasing difficulties in obtaining the raw materials needed in basic production.

In a way Finland is in the same position. Finland also draws a demarcation line vis-à-vis Russia, and the country is working very hard to break loose from the position that became so firmly entrenched during the Cold War. In practice, this has meant less contacts with Russia and intensified attempts at integration with the Western European community. The policy has manifested itself in a willingness to join NATO, in a willingness to participate in peace enforcement operations and also in the decision to purchase American Hornet fighters. All of these reorientations are indicative of an interest to increase national security by military means against Russia. In Russia, one possible way of reading Finnish reactions is that Finland looks upon Russia as an enemy; the impression is that Finland is looking for an enemy on the other side of the border and for a friend on the other side of the Atlantic Ocean.

The Nordic community

After the Cold War there have been increasing difficulties even in traditional Nordic cooperation. In the past, Nordic cooperation was explained by reference to the countries' similar historical experiences, their similar parliamentarian and democratic political systems, their similar systems of social security, i.e. by reference to the Nordic welfare model and cultural homogeneity (Wallensteen, Vesa and Väyrynen, 1973; Hettne, Käkönen, Lodgaard, Wallensteen and Wiberg, 1991). On the basis of integration theories this is a completely feasible interpretation. However, another possible explanation is that Nordic cooperation was motivated by a common interest to stay outside the Cold War confrontation. For Finland, Nordic cooperation had a special value of its own since it was the first post-war link which connected Finland to the Western European community.

Today, with the Cold War over, it is harder to find uniting factors that would bring the Nordic countries together and push them towards closer cooperation. The common Nordic heritage does not seem to suffice as such a factor (cf. Kivimäki, 1992). The diverse interests of the Nordic countries surfaced for the first time when Sweden, a member of EFTA, applied for membership in the EC without informing the other Nordic countries of its intentions. Finland soon followed Sweden's example, as did Norway in 1993. The countries have also had different ideas and initiatives as to the development of cooperation in Northern Europe. Norway and Denmark are mainly interested in East Atlantic or North Sea cooperation, and Norway took the initiative to launch cooperation with Russia in the Barents region. The Barents Region Council, established in January 1993, consists of the three northernmost counties of Norway, the northernmost counties of Sweden and Finland, the Murmansk and Archangel districts of Russia, and the Karelian Republic (Fridjof Nansen stiftelsen, 1992).

The Nordic countries do not enjoy equal status in the different initiatives taken, which clearly reflect national interests. The new ideas for regional cooperation explicate a wider European trend towards regionalization. However, it is also evident that traditional Nordic cooperation no longer offers the same advantages as it did during the Cold War; it is obviously under mounting pressure to change. Nordic cooperation cannot serve as a viable basis for wider Baltic cooperation either.

Baltic Sea cooperation would seem to provide a natural extension to Nordic cooperation (Joenniemi and Waever, 1992). But again there are certain problems. Given the participation of the northern counties and *Länder* of Poland and Germany in the Baltic Sea Council, the German influence in the region is bound to increase. Schleswig-Holstein has been one of the most active areas in initiating Baltic cooperation (Der Denkfabrik Schleswig-Holstein, 1991), fearing that the southern orientation of the Germany economy will leave it in a more or less peripheral position. In the context of Baltic cooperation, Germany would have an excellent opportunity to strengthen its weight and influence in Europe.

Another problem that deserves separate attention here is the imbalance and inequality in development across different parts of the Baltic region. While the Baltic republics and the northern counties of Poland are mostly at the receiving end of the cooperation, the wealthier partners can and do take advantage of the lower labour and production costs in these poor regions. It is indeed hard to see how this cooperation could be organized on principles of full equality; on the contrary it seems more likely that the North-South development gap will leave a definite imprint on regional cooperation. In the field of political development the differences are even more profound. In Poland and in the Baltic republics, the goal is to construct a traditional sovereign and unified state. This means that the state will remain an important actor in post-socialist societies. In the Nordic countries, on the other hand, the role of the state is declining at the same time as they are moving towards the European Union. As was observed earlier, the Baltic republics will probably have to remain outside the Community for at least the next decade.

Future membership in the EC divides the Baltic states into two camps. However, this is at once one of the factors which supports the development of Baltic cooperation in the short term. The EC policy of subsidiarity and regionalization serves to strengthen subregional cooperation, creating as it does new regions — such as the Mediterranean and the Central European regions — within the Community that transcend state borders. In the context of regionalization, the Baltic region would be a neutral unit that would link together the EC members and non-members. At the same time, the Community is showing a definite willingness to support the development of former socialist countries immediately beyond the EC's eastern border. A grey zone with a reasonable level of economic prosperity between Russia and the European Community would have very favourable security effects for Western Europe. All this makes sense from a Western point of view, but from a Russian point of view it may well be interpreted as a strategy to isolate Russia from the rest of Europe.

Indeed the views adopted by the Russian Federation are crucially important with regard to the future stability of the European continent. This is fully appreciated by Western Europe, and therefore both NATO and the EC would want to see closer connections between Russia and Western Europe. At the same time, Western Europe is very much interested in the growth region in Central Europe, which could be a target for refugees from the former Soviet Union. From an economic point of view this region could also offer cheap labour power and growing markets for the Western European economy. Therefore the EC will organize its relations with this region as soon as possible.

At the present time it would seem that once the Nordic countries have joined, the next in line for EC membership are the Christian and Lutheran-Catholic countries of Eastern Europe. Before granting full membership, the Community will have organized extensive cooperation with this region. The Nordic countries will be responsible for supporting the small Baltic states. A suitable framework for Nordic aid to the Baltic economies is provided by Baltic Sea region cooperation. The responsibility of the Nordic countries will also be extended to the Russian regions beyond the Finnish and Norwegian borders, i.e. the Karelian Republic and the Kola region. From the point of view of the European Community, a natural extension for Nordic cooperation would be cooperation in the Baltic and the Barents regions.

The assumed expectations of the European Community have already materialized in the Norwegian initiative for cooperation in the Barents region. This initiative is consistent with Norway's national interests. At the same time, however, it also serves to strengthen Norway's bargaining position in its membership negotiations with the EC in that the natural resources of the Arctic will help to strengthen the European economic region vis-à-vis the rival economic regions of North America and Asia by giving the EC access to Russian Arctic resources.

New challenges

Looking at the above arguments in the light of different strategic choices, it seems clear that there are certain contradictions in the present-day reality; by the same token, the evaluation will necessarily contain some contradictions as well. In a rough generalization, we can identify at least two major contradictory trends in development. The first one presents Russia as a threat. According to this line of reasoning, Russia's neighbours have to arm themselves so that they can defend and protect themselves. From a Northern European point of view, Norway and Finland are the only Western European countries that share a common border with Russia; between the rest of Western Europe and Russia there is a wide zone of engagement. This makes the situation both for the Nordic and for the Baltic countries more serious than it was during the Cold War (Sollie, 1993). This suggests the conclusion that the Nordic countries need a stronger national defence today than they did during the Cold War. A clear indication is provided by the growing defence budgets of Sweden and Finland.

The other trend in development opens up new options for a more cooperative international system. However, insofar as Russia is regarded as a security threat, it seems unlikely that new choices will actually be made. The actions taken by the Nordic countries and particularly by Finland are based on the threat scenario, in spite of the establishment of Barents region cooperation. Finland and Sweden are preparing themselves to counter a threat from the East; this is the only way to understand the military programmes in these countries. We can also see why Sweden and Finland have thrown overboard the old concept of neutrality and why they now want to take part in Western military activities. This process of armament and the clear signs the two countries are giving in terms of their willingness to join Western military organizations, implies a widening gap between Russia and the West, between the Slavic and Orthodox east and the Catholic-Lutheran west. This runs counter to the general Western policy that every effort should be made not to give cause for Russia to think that it is being isolated from the rest of Europe.

The traditional arguments applied in Northern Europe for strong national defence, probably in the context of a military alliance, serve to reinforce the above conclusions in Russia: the argument that defence policy has become more important than foreign policy (cf. Rehn, 1993) is certainly an instance of sending out the wrong signals to the authorities in Russia. The Norwegian initiative for Nordic security cooperation in the autumn of 1992 had the same effect. However, the initiative did not meet with very much enthusiasm in the other Nordic countries. The Finnish authorities, for instance, have made it clear that in the present situation they do not consider it necessary to start on a discussion of new alternatives in security policy; the time will be riper in 1995 when the Nordic countries will probably be taking a stand on a common European security policy (cf. Rehn, 1993).

Behind this growing interest in security policy and the flood of initiatives for closer cooperation, there may lie the changing roles of states and civil societies in relation to each other. By stressing traditional armed security and by adopting an active role in regional cooperation, states and leading state-related elites are trying to strengthen their own power positions. The ongoing power struggle between different power elites is a result of the declining role of nation states since the end of the Cold War and the absence of the common threat of communism to tie together western social and political or sometimes even ethnic forces.

The dissolution of states and state power is further enhanced by the delegation of power from sovereign states to EC institutions. Integration not only changes the role of two central state institutions, but also the essence of politics. In the European Union, defence policy will be coordinated by a single, common organization; at the same time, the duties and responsibilities of ministries for foreign affairs will become a matter of internal policy. This means that national ministries of social security, agriculture or finance will be charged with responsibilities that formerly belonged to the ministries of foreign affairs (Nousiainen, 1992). On the other hand, regionalization is creating new actors in the sphere of international or foreign policy. These regional institutions do not follow traditional state borders, nor do they constitute nationally homogenous areas. In North America, examples are provided by several unofficial institutions that deal with common problems on both sides of the US-Mexican border. Through these joint institutions, it is possible to pursue a common policy on both sides, at the same time as they evade all mechanisms of central control and bring down the locus of power to the local level (see Summit Report, 1989). In the official context cooperation would be coordinated by the state authorities, notably by the ministries of foreign affairs in Washington and Mexico City.

Local communities and towns have also become involved in activities that belong to the domain of international politics, and not only in border regions. This might be an early sign of a fundamental change in the organization of international cooperation and indeed in the whole international system. In the Baltic Sea region, new trends in development are most clearly visible in the Scandinavian countries, whereas the Baltic republics are more conservative in this respect: they are still in the process of building the traditional sovereign state. In other words, there are two contradictory processes under way around the Baltic Sea, presenting an additional challenge for regional cooperation there and in Northern Europe.

With these two different trends in development in the rim states, there are also two possible directions for the development of regional cooperation. First, there is the option of traditional state-centred cooperation, which is grounded in the traditional armed security model. Looking at the official state policies pursued around the Baltic Sea today, it is clear that this model is predominant: the chief concern is quite emphatically with the potential Russian threat and accordingly with traditional security policy. This means that, with the possible exception of Norway, the Northern European countries west of Russia are digging a gap between themselves and their eastern neighbour. At the same time, a growing proportion of social resources is being spent on armed security instead of civic security. This option closes doors to economic cooperation, which would have important benefits to all partners.

The second option involves the development of new fora and new forms of international politics by limiting the role of nation states and by strengthening civic security. The idea is that the money invested in state-centred security could be used for extending cooperation aimed at developing the regions beyond the eastern border of Western Europe. This is a major factor in strengthening civic security. However, this alternative does not enjoy much support in the western parts of Northern Europe. In St. Petersburg, Petrozavodsk and Murmansk, there are far more businessmen from Germany, Italy and Holland than from any Scandinavian country. Even Japanese businessmen have been active in developing joint economic ventures in these Russian regions.

In the Finnish and Baltic cases, the reasons for this hesitancy are quite understandable. Many Finnish companies are still waiting to get their money out of Russia; before they get paid, they will hardly be willing to invest more money in a country where conditions are less than stable. There may be greater willingness among some smaller companies, but they simply do not have the capacity and potential required by the huge Russian economy.

The situation in Russia today is unstable and insecure. However, there have already been some success stories of cooperation, albeit on a small scale. One of these stories is Ben & Jerry's ice cream production in Petrozavodsk in Russian Karelia. Ben & Jerry is a famous ice cream company from Vermont, US. They started production in Petrozavodsk in 1991. From the very outset one of the leading principles of the company has been its social orientation, which traces back to the hippie background of the founders of the company. This helps to explain why the primary aim of the Karelian project has not been to bring back money to the Unites States; instead the operation is run by roubles, the raw material comes from Karelia, and the product is marketed in Karelia. Up until now, all profits have been put back into the company to expand production; some of the money has also been used to develop fishing and wilderness tourism in Karelia. Most of the tourists come from the USA and especially from Vermont, which brings in dollars to Karelia.

The ice cream diplomacy of Ben & Jerry is a useful example which goes to show that it is indeed possible to create an economic growth region beyond the eastern border of the Nordic countries. This region helps to strengthen security and also provides an important boost to the economy on both sides of the border.

Finally, a few words are in order on the contradiction present in the analysis above. In this article I have applied two different approaches at the same time, focusing on both the state and on civil society. While this has made possible a reconstruction of a complex reality, it has also complicated the argumentation. However, the method has the important advantage of avoiding another contradiction that often occurs in analyses of the future of Northern Europe. Official foreign and security policy think tanks usually present separate evaluations of the threats caused by the future development in Russia and the gains of more intensive cooperation. As a result of this divided analysis, cooperation is seen as a positive phenomenon — but it does not do away with the need to maintain a high level of national defence (cf. Sollie, 1993).

In other contexts, the same people representing the same think tanks will say that in the analysis of the preconditions for and the possible results of cooperation, it does not make sense to start out from the vantage-point of conflicts; it is more rational to start from joint interests and from the common aim of minimizing military threats (cf. Sollie 1993). This means that the security and cooperation dimensions rarely meet each other. On this basis it might be wiser to begin from the potential and real conflicts that are immanent in the future development of Northern Europe. With this approach, there is at least the possibility of resolving potential conflicts before they surface. It also stresses the mutual interest of avoiding violent conflicts, and helps to advance the peaceful transformation of international relations in Northern Europe.

The choice is very much one between a state-centred and a civil society-centred approach. However, this not an either-or situation. Instead, we have to look at how these two spheres of interests and goals are related to each other. In both of these approaches the security threats are also different: the threats to civil society in Russia are nuclear catastrophes, industrial pollution, and mass population shifts. None of these are military threats by nature, but they can be translated into military threats (cf. PPN, 1991). However, the militarization of threats to civil society is hardly very helpful as far resolving problems is concerned. Therefore it is also necessary to make the fundamental choice between traditional state-centred armed security and the security of civil society.

Notes

1. This point was emphasized by Russian Foreign Minister Mr. Kozyrev in his double speech at the CSCE conference of foreign ministers in Stockholm in December 1992. In his first, sham speech, Minister Kozyrev raised some of the points that would be high on the agenda of a conservative-led Russia. Before his second speech reports were already out that the Cold War was about to return.

References:

Arrighi, Giovanni (1991), 'World Income Inequalities and the Future of Socialism', *New Left Review*, no. 189.

Bezberezhev, S. (1992), *Venäläisen nationalismin ilmeneminen*, paper presented at Kuhmo Summer Seminar 24.7.1992, Petrozavodsk.

Der Denkfabrik Schleswig-Holstein (1992), *EG-Binnenmarkt '92: Chancen für Schleswig-Holstein*, Der Ministerpräsident des Landes Schleswig-Holstein, Kiel.

Fridjof Nansen -stiftelsen (1992), *Samarbeidet i Barentsregionen — problemer og perspektiver*, Bakgrundsnotat for ekspertkonferanse i Kirkenes 26-27 September 1992, Oslo.

Fukuyama, Francis (1992), *The End of History and the Last Man*, Hamish Hamilton, London.

Hettne, Björn & Käkönen, Jyrki & Lodgaard, Sverre & Wallensteen, Peter & Wiberg, Håkan (1991), 'Norden, Europe and the Near Future. Report from the directors of Nordic Peace Research Institutes', *PRIO Report*, no. 3, 1991, Oslo.

Joenniemi, Pertti & Waever, Ole (1992), 'Regionalization around the Baltic Rim: Notions on Baltic Sea Politics' *Nordiske Seminar- og Arbeidsrapporter*, no. 521, 1992, The Nordic Council, Stockholm.

Kirkinen, Heikki (1991), *Maakuntien Eurooppa ja Suomi*, Otava, Keuruu.

Kivimäki, Erkki (1992), 'Pohjoismainen yhteistyö uuteen vaiheeseen', *UM Taustat*, no. 4, 1992, Ulkoasiainministeriö, Helsinki.

Linzie, Jan & Boman, Dag (1991), *Mälarregionen i ett gränslösa Europa*, Regionplane- och Trafikkontoret, Stockholm.

Los Angeles Times, 25 August 1992, World Report.

McDonnell, Valerie & Ganier-Raymond, Marie (1990), 'Business Cooperation and Development in Border Regions', *Linkage Assistance and Cooperation for the European Border Regions. Working Document.*

Mennola, Erkki (1991), *Euroopan todelliset vaikuttajat*, VAPK-Kustannus, Helsinki.

Meyers, Paul (Raporteur) (1990), 'Report on The Single Market 1992 and its implications for the autonomy of local and regional authorities', *Council of Europe, Twenty-Fifth Session*, Strasbourg, 6-8 March 1990.

Nousiainen, Jaakko (1992), 'Vahvistaako EY-liityntä Suomen presidentin valtaa', *Helsingin Sanomat*, 29 September 1992.

PPN (1991), Parlamentaarinen puolustuspoliittinen neuvottelukunta, *Arvio Euroopan turvallisuuspoliittisesta tilanteesta ja sen kehitysnäkymistä sekä niiden vaikutuksista Suomen puolustuspolitiikkaan*, Helsinki.

Raid, Aare (1992), Finnish-Estonian Round Table Discussions in Tallinn, 7-8 September 1992.

Rehn, Elisabet (1993), Interview, *Rauhantutkimus*, no. 1.

Sollie, Finn (1993), *Security in the Arctic — A View from the Scandinavian North*, A presentation in the Arctic Research Forum Symposium 'Sustainable Development in the Arctic', 10-12 January 1993, Henne Strand, Denmark.

Summit Report (1989), Second U.S.-Mexico Border Governors Finance Summit. Final Report, *San Diego State University. Institute for Regional Studies of California*, San Diego.

Thee, Marek (1992), 'Europe in the Spasm of the System-Change in the East. The pursuit of stable peace', *Tampere Peace Research Institute. Research Report*, no. 46, Tampere.

Ulkopolitiikka, no. 1, 1992, Suomen ulkopolitiikan tapahtumat 1.7.-31.12.1991.

Wallensteen, Peter & Vesa, Unto & Väyrynen, Raimo (1973), 'The Nordic System: Structure and Change, 1920-1970', *Tampere Peace Research Institute, Research Reports*, no. 6, 1973, Tampere.

3 Russian Political Development and Prospects

Jyrki Iivonen

From the Soviet Union to Russia

The Soviet Union collapsed as a super power in a few months during autumn 1991. The collapse, preceded by a political development lasting several years, even decades, has had not only domestic, but also far-reaching international consequences: the demise of the Soviet Union and its alliance system collapsed the bipolar international system formed after the Second World War on the basis of the immanent contradictions between the two superpowers and their respective spheres of influence (Väyrynen, 1993, p. 25). The events of autumn 1991 therefore launched a new period in Russia's foreign political relations and in its international status (see Iivonen, 1992; Laqueur, 1993, pp. 387-420; Remnick, 1993; Rusi, 1991). The events in October 1993, when President Yeltsin crushed his opponents, made the evaluation of Russia's future slightly easier but did not have a similar external impact as those of two years earlier.

The reform policy launched by Mikhail Gorbachev in 1985, better known as perestroika, originally aimed at strengthening the socialist basis of the Soviet society. Another goal was the cautious reform of the structures of the Soviet Communist Party (CPSU) in such a way that its power monopoly would not be endangered. The Soviet economy was to be reformed mainly on the basis of state ownership. In 1986 a new policy of *glasnost* was also started, aimed at encouraging free debate on various social problems, but naturally within certain limits. Beginning in 1987, the democratization of the Soviet political system was added to perestroika. After that, the preservation of traditional socialist structures intact became more and more difficult and finally impossible. When perestroika started to make dramatic changes in the basic structures of society in general and influenced the legitimacy of the system in particular, disagreements inside the highest leadership also started to intensify. The old communist elite *(nomenklatura)* tried to preserve its traditional privileges, leading to a growing conflict between it and the reformers. This tension continued even after 1991 in the activities of the Russian Supreme Soviet (SS) and the Russian Congress of People's Deputies (CPD), leading finally to armed struggle in October 1993.

General Secretary and President Gorbachev tried to maintain a balance between these two main groupings but was successful only for a couple of years. Although in principle he supported the continuation and expansion of reforms, beginning in 1987 he was forced to yield to the will of the conservative fraction in many issues. The goal of Gorbachev's personnel policy was to diminish conflicts inside the highest leadership through a number of replacements. Although the turnover within the highest party and state leadership between 1985 and 1988 was exceptionally high, when several representatives of the old administration were removed, Gorbachev was unable to prevent the continuation and growth of conflicts inside the highest organs (cf. Iivonen, 1989). Along with his equilibrium policy, Gorbachev was gradually alienated from the supporters of reform policy and especially from the ambitious Russian leader Boris Yeltsin, his former ally (Morrison, 1991). Yeltsin's position only become stronger in June 1991, when he became the first freely elected president in the history of Russian Federation.

Yeltsin's election victory alarmed the most conservative forces in the Soviet leadership. The primary goal of the August 1991 coup attempt was to prevent the further extension of political and economic reforms, because they were believed to be a serious threat to the continued existence of the socialist system. The initiators of the coup obviously wanted to replace Gorbachev (although he was first promised a position in the new government), whom they found ineffective. But in particular they wanted to replace all reformers in the highest leadership. After the coup failed, Gorbachev still retained his position of leadership for some months, but by this time he was already virtually without the power that had earlier belonged to him. The actual leader from now on was Yeltsin, the organizer of the resistance against the coup, a new symbolic figure, who with his allies now started to construct his own power apparatus, replacing old Soviet institutions by new Russian ones. One of his first measures after the coup attempt was to outlaw the activities of the CPSU.

Russian political developments during autumn 1991 were characterized by Yeltsin's efforts to suppress those Soviet political structures that were still seen as an obstacle to his own aims. The Commonwealth of Independent States (CIS) was created in December 1991 after the failed attempt to conclude the new Union Treaty that would have guaranteed Russia's leading position in the future as well. The final reason for the failure was the Ukrainian referendum, leading to the Ukraine's declaration of independence. In this situation Russia's leadership wanted to create a political arrangement, in which the manoeuvring room of the various new republics would be larger than before but where power and power resources would still belong to the Russian-dominated central leadership to be located in Moscow.

In this new situation, Russia desired international recognition of its position as the legitimate heir of the Soviet Union. At the international level it was rather successful. According to the leading Western powers, the formation of the CIS was rather a question of a transition of power from one person to another than a profound social transformation as such (see Mullerson, 1993). The prohibition of the CPSU and the founding of the CIS only partly solved the problems that had led to the dissolution of the USSR. The prospect of having Russia as the lawful heir of the USSR did not please all former Soviet republics. Estonia, Latvia and Lithuania had issued their independence declarations immediately after the failed coup attempt, receiving international recognition within a few weeks. In the same way, republics with extensive economic and military resources (especially Ukraine and Kazakhstan) questioned the idea of Russia replacing the USSR on its own terms. The starting point of the CIS was therefore problematic and this explains why several conflicts concerning the division of the Soviet inheritance have characterized its first steps. Both foreign debts as well as the reorganization of the Soviet armed forces have been on the agenda in the discussions. Internationally the most difficult problem has been the future of Soviet nuclear arms.

The finding of solutions to Russia's domestic problems has not proceeded as rapidly as was originally expected and wished. Many of the problems inherited from the Soviet system have remained unsolved. Yeltsin, emphasizing his democratic state of mind, tried to continue the policy of centralized leadership, based on what could be called a *dekret*-policy[1], where the possibilities to choose between different alternatives were rather limited. This was the situation up to autumn 1993. The separation of powers, one of the basic principles of Western democracy, was not carried out in a satisfactory way. Instruments of resolving social conflicts were also absent, adding to the instability and insecurity (cf. Olson, 1993). Because the Russian parliament was elected already in 1990 during the Soviet period, one could not find a genuine multiparty system in Russia. Rather, the political organization was still based on separate individual leaders rather than on the explicitly defined political ideologies or social classes as in the West (cf. Rogatshi, 1992; Pribylovskii, 1992). This politically ambiguous situation was reflected in the economic sector as well, where, due to the lack of jointly approved programmes and rules, it was practically impossible to carry out a consistent reform policy. The political elimination of the old Russian parliament has, with a very high probability, removed many of these political obstacles. At least it has made it much easier for Yeltsin to get his political plans approved and executed.

This domestic instability can also be seen in the discussion on Russia's foreign policy goals and methods. The separation into *Zapadniks* and Slavophiles, dating back to the first half of the nineteenth century, has remained relevant even in today's Russia (see e.g. Schapiro, 1967; Walicki, 1980; Vihavainen, 1990). On one hand, there are those who believe that only a complete and unconditional adaptation to Western political and economic models and ideas is the best way to pull Russia out of the present crisis. On the other hand, there are those who insist that Russia either must turn inwards to look for security in traditional Russian values or find allies in Asia and in the Islamic world. They further believe that the defence of Russian national interests must become the main task of Russian domestic and foreign policy.

In theory, it is possible to distinguish four different schools in Russian foreign policy. The Westerners emphasize close relations with the West, seeing it as Russia's natural ally. The nationalists are anti-Western, intent on the strengthening of the Russian imperial tradition. Neo-Eurasians see Russia as Eurasian rather than European power and stress the need to cooperate with China and the Islamic world. The realists, finally, tend to think in terms of geopolitics, believing that the conflicts with the West have not disappeared, that new threats (Islam) have appeared and that Russia's first task in foreign policy is to defend the interests of Russians wherever they live (Matveyev, 1992, p. 81; see also Alexandrova, 1993).

Leaving these schools aside, it can be said that since 1992 Russian foreign policy has been dualistic in nature. In relations to the West, Russian leadership has continued Gorbachev's 'new thinking'. Partly this has led to Russia's growing economic dependency. By having good relations with the West, Russia has been able to preserve the high level of economic and technological aid. Consequently, Russia has in most cases followed the will of Western powers and international economic organizations (IMF, World Bank) (Sachs, 1993). The socialist alliance system, earlier a great economic burden to the USSR, does not exist any longer. Russia has also ceased to support both Eastern European countries as well as several governments in the Third World (Cuba, Iraq, Afghanistan, North Korea, Ethiopia, etc.). The dissolution of the Warsaw Treaty Organization has led to the creation of the North Atlantic Cooperation Council (NACC), and some Russian leaders have even spoken of the possibility of applying for NATO membership. In foreign trade and economic cooperation Russia's main aim has been, after the dissolution of the CMEA, to improve relations with the EC. In the United Nations, Russia along with other CIS countries has almost without exceptions accepted the policy line of the USA in international crises such as the Gulf War and the Yugoslavian war. However, there has been a lot of confusion concerning the present foreign political decision-making apparatus. In other words, it has been very difficult to know who really is in charge (Halliday, 1993).

In many quarters it is believed, however, that a more isolated (or independent) foreign policy, emphasizing Russian national interests, would better serve Russia's present situation and needs. From that point of view, Russia's Western-oriented foreign policy has been severely criticized (the main target of criticism has been Kozyrev rather than Yeltsin, who has avoided identifying too strongly with the statements of his foreign minister). Demands have been put forward that in keeping with the new orientation, allies should be sought in other places than in the West. The main aim of Russia's foreign policy should, according to these demands, be the defence of interests and positions of Russians living in former Soviet republics. Russia, in other words, would rather be understood as an ethnic than as a geographical concept. A re-evaluation of the present foreign policy has been demanded not only by right-wing nationalistic politicians but also by some very close to Yeltsin, among others his personal adviser since 1991, Sergei Stankevich, who in March 1992 wrote as follows: 'The attitude towards the Russian population and Russian heritage in a given country is from Russia's point of view the main criteria when deciding whether that country is regarded as a friend or not' (Stankevich, 1992; see Zubok, 1992). In the same connection, he especially criticized the Baltic states for discriminating against their Russian minorities. The dissatisfaction with the Baltic citizenship laws has already influenced the timetable according to which Russia is withdrawing its troops from the area (e.g. Wettig, 1993).

It is true that in some instances Yeltsin was compelled to yield to some of the nationalist, even chauvinist, demands. For example, several times he cancelled his visit to Japan after the latter made repeated demands for the return of the Northern territories annexed by the USSR during the last days of the Second World War. Yeltsin has also criticized Estonia's and Latvia's citizenship laws and threatened to stop the withdrawal of Russian troops from the area. Foreign minister Kozyrev has temporarily been even more outspoken. On the other hand it must be remembered that these moderate leaders have also emphasized the possibility of finding jointly acceptable solutions, whereas some more conservative critics have found no reason whatsoever for any compromises or negotiations.

Why was the USSR dissolved?

Because today's Russia continuously tries to solve the problems inherited from the Soviet period, it is necessary to analyze in detail the factors that contributed to the disintegration of the socialist system. It is not possible to find one grand explanation but, rather, attention must be paid to the simultaneous effect of several different factors. In this chapter, the dissolution is explained by five different factors (for a more detailed analysis, see Iivonen 1992, chapter 9). Ultimately the decline and fall of the Soviet Union occurred after several separate crises came to a head at the same time so that their effective solution became impossible.

First of all, the fall of the Soviet Union was caused by several ideological factors, especially by the fact that the social goals expressed in various ideological declarations were not materialized and that the discrepancy between the image expressed in the official ideology and its promises for the future and concrete reality grew larger and larger. The policies of perestroika tried to reduce this discrepancy, but too late, leading to the collapse of the entire socialist world system (cf. Chafetz, 1992). The original promise of the Marxist-Leninist ideology had been to transform a backward Russia into the most developed country in the world, a country in which the standard of living of the ordinary people would be higher than in any other industrialized Western country. In numerous declarations it was also promised that the Soviet power would rapidly develop into a global system. As a compensation for future welfare, for the prospect of having one day a 'paradise on earth' (i.e., the communist society) Soviet citizens were asked (or rather expected) to accept the suppression of their political rights, the suppression of their individual liberty. This was explained to be especially important because Soviet Russia after the revolution was surrounded by a group of 'hostile imperialist powers'. In this way, Soviet thinking was right from the beginning strongly attached to the categories of 'good' and 'bad', through which reality and its phenomena were then explained (Harle, 1992). All this meant that Soviet communism played its ideological role more and more poorly, becoming at a certain point an obstacle to all development efforts (Nowak, 1993). A great many observers have emphasized the fact that there was actually no connection between Soviet communism and original Marxism (Avineri, 1993).

The socialist experiment in Russia failed in the economic sphere as well. The centrally led socialist planning economy with its ideal of the equality of wages did not offer private citizens incentives that would have created prerequisites for permanent economic growth and the rationalization of production. The efforts to raise the level of productivity, i.e. to compensate for extensive growth by intensive growth, were doomed to fail right from the beginning. The stabilization of economy was also made difficult by the fact that the role of the military production was, from the point of view of the national economy, much too central (see Cooper, 1991). In addition, at the beginning of the 1980's as well as during the first years of perestroika the fatal mistake was made of assessing economic prospects too optimistically, resulting in the adoption of reform projects which were too extensive and too expensive. When the economic situation then rapidly deteriorated, there were no longer any real possibilities of carrying out these reforms. (On economic development during perestroika, see Åslund, 1991, and Verdery, 1993.)

The complete economic failure has been linked to the rapidly growing environmental crisis with its several negative implications in the former Soviet Union (Feshbach & Friendly, 1992; Turnbull, 1991). The seriousness of environmental problems was first realized during the last years of the Soviet power, along with the activation of public discussion on various problems in the Soviet Union. Before that the uncritical assurances from the ideological apparatus that in a scientifically led socialist society there was no room for environmental problems were widely believed both at home and abroad. The adoption of the Maxist-Leninist scientific world view gave Soviet society a right to use and exploit nature for the satisfaction of its needs in a planned and balanced way. In other words, ecological problems in a socialist society were impossible already by definition. However, this definition has proved to be fatally erroneous, as the Chernobyl accident in 1986 showed. After that the state of environment has dramatically deteriorated in various parts of the country, leading, for example, to a number of serious health problems.

The third factor to be mentioned is the failure to create a unified Soviet nation, that is, the failure of the official national policy. In the 27th Party Congress of the CPSU in February 1986, General Secretary Gorbachev was still giving assurances that the Soviet Union had permanently eliminated national suppression and inequality in all its manifestations (Gorbachev, 1986). However, less than one year later, violent national clashes started to occur in different parts of the country, taking soon openly political forms. As soon as the old party-led ideological apparatus collapsed, nationality (ethnicity) — in addition to religion — quickly became the most important focal point of political identification for the ordinary man in the street, determining to a very high degree his political behaviour as well.

Because a process of ethnic diversification had taken place in different parts of the country during the Soviet period, formal preconditions for extensive ethnic conflicts existed. The increasing national heterogeneity of the Soviet Union was due to (a) the deliberate official development and labour policy of the state (industrialization through Russian/Slavic workers), (b) the linking of border regions to the central powers by importing the Russian administrative and party elite, and (c) forced deportations of smaller national groups to completely new territories.

An additional reason for the growth of ethnic conflicts was the weakening of the all-union institutions and mechanisms that earlier played a central role in balancing various social interests and in settling disputes. According to recent Russian estimations, in the territory of the former Soviet Union there are at the moment about 30 armed conflicts. In addition, there are at least 40 situations that could develop into armed conflicts in the future (Fadin, 1993). While it has been difficult for Russians to admit the disappearance of its empire it can be anticipated that relations to former Soviet republics will remain tense. Especially critical in this respect are the Russian-Ukrainian relations (Solchanyk, 1992).

The fourth factor in the dissolution of the Soviet Union has been the collapse of the moral basis of the socialist society, in other words, its complete failure to create a new societal morality and a new man *(homo sovieticus)*. Instead of creating a collective man, devoted unselfishly to the socialist cause, a social apparatus based on coercion has driven people to utmost selfishness and neglect of others. The education that formally emphasized internationalist values led to the emergence of chauvinism, and enforced formal equality led to the collapse of the standard of living and thereby to exaggerated self-interest (Collias, 1991; Hayek, 1972, p. 102). The removal of these behavioural traits will be an exceptionally difficult process that very likely will last for several generations (see Heller, 1988; Rogatshi, 1991; Erasov, 1991).

Finally, various foreign political and international factors also speeded up the disintegration of the Soviet Union. Above it was mentioned that the Soviet economy was thoroughly militarized. The main reason for the disproportionate size of the military sector was the determination of the Soviet leadership to make their country — whatever the costs would be — militarily as powerful as the USA. Productive and technological resources necessary to reach this goal were, however, clearly more restricted than in the USA. After Ronald Reagan had been elected president of the USA at the end of 1980, the Soviet Union first tried to participate in the new round in the armaments race. The consequences became fatal, however. In a few years, the Soviet Union was forced to give up not only its military parity vis-à-vis the USA but also its alliance system in Eastern Europe and in the Third World. The political and military expansion of the Soviet Union in Ethiopia, Angola, Cambodia and Central America during the latter half of the 1970's proved to be a Pyrrhic victory. The positive image gained by the Soviet Union during the Vietnam war disappeared almost overnight. In many respects, the Soviet over-expansion therefore recalls that of the Roman and Ottoman empires (cf. Kennedy, 1990, p. xvi).

The state of the Russian political system

It can be argued that until autumn 1993, dramatic qualitative changes in reforming the Russian political system have so far been few. Formally many things were, of course, quite different compared to the situation before 1991. However, many of the changes remained only partial. Although Russia has adopted a multi-party system, the structures of the old socialist system are still effective, in particular at the local level. Even after the prohibition of the CPSU, former party leaders have often remained in power so that the majority of the leaders in the former Soviet republics are ex-communists. This shows that the creation of a civil society in Russia has been a much more difficult process than expected (see Lapidus 1989; Alapuro, 1993). All all-union organizations, that is, those functioning throughout the territory of the former Soviet Union, were naturally suspended. The original idea in December 1991 was to replace them by creating common defence and security forces as well as a partly centralized economic coordination and planning system for all CIS states.

The legislative and executive institutions of the newly independent former Soviet republics were in most cases direct copies of the respective institutions during the last years of Soviet power. Russia, for example, elected its own Congress of People's Deputies (CPD) in spring 1990. Its composition as well as functions were the same as those of the all-union CPD. While in many cases the members of the political elite are the same as before August 1991, the breakthrough of the new elite has so far been very difficult for many reasons (cf. Kagarlitsky, 1992; Burbach, 1993). In Russia, this competition between elites has been the main cause of the current severe political crisis: most of the members of the Russian CPD were very conservative opponents of Yeltsin's efforts to continue extensive political and economic reforms. Throughout the first half of 1993 Yeltsin seemed to lack the necessary leverage to organize new parliamentary elections.[2]

Yeltsin's domestic strategy between early 1992 and fall 1993 was based on two tactics. First, he tried to concentrate as much power as possible in his own hands either by assuming personal responsibility for important tasks or by appointing his supporters and allies to key posts. It was quite expected that the centralization of power in his own hands would soon lead to growing criticism — and this also happened. During the first months after the dissolution of the Soviet Union, Yeltsin acted as Russia's president, prime minister and minister of defence. In the CPD he was therefore repeatedly accused of deliberate efforts to increase his personal power.

Yeltsin's second tactic, attempted unsuccessfully by Gorbachev before him, was an equilibrium policy. In spite of his former critical stance towards Gorbachev and the conservatives, Yeltsin clearly avoided identification with one political group only and several times he compromised with the political centre. In December 1992, for example, he was ready to sacrifice his personal favourite Egor Gaidar as prime minister, agreeing instead to the election of Viktor Chernomyrdin — then thought of as a technocrat.[3] Simultaneously with the domestic balancing policy, Yeltsin several times appealed to Western governments for extensive economic and technological aid. He has warned that without this aid his administration is in danger of collapsing and that the conservatives would correspondingly be on their way to power. For the present, Western powers have acted accordingly. During the September-October 1993 crisis, for example, all Western governments supported Yeltsin's measures, providing that the dissolution of the CPD would not lead to the violation of human rights and the principles of democracy (New York Times, 23 September 1993). The immediate prohibition of a number of political organizations, newspapers and journals has not been seen as such a violation. The USA has more or less openly drawn a parallel between Yeltsin's presidency and US national interests (see Malia, 1993; Cohen, 1993).

Even after the defeat of the Parliament, Russia is still facing several problems concerning the reconstruction of the political system. First of all, the legislative reform is still badly incomplete. A new constitution was under preparation for several years, but no parliamentary discussion took place (see e.g. Topornin, 1993 and Senyakin, 1993). Yeltsin's original draft was rapidly followed by several competing texts and plans. It was assumed that as long as Russia had no new constitution confirming the democratic basis of the new society, the power struggle in the highest leadership would continue. It was obvious that conservative deputies in the CPD were not willing to enact such a constitution that would have deprived them of their power. Yeltsin's plan to promulgate a new constitution through direct negotiations with the regional and local bodies would naturally have made it possible to avoid the discussion in the CPD. With the support of the Constitutional Court the plan was able to contain most of the reform proposals (see Luchterhandt, 1993, and Brzezinski, 1993). This kind of negotiation process is an illustration of the art of compromise as an essential feature of Yeltsin's policy-making. But if it had continued in this form, an insecure state of dual power would have remained, in the same way as between the February and October Revolutions in 1917. Yeltsin's decisiveness in October 1993 showed, however, that comparing him to Alexander Kerensky is not appropriate.

Due to the difficulties in enacting the new constitution, all other legislative work has also remained substantially unfinished and incomplete. Several new laws were naturally enacted, but laws concerning such central activities as property rights, taxation, the banking system, citizen's basic rights and the position of minority nationalities have still remained ambiguous and left room for a variety of different interpretations and practices. The respect for law and order has also declined, as is shown by a growing crime rate (e.g. A Long Bloody Summer, 1993). As long as the situation remains like this, it was not possible to speak of the fundamental reform of Russia's political and legal system.

Furthermore, several references have already been made to the weaknesses of the Russian multi-party system. There has been a huge number of political parties and organizations in the country as such, but not a proper party system in the Western sense of the word. Russia's present political parties are not based on different ideologies but have rather been instruments for individual political leaders to strive for power. The situation has been quite similar in all former socialist countries in Eastern Europe (see Roskin, 1993). This might also explain why the total number of political parties in Russia can be estimated in hundreds rather than in dozens. For some time it has been obvious that their number will not decline without all-Russian parliamentary elections. Only the problem has been that until October 1993 it was difficult to find political groups influential enough to push for new elections. The Russian parliament was more than happy with the old situation because after new elections a large number of its members would very likely have lost their seats. Recent political parties, being organizationally still weak and having very limited resources, were also not ready for extensive election campaigns. Finally it must be remembered that the Russians, living in a permanent state of economic insecurity, were obviously much more interested in their daily living than in political contests, which — as many people think — did not really affect their daily life at all. This has been seen in several opinion polls, in which the credibility of the leading politicians and of the whole political system has remained exceptionally low (e.g. Byzov & Lvov, 1993).

In the territory of the former Soviet Union, ethnic conflicts have been one of the most difficult problems. Russian expansionism and efforts to dominate smaller nationalities and national groups have long historical roots dating back to medieval times (see Iivonen, 1994). Russians started to build an empire — a conglomeration of several nationalities — after the so-called Tatar yoke was lifted during the latter half of the fifteenth century. Russian expansionism to the East was strong during the sixteenth century and to the West since the reign of Peter the Great at the beginning of the eighteenth century. The idea of Moscow as 'the third Rome' gave Russians a divine right to acculturate smaller nationalities and extend the empire beyond them (see Agursky, 1987). Today some Russians believe that it is Russia's religious duty to support the Orthodox Serbs in the Yugoslav civil war. Along with the Bolsheviks' rise to power this divine right to rule over smaller nationalities found its expression in the Third or Communist International as well as in Soviet national policy, based formally on the principle of national self-determination. But what did this self-determination actually mean? According to Lenin, only two national groups within the Russian empire were mature and developed enough to be defined as nations in the spirit of the official Bolshevik definition formulated by Stalin in 1912 and therefore eligible to create a nation state of their own, namely Poland and Finland (Lenin, vol. 23, p. 315). For all other non-Russian national groups inside the Russian empire, self-determination actually meant only a right to join the victorious socialist revolution and assist the Soviet Russian state in building a developed socialist society and finally to reach the stage of communism, in which all ethnic differences and borders would gradually wither away.

Stalin — himself a Georgian — was the cruellest and most important Russifier of non-Russian nationalities (cf. Bullock, 1993). But even during other periods of Soviet rule, the Russian-dominated, all-union leadership in Moscow determined in a detailed way how the preservation of the ethnic identity of non-Russians would take place. Soviet national policy was in many ways something which could be called a 'folk dance national policy', in which only politically harmless forms of ethnic consciousness were allowed. If ethnic consciousness led, for example, to demands to divide power in a new way between Moscow and the regions, it was easily defined as bourgeois nationalism and was therefore something that had to be resisted by all available means. Both the formation of a new type of Soviet man, *homo sovieticus*, as well as the formation of the unitary Soviet people were utopias that could not be realized. They were only efforts to disguise the Communist monopoly of power and the Russification of non-Russian nationalities and ethnic groups. Because of that, old national symbols have been psychologically very important for non-Russian nationalities (see e.g. Krawchenko, 1990).

The national political system of the Soviet Union collapsed in a surprisingly short time. The movement for more extensive national rights proceeded in a very consistent way and without the all-union leadership being able to stop it. The first demands dealt with the right of different regions to have a larger say especially in economic decision-making. Later demands were extended to the domain of cultural identity and history. Beginning in 1988 various national fronts were formed in different republics and regions, then in 1989-1990 a new treaty of a union on a confederative basis was discussed (but not concluded). Finally, in 1991 political independence became the main goal of various national movements in non-Russian territories. During this process the Russians were more or less confused. They understood the demands for wider autonomy, but outright political independence was a demand that was very difficult for them to accept. In many statements Russia was seen as an altruistic helper of less developed non-Russian nationalities, whose will to independence was therefore interpreted as an outright expression of ingratitude.

This kind of thinking gave fresh nourishment to the growth of Russian national consciousness, which soon took on quite radical forms as well. This was seen already some years before the dissolution of the Soviet Union (see Szporluk, 1989). The so-called red-brown alliance, a pact between the left-wing communists (Stalinists) and the nationalist right, emerged in 1992. It is highly improbable that such an alliance was more than a tactical measure; it has even been argued that it was exactly the emergence of this alliance that showed that neither of these groups had enough power to have an impact on political developments (Bukowsky, 1993, p. 36). Since December 1991 this mood has had an inhibiting impact on Russia's relations with the former Soviet republics as well (see Motyl, 1991). Now that Yeltsin has been able to crush his opponents, it is possible to lift Russian relations with the former Soviet republics to a new level. However, the improvement of relations will not be an automatic process. So far we cannot know for sure what Yeltsin's foreign policy toward these new nations will be when internal constraints have disappeared. It might be that Russia wishes to conclude with them a 'special relationship' of the sort that it earlier had with East European socialist countries.

The stabilization of the Russian political system was further disturbed by the uncertainties of institutionalized cooperation with the former Soviet republics. Usually it has been believed that in the future the CIS cannot have more than a symbolic role, that it will be extremely difficult to create any institutional structures for it. Because of the difficulties in cooperation, the idea of the CIS as some kind of Eastern counterpart to the European Union has sounded too ambitious. One concrete piece of evidence was the failure to create joint armed forces for the CIS. The dispute between Russia and Ukraine regarding the principles of dividing the Soviet army still in the Ukraine is one example of several difficulties that can become very problematic in the future. Russia has therefore started to strengthen its ties to its newly independent neighbours in the southeast in particular, perhaps because they have no other options than to cooperate with Russia (Barylski, 1993; Rumer, 1993).

Finally it is necessary to recall once more several disagreements concerning the new Russian foreign policy still under formation, with regard to its basic principles as well as its procedures. The central question is, as mentioned before, whether Russia should concentrate on improving its relations with the West or whether it should pay more attention than before to its national interests and the position of Russian minorities in the former Soviet republics — or the 'near abroad' as they are now called (Kanet & Sounders, 1993; Cullen, 1993; Timmermann, 1993). Russian relations vis-à-vis other former Soviet republics have occasionally been rather tense. Russia still regards itself as a great power and wants to control developments in the neighbouring areas. Other republics feel uneasy when thinking of Russia's possible imperialist aims and the military resources at its disposal. The speech of foreign minister Andrei Kozyrev in December 1992 in the CSCE meeting in Stockholm can therefore be interpreted as one of several warnings of the worst case scenario for the future of Russia. Kozyrev especially warned about the growing strength of nationalistic thinking in Russia (Helsingin Sanomat, 16 December 1992).

Russia's development alternatives

The evaluation of Russia's various development alternatives has been exceptionally difficult due to the transformation of the development logic of both Russia and the whole international system. The socialist system with its one-party rule and command economy projected externally an image of high stability, the societal processes were permanent and the mechanisms regulating various disputes, based on coercion, seemed to function well. The situation changed, however, after Gorbachev launched his reform policy, when the sphere of politics was extended (politics was also extended beyond the sphere of pure administration) and, in the name of glasnost, political decision-making was made more open. During the first years of perestroika, the transformation still seemed to be quite deliberate and controlled. The situation

changed completely in August 1991, when insecurity and unpredicta-
bility became dominant features of Russian politics.

Because of the existence of several factors of uncertainty, the scenarios
presented in this article cannot be fixed, absolute or exclusive (cf. e.g.
Remes, 1990). The longer the time to be covered is, the larger the
number of these factors, making the presentation of reasonable alternatives more difficult and analysis more speculative. Because of these
uncertainties the scenarios in this article are limited to the next few
years. They are by their very nature not absolute — it is hardly probable
that they would be realized in a pure form. In addition, even rapid
transitions from one scenario to another are possible and even probable, as was shown in October 1993. The main function of these scenarios is, therefore, only to offer material for the evaluation of concrete
development during the next few years.

When discussing Russia's various development alternatives, it must
be remembered that many of its problems have been quite chronic and
therefore cannot be solved in a short time. This means that within the
next few years possibilities of solving certain problems are rather
limited. This has been especially true of Russia's economic depression
or chaos, which is bound to continue independently of the extensive
resources that Russia and some of the other former Soviet republics
have within their territories. The sad state of Russia's economic infrastructure has led to a situation in which certain export products (oil and
gas in particular), very important as means to obtain foreign currency,
have not been delivered to international markets. There have even been
problems in getting these products to domestic markets in adequate
amounts. In addition, the scarcity of capital and the difficulties in
re-educating the labour force can be mentioned as explanations for the
present situation.

In principle, Russia has five different development alternatives. Scenarios one and two represent varieties of non-controlled development
and scenarios three, four and five varieties of controlled development.

1. The zero option, which would mean that the present chaotic
   situation will continue more or less unchanged;

2. Fragmentation, which practically would mean that the central
   administration would become weaker vis-à-vis the regional level;

3. Continuation of a reform policy with a successful transition to political democracy and market economy;

4. A corporate agreement between different interest groups on the division of power and resources as well as an agreement on slowing down the most radical part of the reform policy;

5. The return to totalitarian rule on a nationalist, communist or bureaucratic-administrative basis.

Scenarios of non-controlled development

The zero option, that the situation would remain unchanged, would in practice mean a gradual decline of Yeltsin's position and the regionalization of power without any strong and organized opposition to him. The political development in the Soviet Union during the last years of perestroika (from 1988 to 1991) showed that it is not possible to preserve the balance of power in a situation where the social and political institutions are in a state of constant change. The zero option cannot be permanent because it presupposes immutable relations between different political powers as well as clear rules of the game. Neither of these have existed in post-communist Russia. If Russia's economic and political problems remained unsolved, pressures towards either increasing centralization or increasing disintegration would at a certain stage become too great to be contained. In such a case either the leadership would almost inconspicuously be replaced by a new one or its policy would become more conservative. Viktor Chernomyrdin's election as the prime minister in December 1992 was first mistakenly interpreted as a proof of the latter alternative.

Even continuing fragmentation in Russia would not necessarily lead to Russia's dissolution as an independent multinational state. It is completely possible that fragmentation would only mean more extensive regionalization of the decision-making power in such a way that the possibilities and eagerness of central authorities to intervene in regional decision-making would decline sharply. During the crisis of September 1993 regional leaders were more determined than ever to add to their earlier power. Yeltsin had already earlier tried to out-manoeuvre his conservative opponents by granting more decision-making to the regional level. The political and economic consequences of this decentralization could even be positive in nature. From the point of view of Russia's old neighbours, the so-called border cooperation and trade would receive much greater importance than before. Yeltsin's plans for future political arrangements imply that he is ready to increase the regional authority in order to preserve some kind of a federation between various parts of the country.

If the central leadership wanted to stop this fragmentation process, it would need adequate power resources and both the ability and the willingness to use them. President Yeltsin has had a lot of formal power in his hands; at certain stages he even had special authority to bypass the decisions of legislative bodies. In spite of the narrow legitimate basis of the CPD, it was able to slow down the reform process effectively. Even with his special authority Yeltsin was not always able to have his way. An example of this was the so-called Chechenian crisis (see Fuller, 1992). Yeltsin has also been unable to stop the growth of separatist ideas in certain autonomous areas inside Russia (e.g. in Tatarstan and Bashkortostan as well as in the republics of Tuva and Saha in Siberia), movements with even local Russian participants (see e.g. Vorontsov and Muradyan, 1992, and Davydov and Trenin, 1993).

Russia has also been unable to restrain the spreading violence and armed clashes in certain former Soviet republics; in autumn 1993 both Georgia and Tadzhikistan were in a state of civil war. There has, on the contrary, been a danger that Russian troops would also be drawn into the fighting. Especially Georgia has accused Russian troops (not necessarily government troops, however) of taking part in the struggles in Abkhazia. In the same way, in the Tadzikhistan civil war in 1993 Russian 'peace keepers' were active in the area so that fears of even an outright war between Tadzhikistan (Russia) and Afghanistan have gradually been growing.

If the fragmentation inside the Russian federation led to extensive armed conflicts, as has already happened in the Caucasus and the Central East, then this scenario would be rather unpleasant. In addition, several economic and environmental problems would also continue, slowing down the economic recovery and thereby affecting social conditions as well as environmental protection. In the field of foreign policy, this scenario would not automatically lead to either isolation or increasing cooperation. The international and national consequences of this scenario depend to a very high degree on the

extent to which the centrifugal development inside the Russian federation can be controlled.

Scenarios of controlled development

Controlled development in Russia can in principle be realized in three
different ways. The third alternative above, the continuation of the
reform policy, would mean that in Russia (and possibly in some other
former Soviet republics as well) a new civil society would emerge,
based on principles of political democracy, private property and freedom of enterpreneurship. The reform policies would continue at best
as some sort of liberalist transition to a market economy with rapid
privatization and the liberation of prices and wages. This would mean,
however, that it would not be possible to control certain social problems
of the transition period efficiently, because of which inequality and
other social disturbances would increase at least temporarily. Very
many observers find this to be unavoidable, if real improvement is to
take place in the economies of former socialist countries (see Bouillon,
1992).

According to the fourth scenario, the Russian political and economic
system would be developed on the basis of a collective interest group
agreement. It would mean that the most influential interest groups
(state-led industrial enterprises, labour unions, the bureaucratic apparatus, army and security organs, etc.) would jointly agree on the new
division of economic and political resources. The goal would be to
create for Russia a new guidance mechanism that would permit the
centralized allocation of scarce resources and thus push the development in the desired direction. A central role in this respect has been
played by the Civic Union (*Grazhdanskii Soyuz*). Its goal has been to act
as an organizational basis for such an agreement. Especially in 1992 it
was able to exert a lot of influence on Russia's political development.
One of its most influential figures has been Arkadi Volsky, chairman of
the influential Russian Union of Industrialists and Entrepreneurs. In
November 1992 Volsky declared: 'Power belongs to those who have
property and money. At present it is not the government but the
industrial managers who have both' (Financial Times, 2 November
1992). It is worth noting that during the October coup attempt, the Civic
Union assumed a very low profile.

Russia's first experiences with a genuine party system date back to the first decade of the twentieth century, to the time when the modern party system emerged in Europe in general. In spite of certain limitations of its political system at that time, Russia had quite a variety of political parties, usually based on a variety of ideological preferences. These parties took part in several Duma elections and soon after the October Revolution also in the election of the Constituent Assembly. The aim of the Bolsheviks — a minority group in the freely elected Assembly — was to gain the monopoly of power. It led to the creation of a one-party rule in the beginning of the 1920's (see Carr, 1950, vol. 1; Walicki, 1980). After that the Soviet Union became a one-party state, in which not only competing parties but even fractions inside the ruling party were declared illegal and their membership was severely punished, especially during Stalin's reign. The one-party system ruled up to the end of the 1980's, when the sixth paragraph of the Soviet Constitution was finally rewritten so that other political parties, in addition to the Communists, became legal. But even then it was believed that the Communist Party would still be the leading party.

As said before, during the last three or four years a huge number of different political parties have been formed in Russia (Pribylovskii, op. cit.). It is very difficult to state unambigiously their exact number, but the most common figure seems to be around 400. These 400 parties are not, however, political parties in the Western European sense of the word. First of all, Russian political parties are not usually based on ideological premises. They have often adopted very Western-type names (such as the infamous Liberal-Democratic party of Vladimir Zhirinovsky), but they have no resemblance to similar parties in the West. Second, the programmes of these parties are either ambiguous or totally non-existent. Third, the parties do not have unambiguous rules according to which they function. Fourth, the legislation on political parties and their activities is inadequate. Fifth, Russian parties are very small in size — very often they have only from twenty to fifty members. Sixth, because of their small size, the parties are territorially limited and very few of them have effective organizations throughout Russia. Finally, because Russian parties are not based on ideological premises, they concentrate very heavily on a few individuals, political leaders who want to have their own political movements to support their own desire for power. Russian politics all in all is very leader- or person-oriented, people make their political choices (whenever they have an opportunity to do it) between different individuals (or their images), not between different ideologies or social and political programmes. Russian parties are organizations, created with the purpose to support their leaders in their efforts to gain more power and influence.

Because Russian political parties in general are leader-oriented and both ideologically and programmatically ambiguous, their ability to reflect various social interests is also relatively low. And because the parties do not have a broad membership basis, their internal administrative structures are very underdeveloped as well. In such a situation conflicts between different leaders inside a party can have very fatal consequences; no efforts have been made to conciliate conflicts. Instead, they are solved through expulsions from the party. Because of that, the whole party system is in a state of constant flux and unable to take a leading role in the construction of the new society. In addition, nothing seems to imply that the situation would soon improve. Only democratic and free all-Russian elections will force political parties and their leaders into real cooperation, leading to an overall rationalization of the party system.

The underdeveloped character of the party system is not the only political problem Russia should solve as soon as possible. Another political problem has been the low credibility of political leaders and organizations, even the credibility of the whole post-communist political system. After the power struggle flared up again in spring 1993, Yeltsin seemed more and more to be the only politician who has at least some kind of political credibility. But even that does not make him irreplaceable — Gorbachev was also believed to be irreplaceable up to August 1991, and today he is one of the least liked politicians in Russia. All politicians except Yeltsin are either strongly disliked or ignored by the majority of the population. Yeltsin and his allies have, on the other hand, been extremely disliked among certain Russian politicians (Rutskoi, 1993). When the dispute with the parliament seemed to drag on and on, even Yeltsin's credibility was more and more on the agenda. It is therefore quite possible that his determination in this crisis situation has brought him new supporters.

According to the fifth scenario, the perpetual disintegration of administrative and economic structures could be stopped by constructing a new totalitarian system of government, which can be based — as stated before — on a nationalist, communist or bureaucratic-administrative restoration. This scenario could not be realized without calling off extensive political and economic reforms that have been begun during the last few years. The possibility of a totalitarian restoration was on the agenda already before the coup attempt in 1991. In principle, totalitarian restoration could be carried out in three ways or rather by three different organized groups. First, it could mean the revival of various communist organizations to such a degree that they can take advantage of the internal turmoil in Russia and return to power. Second, totalitarian restoration could take place through a military coup and administration, for example, as a joint effort of the army and the security organs (see Barylski, 1992). Third, totalitarian rule could be based on a radical chauvinist (great-Russian) administration.[4] All kinds of coalitions between these three forces are also possible, at least theoretically.

In spite of several speculations on the matter, the possibilities of a totalitarian restoration seemed limited, although not completely impossible, already before October 1993. A number of factors spoke against it. First of all, it must be remembered that the support of these forces and groups has been rather low. Old communists and various ultra-national groups have now and then been able to organize visible demonstrations which have been widely reported in the world media. In various opinion polls their support has been very limited, however, and their leaders have regularly been the most unpopular politicians in the whole country. The communists have split into several competing organizations after the CPSU was outlawed (Medvedev, 1992).

It is also obvious that some of Yeltsin's earlier political moves have effectively restricted the manoeuvring room of these groups. Especially his compromise with the Civic Union in December 1992 prevented a strong anti-government coalition from emerging. The referendum in April 1993 was another occasion where Yeltsin won a victory over the totalitarian forces. Although because of some constitutional tricks he did not get enough votes to declare new parliamentary elections, he got enough votes to start new processes (new constitution, etc.) that in due time made it even more difficult for the totalitarians to regain power. Finally in October 1993 it became clear to everyone that these groups did not have support even inside the Russian army.

What about the role of the army and security organs in the future? The events of 1991 showed that the Soviet army no longer constituted a compact force and interest group. It had become clear to its members that the armed forces had lost their former privileged status in society and in the allocation of resources. While some of the highest army and KGB leaders had supported the coup, at lower levels there was enough opposition to prevent their open involvement. After that there was a virtual purge inside the army and security organs. After some new institutional arrangements (the KGB was divided into four new organizations, etc.), the army and security organs have effectively been stripped of their former power (Yasmann, 1992). There are some officers and organizations inside the army that still have a very critical attitude towards Yeltsin's policy, but they are in no position to prevent or seriously limit his activities. Quite the contrary, he seems to have succeeded in occupying most central positions with his allies, one reason for his victory in October 1993. It is, in other words, highly probable that none of these three 'conservative' groups, either separately or together, could have prevented democratization and market reform in Russia. The totalitarians have, no doubt, been loud and visible, but politically weak and heterogeneous. In spite of that, these groups have been able to considerably slow down Russia's gradual development towards political democracy.

As a conclusion it can be said that two scenarios presented above seem to be most obvious after Yeltsin crushed his conservative opposition in October 1993, namely 1) the collective interest group agreement on one hand or 2) the fragmentation of political power on the other. While political parties still are incapable of policy-making, real power is necessarily concentrated in the hands of various interest groups, the central administration led by Yeltsin being the most powerful of them. But even Yeltsin is dependent on certain interest groups — army, security organs, the central bureaucracy and industrialists — and therefore still in a vulnerable position. It must also be remembered that Russia's recent economic problems are so large that the central administration in Moscow will have enormous difficulties in solving them. Various regions, after gaining more independence than ever before in history, are certainly unwilling to yield it back to Moscow. They are convinced that they themselves have the best possibilities of solving these problems and of guaranteeing that the income from their resources will be used in an appropriate way. This means that with a very high probability fragmentation will continue although it will not necessarily lead to the complete dissolution of Russia in the same way as in the case of the Soviet Union.

Notes

1. Soviet policy immediately after the October revolution was based on issuing various decrees *(dekrety)*, because other organs of power were still absent. In such a decree policy there is no clear separation between the legislative and executive powers.

2. On 21 September in a TV speech Yeltsin announced that he had decided to dissolve the parliament and set 11-12 December as a date for new elections (New York Times, 22 September 1993). Two days later he announced that new presidential elections will be held in June 1994 (New York Times, 24 September 1993). Ten days later, this announcement led to an armed coup attempt by the parliament.

3. Against several expectations, Chernomyrdin has remained exceptionally loyal to Yeltsin's reform policy and is nowadays severely criticized by the conservatives. His popularity has also been relatively high. Gaidar succeeded in getting a position in the government in September 1993, becoming the first deputy prime minister.

4. A central role in the revival of Russian nationalism has been played by the Nobel laureate Alexander Solzhenitsyn. His relatively moderate programme has received a lot of support (Ericson, 1992; Davis & Byrd, 1992). In October 1993 he demanded that the communists should be purged from Russian politics (New York Times, 5 October 1993). For a general introduction to Russia's nationalist movements, see Laqueur, 1993.

References

Agursky, Mihail (1987), *The Third Rome. National Bolshevism in the USSR*, Westview Press, Boulder.

Alapuro, Risto (1993), 'A Civil Society in Russia?' in Iivonen, Jyrki (ed.), *The Future of the Nation State in Europe*, Edward Elgar, Aldershot.

Alexandrova, Olga (1993), 'Entwicklung der Aussenpolitischen Konzeptionen Russlands', Berichte des Bundesinstituts für ostwissenshaftliche und internationale Studien, no. 8/1993.

Avineri, Shlomo (1992), 'Capitalism Has Not Won, Socialism Is Not Dead', *Dissent*, Winter 1992.

Barylski, Robert V. (1992), 'The Soviet Military before and after the Coup: Departization and Decentralization', *Armed Forces & Society*, vol. 19, no. 1, Fall 1992.

Barylski, Robert V. (1993), 'Central Asia and the Post-Soviet Military System in the Formative Year 1992', *Central Asia Monitor*, no. 6/1992.

Bouillon, Hardy (1992), 'The Postcommunist Sociopolitical System of Eastern European States', *International Journal of World Peace*, vol. 9, no. 2, June 1992.

Brzezinski, Mark F. (1993), 'Toward "Constitutionalism" in Russia: the Russian Constitutional Court', *International and Comparative Law Quarterly*, vol. 42, part 3, July 1993.

Bukowsky, Vladimir (1993), 'Boris Yeltsin's Hollow Victory', *Commentary*, vol. 95, no. 6/1993.

Bullock, Alan (1993), *Hitler and Stalin. Parallel Lives*, Fontana Press, London.

Burbach, Roger (1993), 'Russia's Upheaval', *Monthly Review*, vol. 44, no. 9, February 1993.

Byzov, L. & Lvov, N. (1993), *Referendum: byt ili ne byt? Obzor rezultatov issledovaniia, provedennogo Fondom 18-23 Fevralia v razlichnih regionah Rossii*, Rossiskii Fond Kostitutsionnih Reform, mimeo.

Carr, E.H. (1950), *The Bolshevik Revolution 1917-1923*, vol. 1, Macmillan, London.

Chafetz, Glenn R. (1992), 'Soviet Ideological Revision and the Collapse of Communism in Eastern Europe', *International Relations*, vol. XI, no. 2, August 1992.

Cohen, Stephen F. (1993), 'Illusions and Realities: American Policy and Russia's Future', *The Nation*, 12 April 1993.

Collias, Karen A. (1991), 'Patriotic and Internationalist Education in the Formation of a Soviet State Identity' in Huttenbach, Henry R. (ed.), *Soviet Nationality Policies. Ruling Ethnic Groups in the USSR*, Mansell, London.

Cooper, Julian (1991), *The Soviet Defence Industry. Conversion and Reform*, Frances Pinter, London.

Cullen, Robert (1993), 'Russia Confronts Its "Near Abroad"', *The Nation*, 20 September 1993.

Davis, Beth & Byrd, Richard W. (1992), 'From the Czars to the Commissars: The Growth of Dissent inside Russia and the Impact of Alexander Solzhenitsyn on the Disintegration of the Soviet Union', *Lamar Journal of the Humanities*, vol. 18, no. 2, Fall 1992.

Dawydow, Jurij P. & Trenin, Dimitrij W. (1993), 'Ethnische Konflikte auf dem Gebiet der ehemaligen Sowjetunion. Muster, Aussichten und wahrscheinliche Konsequenzen für das Ausland', *Europa-Archiv*, 48. Jahr, no. 7/1993.

Different Development Alternatives in Russia and their Influence on Finnish-Russian Relations in the 1990's (1992), Finnish Institute of International Affairs, Helsinki.

Erasov, Boris (1991), 'Russia and the Soviet Union: Civilizational Dimensions', *Comparative Civilizations Review*, no. 25, Fall 1991.

Ericson, Edward E., Jr. (1992), 'Solzhenitsyn and the Rebuilding of Russia', *The Intercollegiate Review*, vol 27, no. 2, Spring 1992.

Fadin, Andrej (1993), 'Spasmen der Gewalt. Der soziale Sinn der Postsowjetischen Kriege', *Blätter für deutsche und internationale Politik*, Heft 7/1993.

Feshbach, Murray & Friendly, Alfred Jr. (1992), *Ecocide in the USSR. Nature under Siege*, Basic Books, New York.

Fuller, Elizabeth (1992), 'Georgia, Abkhazia, and Checheno-Ingushetia', *RFE/RL Research Report*, vol. 1, no. 6/1992.

Gorbachev, Mihail (1986), *Muutosten aika. Puheita ja kirjoituksia*, Weilin & Göös, Espoo.

Halliday, Fred (1993), 'Russian Foreign Policy: Who's Driving the Troika?', *The Nation*, 8 March 1993.

Harle, Vilho (1992), *Hyvä, paha, ystävä, vihollinen*, Rauhan- ja konfliktintutkimuslaitos, Tampere.

Hayek, Friedrich v. (1972), *Road to Serfdom*, The University of Chicago Press, Chicago.

Heller, Mihail (1988), *Cogs in the Wheel. The Formation of Soviet Man*, Alfred A. Knopf, New York.

Iivonen, Jyrki (1989), 'Gorbachev's Personnel Policy' in Hill, Ronald J. & Dellenbrant, Jan Åke (eds.), *Gorbachev and Perestroika*, Edward Elgar, Aldershot.

Iivonen, Jyrki (1992), *Neuvostovallan viimeiset vuodet*, Gaudeamus, Helsinki.

Iivonen, Jyrki (1994), 'Expansionism and Russian Imperial Tradition' in Forsberg, Tuomas (ed.), *Contested Territories. The Post-Cold War Position of the Territories Annexed by the Soviet Union in the Second World War*, Edward Elgar, Aldershot (forthcoming).

Kagarlitsky, Boris (1992), *Disintegration of the Monolith*, Verso, London.

Kanet, Roger E. & Sounders, Brian V. (1993), 'Russia and Her Western Neighbours. Relations among Equals or a New Form of Hegemony?', *Demokratizatsiya. The Journal of Post-Soviet Democratization*, vol. 1, no, 3/1993.

Kennedy, Paul (1990), *The Rise and Fall of Great Powers. Economic Change and Military Conflict from 1500 to 2000*, Fontana Press, London.

Krawchenko, Bohdan (1990), 'National Memory in Ukraine: The Role of the Blue and Yellow Flag', *Journal of Ukrainian Studies*, vol. 15, no. 1, Summer 1990.

Lapidus, Gail (1989), 'State and Society: Toward the Emergence of Civil Society in the Soviet Union' in Bialer, Seweryn (ed.), *Politics, Society, and Nationality inside Gorbachev's Russia*, Westview Press, Boulder.

Laqueur, Walter (1993), 'Gorbachev and Epimethus: The Origins of the Russian Crisis', *Journal of Contemporary History*, vol. 28, no. 3, July 1993.

Laqueur, Walter (1993), *Black Hundred: The Rise of the Extreme Right in Russia*, Edward Burlingame Books, New York.

Lenin, V.I., 'Tezisy po natsionalnomu voprosu', *Polnoe sobranie sochinenii*.

'A Long, Bloody Summer', *Newsweek*, 30 August 1993.

Luchterhandt, Otto (1993), 'Vom Verfassungskomitee der UdSSR zum Verfassungsgerich Rußlands', *Archiv des öffentlichen Rechts*, 188. Band, Heft 2, Juni 1993.

Malia, Martin (1993), 'Apocalypse Not', *The New Republic*, 22 February 1993.

Matveyev, Vladimir (1992), 'New Russian Diplomacy: The First Months', *International Relations*, vol. XI, no. 2. August 1992.

Medvedev, Roy (1992), 'After the Communist Collapse. New Political Tendencies in Russia', *Dissent*, Fall 1992.

Morrison, John (1991), *Boris Yeltsin. From Bolshevik to Democrat*, Dutton, New York.

Motyl, Alexander J. (1991), 'Russian Hegemony and Non-Russian Insecurity: Foreign Policy Dilemmas of the USSR's Successor States', *The Harriman Institute Forum*, vol. 5, no. 4, December 1991.

Mullerson, Rein (1993), 'The Continuity and Succession of States by Reference to the Former USSR and Yugoslavia', *International and Comparative Law Quarterly*, vol. 42, part 3, July 1993.

Nowak, Leszek (1993), 'Real Marxism in Real Socialism', *The Centennial Review*, vol. 37, no. 1, Winter 1993.

Olson, Mancur (1993), 'Dictatorship, Democracy, and Development', American Political Science Review, vol. 87, no. 3, September 1993.

Pribylovskii, Vladimir (1992), *Dictionary of Political Parties and Organizations in Russia*, PostFactum/Interlegal, Moscow.

Remes, Seppo (1990), *Neuvostoliiton tulevaisuuden vaihtoehtoiset skenaariot. Vaikutukset ulkomaankauppaan ja suomalais-neuvostoliittolaisiin taloussuhteisiin*, Turun kauppakorkeakoulun julkaisuja, sarja A, Turku.

Remnick, David (1993), *Lenin's Tomb: The Last Days of the Soviet Empire*, Random House, New York.

Rogatshi, Inna (1991), *Särkynyt sukupolvi. Kymmenen käskyä Neuvostoliitossa*, Otava, Helsinki.

Rogatshi, Inna (1992), 'Katsaus nyky-Venäjän poliittisten puolueiden kirjoon', *Ulkopolitiikka*, no. 2/1992.

Roskin, Michael G. (1993), 'The Emerging Party Systems of Central and Eastern Europe', *East European Quarterly*, vol. 27, no. 1, Spring 1993.

Rumer, Boris Z. (1993), 'The Gathering Storm in Central Asia', Orbis, vol. 37, no. 1, Winter 1993.

Rusi, Alpo (1991), *After the Cold War — Europe's New Political Architecture*, Macmillan, London.

Rutskoi, Aleksandr (1993), 'Rossiia, skazhi mafii "net"!', *Molodaia gvardiia*, no. 7/1993.

Sachs, Jeffrey (1993), 'Moscow Meltdown', *The New Republic*, 23 & 30 August 1993.

Schapiro, Leonard (1967), *Rationalism and Nationalism in the Nineteenth Century Russian Thought*, Yale University Press, New Haven.

Senyakin, I.N. (1993), 'Problemy spetsializatsii i unifikatsii rosiiskogo zakonodatelstvo', *Gosudarstvo i pravo*, no. 5/1993.

Solchanyk, Roman (1992), 'Back to the USSR?', *The Harriman Institute Forum*, vol. 6, no. 3, November 1992.

Stankevich, Sergei (1992), 'Russia in Search for Itself', *The National Interest*, no. 28. Summer 1992.

Szporluk, Roman (1989), 'Dilemmas of Russian Nationalism', Problems of Communism, vol. 37, July-August 1989.

Timmermann, Heinz (1993), 'Die Außenpolitik Rußlands. Ausdruck der Suche nach einer neuen Identität', *Berichte des Bundesinstituts für ostwissenschaftliche und internationale Studien*, no. 20/1993.

Topornin, Boris (1993), 'Problems of Constitutional Reform in the Former USSR', *Coexistence*, vol. 30, no. 1, March 1993.

Turnbull, Mildred (1991), *Soviet Environmental Policies and Practices. The Most Critical Investment*, Dartmouth, Aldershot.

Walicki, Andrzej (1980), *A History of Russian Thought from the Enlightenment to Marxism*, Oxford University Press, Oxford.

Wettig, Gerhard (1993), 'Der russische Truppenrückung aus den baltischen Staaten', *Berichte des Bundesinstituts für ostwissenschaftliche und internationale Studien*, no. 8/1993.

Verdery, Katherine (1993), 'What Was Socialism and Why Did It Fall?', *Contention*, vol. 3, no. 1, Fall 1993.

Vihavainen, Timo (1990), 'Russia and Europe: A Historiographic Aspect' in Harle, Vilho & Iivonen, Jyrki (eds.), *Gorbachev and Europe*, Frances Pinter, London.

Vorontsov, V. & Muradyan, A. (1992), 'Far Eastern Regionalism', *Far Eastern Affairs*, no. 1/1992.

Väyrynen, Raimo (1993), 'Kylmästä sodasta uuteen maailmanjärjestykseen. Suomen ulkopolitiikan kansainvälinen ympäristö' in Forsberg, Tuomas & Vaahtoranta, Tapani (eds.), *Johdatus Suomen ulkopolitiikkaan*, Gaudeamus, Helsinki.

Yasmann, Viktor (1992), 'The KGB and Internal Security', *RFE/RL Research Report*, vol. 1, no. 1/1992.

Zubok, Vladislav (1992), 'Tyranny of the Weak: Russia's New Foreign Policy', *World Policy Journal*, vol. IX, no.2, Spring 1992.

Åslund, Anders (1991), 'Gorbachev, Perestroika, and Economic Crisis', *Problems of Communism*, vol. 40, January-April 1991.

4 The Economic Transition in Russia

Pekka Sutela

The presentation in this chapter is intentionally simplifying and general. The chapter is limited to a four-part discussion of Russian economic transformation in the narrow sense of the word 'economic'. First we outline the prevailing orthodoxy on transition from a centrally managed economy to a market economy. Russian economic policies in 1992-93 are then outlined against this background, followed by a discussion of the reasons for the failure of orthodoxy in Russia. The article ends with cautious guesses concerning the future.

The IMF orthodoxy

Almost immediately after 1989, a widely shared opinion emerged on how to transform previously centrally managed economies (PCMEs) into market economies (MEs). Even if the emerging orthodoxy also has had its critics, it still determines economic policies in most transition economies, in particular in those with the best degree of success so far. As the orthodoxy is most explicitly set down in those criteria of economic policy conditionality that a client country has to fulfil in a stabilization programme in order to be eligible for International Monetary Fund financing, these views will here be called IMF orthodoxy.

The existence of a stabilization programme is usually a precondition for all foreign official lending. Practice has also shown that private financing does not often reach countries pursuing policies fundamentally at odds with the views of the Monetary Fund. The role of the IMF as a gatekeeper is much more important than the rather humble amounts of finance available through the Fund might seem to imply. It would, however, not seem appropriate to conclude that what we see is just another imperialist plot to force ignorant, stupid, corrupt or just weak governments into the capitalist cobweb of the world economy. IMF support — as any other outside support — can be effective in reaching its goals only if domestic governments have really and credibly committed themselves to a policy line seen to be fundamentally sane. Understanding this is of particular importance in discussing Russia.

The roots of the IMF orthodoxy are not difficult to fathom. The organization has had much experience with economic stabilization in Latin America and elsewhere. The practical results of this policy have not been uniform, but a basic alternative has failed to appear. There is also a degree of experience with programmes of partial economic liberalization and privatization in various corners of the world. Furthermore, we know quite a lot about the way in which PCMEs used to function, how they were reformed, and how these reforms succeeded and failed. Finally, one uses both common and economists' sense on how centrally managed economies differed from MEs, how possible changes are interconnected and which are the economic, political and social preconditions under which policies have to be planned, implemented, appraised, and corrected.

The prevailing orthodoxy on transition is a fresh one. It first came into being in Poland after the autumn of 1989. There is no typical country in transition, and Poland also had its important peculiarities. The country was in hyperinflation or just about to lapse into one. That means that the local currency, the zloty, was about to lose its credibility, not only as a store of value but also as a means of exchange, and currency substitution, dollarization, was far advanced. Control over money supply is, however, most useful for economic policy, and stopping hyperinflation by restoring the lost honour of the zloty was therefore of prime importance. Another Polish peculiarity was a private sector of notable size. The necessary preconditions for normal capitalist development had to be created for it. The economy, thus, had to be liberalized. Opening up to foreign competition was also of great importance. The population of the country accepted the necessary, even if to a high degree bitter policy measures for many reasons. Among them was the crucial recent change in the politics of the country, which gave the government strong, even if not everlasting support among the people.

The Polish stabilization programme had many fathers. Most if not all of them agreed on most of its ingredients. Essentially it was a home-made programme created under the leadership of Leszek Balcerowicz, the minister of finance. The advice of international financial organizations was important, especially in deciding upon the technicalities of policy measures. Other foreign advisors had an important role in particular in securing international visibility and support.

About a year later a very similar programme was accepted for Czechoslovakia. This is interesting, as Czechoslovakia did not need to grapple either with hyperinflation or dollarization. Neither could opening up of the economy — for many reasons — have the same priority as in Poland. Hungarian economic policies have had yet another rhetoric and background, but on the level of actual policies the differences between these three Eastern Central European countries are substantially smaller than often assumed.

Transition is a recent phenomenon. Still, it already has its myths. The notion that the hand of Jeffrey Sachs, the Harvard economist, is directing everything is one of them. The portrayal of Hungary and Poland as the ideal types of gradualism and shock therapies is another of the myths of transition.

It is useful to characterise the IMF orthodoxy as a menu of four courses. The meal consists of stabilization, liberalization, privatization, and structural change. In the case of newly independent countries, a fifth course also emerges, that of independence. The orthodoxy also contains views on the sequencing of these courses into a consistent process over time.

Stabilization

Consider, for a moment, the fundamentals of economics. Put very simply, the existence of a market economy presupposes (a) the existence of economic agents with sufficient independence that they can react consistently and in a foreseeable way to signals encountered, (b) the existence of institutions facilitating communication and the emergence of signals and (c) the emergence of an information system transforming signals into a whole. The first point is an issue of property rights, the second an issue of markets and prices and the third concerns money.

These points are not just of academic importance. As we shall see later, the basic problem in the Russian economy recently has been the non-existence of well defined property rights and money. Therefore, markets have not been able to function properly.

Centrally managed economies were, as defined by Janos Kornai, economies of shortage. Their inherent imbalance worsened with the implementation of the kind of economic reforms which typically meant the increasing of insider — managerial and partly employee — prerogatives without substituting the former hierarchic discipline by constraints created by markets, competition, and effective demand. Plants utilized their newly-found rights by raising prices and wages. Paying taxes was often neglected. Consequently, budget deficits ballooned. Inflation was fed directly by the wage-price spiral and indirectly by monetizing budget deficits in the absence of other possibilities of finance. Inflation was partially open, but in as far as price fixity was maintained, inflation became repressed by creating purchasing power without sufficiently desirable objects. At worst, political and institutional instability led to the brink of hyperinflation, as evidenced by Poland in 1989 and by Russia in 1991-92.

The principles of stabilization are well-known and almost beyond doubt. If a country has monetary overhang due to repressed inflation, this overhang has to be neutralized either by offering new supplies, by instituting a confiscatory monetary reform or by accepting open inflation. So far at least, the first alternative has been impractical. All countries in transition have until now selected the last alternative to solve this, the so-called stock problem of imbalance.

But there is also a flow problem of imbalance, the ongoing reproduction of imbalance. Two economically fundamental but politically and socially often inconvenient actions are needed here. Money supply must be brought under control. The central bank must identify stabilizing the monetary supply, not for instance creating jobs or maintaining production, as its task. On the other hand, the budget must be brought into balance, or at least nearly so. Typically, both drastic cutting of expenses and the creation of such a taxation system that would be simple, transparent and perhaps based on taxing expenditure, are needed. Third, statistical real wages have to be cut and the emergence of a wage-price spiral must be prevented. This is usually best done through incomes policies.

Contrary to recurrent claims, a drop in statistical real incomes — nominal incomes divided by a suitable price index — does not necessarily imply a drop in consumption or welfare. One must also keep in mind any changes in the availability and quality of goods, in the distribution of consumption possibilities, in the time used for securing commodities and in the general quality and security of living. Arguing that the Russian standard of living at the end of 1992 was one half of that a year earlier is outright ridiculous, even if one might find some corroboration for that in published real income statistics.

One may also wish to note that stabilization à la the IMF orthodoxy is not a monetarist or liberalist doctrine. Things like incomes policies do not go well together with these doctrines.

The experiences which we have had show almost beyond doubt that the idea of gradual stabilization is usually neither economically nor politically realistic. Stabilization is simply best done as a shock. But experience also shows that stabilization is usually beyond the powers of weak governments. Therefore it must be embarked upon when the popularity of the government is at its strongest and resolve most determined. If ever, these conditions may be best fulfilled immediately after fundamental political change.

Purely economical reasons also dictate that stabilization should be implemented right at the beginning of transition policies. It is, after all, a question of credible money and foreseeable prices. Almost nothing can function properly in a market economy in the absence of these fundamentals. A comparison across economies in transition shows that those countries with the strictest stabilization programmes — Poland and the Czech republic — have not only the best inflation record but also the least losses in terms of production. Furthermore, hyperinflation, privatization and structural change simply do not go together. It is sometimes argued that Russia should have privatized and demonopolized the economy before attempting stabilization. This is a castle in the air, built without any regard for its chances of survival.

Liberalization

Another series of actions to be sequenced towards the early phase of transition is the liberalization of prices, entrepreneurship, and foreign trade. Market-based prices are quintessential for a market economy. Because price liberalization is in any case inevitable, it should be for both economical and political reasons undertaken as early as possible. Stabilization and liberalization belong together. Stabilizing the budget may well be impossible without abolishing price subsidies, which have in some cases grown immense. But the connection also runs the other way: liberalization without stabilization is a recipe for hyperinflation.

Entrepreneurship should be liberalized, because an inordinate share of normal economic activities were forbidden under the old regime. And finally, there are many reasons for liberalizing foreign trade. Among them are subjecting domestic monopolies to import competition, minimizing unnecessary administration and ensuing rent-seeking and corruption, the importance of technology and know-how as well as integration into the world economy, which is deemed necessary also for political reasons.

The liberalization of foreign trade has probably been the major source of welfare during the last centuries. Import substitution policies for a closed economy have thoroughly failed to deliver welfare. This is the substance of the so-called Washington Consensus in development economics. Still, the position of foreign trade liberalization in transition sequencing is probably that part of the IMF orthodoxy which has been under debate for the best reasons.

The Washington Consensus on speedy opening up, foreign sector liberalization and currency convertibility has come under increasing criticism. Critics usually refer to the success of the Southeast Asian tigers. Developments there have been based both on government activism and on import substitution, especially in the early phase of industrialization.

The experience of Eastern Central Europe shows that rapid opening up is feasible. Already in a couple of years, the ensuing export growth can become an engine of growth, and access to Western markets correspondingly an important constraint. This seems to have been the case both in Poland and in the Czech republic. On the other hand it is obvious that countries vary in their capacity to bear the risks of opening up. One thing should be obvious, though it is far from being that. Russia and other former Soviet republics (FSRs) are no Southeast Asian countries. They fail to have a far-reaching consensus on the social end state aspired to. Their governments seldom have the resources needed for state activism, as even tax collection may be beyond their powers. Neither would they seem to have the capacity to decide upon the structural change needed for active industrial policies. And how could they possibly direct their foreign trade 'as the Japanese do,' as the FSR's seem to be even incapable of providing basic trade statistics. And quite obviously, Russia has not been blessed with political leaders that would — as some of the Asians have done — discipline the students but let the tradesmen trade. The Russian inclination has rather been the opposite one.

Yes, even some of the best-known Russian social scientists have dreamed of a Southeast Asian way in Russia. That should be seen as a sad comment on the state of social analysis in that country.

Privatization

Market economy needs sufficiently independent economic agents, not necessarily ones that are privately owned. Would market socialism, a combination of state ownership and markets, have been possible? Is privatization primarily a politically-motivated goal?

Paradoxically enough one might argue that Eastern Central Europe has recently lived under market socialism. Markets have developed much faster than privatization. In Poland, most of the recent handsome export growth has come from state-owned companies. Still, saying that these countries have lived under market socialism would be misleading. What we see is a peculiar state of transition only made possible by governments in principle very strongly opposed to socialism.

What is important, though, is the fact that state enterprises are not all similarly hopeless cases. Even without privatization many of them can reform themselves, and this should probably have had more weight in judging policy alternatives than has been the case so far. State desertion, the neglect of existing capacities, goals, and possibilities may become an expensive mistake.

Janos Kornai has given what is possibly the most widely accepted rationale for privatization in PCMEs. Socialist plants used to live under soft budget constraints. They had few incentives to react rationally to price signals, as eventual losses used to be more or less routinely covered by budget subsidies or soft bank loans. Bankruptcies were impossible and employees had what amounted to a guaranteed right to their present jobs. The natural consequence was insensitivity to cost calculation and therefore even massive wastage. The economic reforms implemented did not do away with this mainspring of inefficiency. The peculiar paternalistic umbilical cord between plants and the socialist state was still maintained.

The most important economic rationale for privatizing existing state-owned companies is therefore that the probability for hardening budget constraints is not sufficiently high as long as state ownership remains predominant in some of its forms. There are also other economic arguments for privatization. Theoretically and perhaps also empirically, the most intriguing among them concentrate on asking how efficiently capital markets function under prevalent state ownership. Western experience with state enterprises within a market economy environment does not really answer this question for economies in transition. There, the issue concerns just the creation of institutional preconditions for a market economy. Changing property rights as such may be far from enough if the whole institutional framework, including capital markets and the whole financial system, is not recreated more or less at the same time.

The simple, even if somewhat unfortunate fact seems to be that there is no method of privatization that would be simultaneously fast, economically efficient, and socially acceptable. Privatization can therefore not have priority in sequencing over stabilization and liberalization. True enough, there are no particular problems concerning small-scale privatization, involving shops, kiosks, and service establishments. They should be speedily sold to the highest bidder. The problems in large-scale privatization, involving major state-owned plants, on the contrary, are formidable.

Before starting privatization one should preferably be able to pick out the losers, even if one would not believe in the state's capacity to pick out the winners. One should try to decide which of the existing capacities are worth maintaining, worth giving a chance. This is far from being easy or noncontroversial. Also, as the point of departure one should determine which property rights are to be taken. One of the major economic problems of late socialism was the lack of clarity of existing property arrangements. They should be clarified.

Basically, large-scale privatization has two alternatives, selling property or giving it away. Privatization by sales gives the state much-needed revenue. It is also a slow-moving, complicated, and politically debatable process. One has to decide to whom to sell, for which price to sell and on which conditions to sell. Not surprisingly Hungary, the most consequent country in its strategy to privatize by sales, has so far only been able to sell some one tenth of its state industries.

Give-away privatization does not raise revenue, but it may seem fast and may be — especially if property is distributed among the whole of the population — deemed socially just. Still, give-away privatization may prove to be devilishly complicated in practice, and the outcome may prove to be a far cry from what was expected. In the Czech republic, a small number of mostly bank-controlled investment funds emerged as the main owners after give-way privatization.

In this light it is probably not surprising that most countries tend to combine different methods of privatization. Still, progress has been generally less than expected. Enterprising people — in particular those who are insiders to plants and the traditional power structures — have utilized the situation and taken over state property in so-called spontaneous or nomenclature privatization. It can be seen as a form of primary accumulation of capital taking place in a spontaneous, 'private' way through the civil society. As such it is a part of liberalization. It also has economic advantages.

The social problem with spontaneous privatization is in its questionable equity. It also has an economic problem. Making companies the property of their insiders significantly weakens the crucial capitalist conflict between labour and capital on the enterprise level. It may be that the badly needed structural changes are becoming almost impossible if everybody has a vested interest in existing production, employment and wages, and nobody cares sufficiently for the long-term capital value of enterprises. In a way, a parasitic casino capitalism would be established on the ruins of socialism. As will be soon seen, this possibility is of special importance in the case of Russia.

Structural change

As we saw, the popular counterposing of gradualism and shock therapies is almost without actual contents. Basically, stabilization and liberalization succeed best when implemented swiftly. Privatization, on the other hand, is of necessity a gradual process. This is even more true of structural change, the creation of an economy which, through its efficiency and competitiveness, is able to provide a sufficiently high standard of living distributed in a way acceptable to society. In the end, all the rest in the orthodoxy is just a means for attaining this goal.

Even attempting to enumerate the ingredients of structural change would be futile. It is clearly a matter of competition, technical change and investment, but the development of a cultural basis and social relations typical for the contemporary society also belong here. While discussing structural change, one inevitably crosses the implicit border between conscious policies and the mainstream of autonomous societal development, the actual contents of human existence. At the same time, one really enters areas with no schedules or earlier models to follow.

The spirit of capitalism does not seem to need Protestant ethics. Markets are able to adapt themselves to the most divergent historical and cultural environments. The development of South Korea was truly not totally handicapped by its inheritance, though the best and brightest among American social scientists may have argued so in the early 1950's. Russian capitalism will differ from German or French capitalism. Its embryos are now called — making a huge mental transfer — mafia. For an American who remembers New York local politics or Chicago in the 1920's and Mississippi a decade later, Russian capitalism in its bud evokes many memories. That is also true of those who have looked behind the facades of Tsarist economic growth.

The Gaidar programme

Russian policies of transition since late 1991 are for the most part in line with the IMF orthodoxy. Still, this is not something force-fed from the outside. Jegor Gaidar and other reformist ministers supported similar ideas long before they became members of the Russian government. Naturally, Russian policies and the orthodoxy differ in technical detail, and the government has been unable to implement many of the common features. There are also three important differences of principle. Each one of them actually emphasises the gradualist features in Russian policies. This has been true of price liberalization, where gradualism has been economically devastating. The same applies to rouble convertibility. The peculiarity of Russian policies of privatization, though this is seldom emphasised, is in the degree of privileges given to company insiders.

The first year of Russian transformation has already shown that many deeply-rooted conceptions about Russia amounted to nothing more than prejudices. The first thing must be underlined: change in Russia is not only possible but also irreversible. A return to the *ancien regime* has become impossible, and even proposing something like that is not likely to arouse electoral support. Transformation has also taken place without violence or large-scale social disturbances. Citizens still support continued reforms. Many of them have even found legal ways of benefiting from the new liberties. Opposition to change naturally exists, but it has not been crystallized into a credible and consistent alternative.

All of this must be emphasised, because this is not how many thought it would be.

The great failure

Still, the change has been far from that aspired to by the government or the IMF orthodoxy. Liberalization, especially that of the foreign sector, has been overly partial. There is little evidence of the structural change needed. Privatization is progressing, especially fast in 1993, but its impact on the economy and society remains to be seen. Most worrisomely, stabilization has failed on a grand scale. At Christmas 1992, the economy was even closer to hyperinflation than a year earlier. After relative calming down, the imbalances again seemed about to explode in the autumn of 1993.

There are many reasons for this great failure. One of them was the particularly bad shape of the economy when stabilization was first attempted. In late 1991 and during all of 1992, general government budget deficit was somewhere around 20-30 per cent of GNP, depending on calculations. Solving this equation during a steep decline of production would be a gargantuan task for any government, in any country. And the Russian government faced a particularly awkward hurdle. It only had an indirect mandate through a president elected by popular vote. Many of the decisions had to be seen through a hostile parliament with no programme and no strong leaders, a parliament concentrating only upon politicking, maintaining privileges, and blocking the government. The central bank is subordinated to parliament, and its policies have been geared first towards controlling payment flows and then towards supporting enterprises — towards almost anything but stable money.

The economic basis of politization

The reformist government made its share of mistakes. Perhaps the biggest one, at least in the first phase, was in a technocratic refusal to create a political base. Originally, the ministers felt themselves technocratic officials who would do their job and then go. The art of politics was left aside. Therefore, it was no great surprise that the government was almost toothless when proper political mobilization was started in the country against its stabilization policies. As in the other countries in transition, state enterprises reacted to more stringent monetary and financial policies by accumulating payment arrears both vis-à-vis one another and to banks. This was essentially a way of financing such production and jobs for which nobody was willing to pay. At worst, more than half of industrial production was based on unpaid bills. The enterprises demanded more money and duly organised a political movement for industrial insiders, the Civic Union (*Grazhdanskii Soyuz*).

In the summer of 1992 the government and this movement stood opposed, and the government blinked first. This was the end of proper stabilization policies. Government policies went adrift, industrial subsidies ballooned, and compromises were increasingly seen as the way of creating a political base of support. But this was late, an attempt to consolidate positions of defeat already suffered.

Undaunted, the government followed a manuscript drafted earlier and announced that the first phase of transition, that of stabilization, had been already successfully passed, and the time for privatization and structural change had come. Ambitious blueprints for industrial policies were laid out without too much concern for such details as that the government had neither conceptual clarity, resources nor actual policy impact to implement them. At the same time, an exceptionally wide-ranging and ambitious programme of privatization was embarked upon. As the government preferred to emphasize the give-away elements involved, a conflict with insider interests seemed to be developing. When due regard was given to the insider privileges actually involved, this seed of discord seemed to fade away.

The problem of a missing political base remained, and it was not made easier by the factual dissolution of the Civic Union after the end of 1992. The reformist course was supported in a referendum in April 1993, but the proper build-up of political change was again thwarted. By the autumn of 1993, the government and the parliament were increasingly at loggerheads, unable to agree upon constitution, elections or policies. At the same time, politics in general was overshadowed by numerous accusations of corruption and worse. The economy seemed to be losing what governability it still had. The dissolution of the parliament in October 1993 put, at least temporarily, an end to this stalemate, and the new constitution granting the president considerable powers may provide a far more stable environment for economic policy.

The Soviet heritage

Another of the great failures of the reformist government was its inability to face the institutional and political heritage bequeathed by the Soviet Union. The government came to power as Russia wanted its independence from the USSR. In late 1991, plans for a future economic union were abandoned, as they would still have left some justification for the continued existence of the central institutions left by the Soviet Union. No new arrangements proper could be substituted for the earlier intergovernmental institutions. Little by little, attempts at creating new rules of the economic game for the Commonwealth of Independent States became more serious, but at the same time their repeated failure seriously undermined any credibility that might have existed.

It must be admitted that the challenge facing the Russian government was not among the easiest ones. One had to negotiate with other inexperienced states, some of which pursued totally irresponsible economic policies. Also, the issue concerned the whole inheritance left by the Russian empire and the USSR. For the last centuries, attitudes to the geographical environment have been among the great unresolved problems in Russian politics. Russia has never been equal to current Russian federation. It was actually founded in Kiev, which is now supposed to be the capital of a foreign country. Small wonder that the Russian authorities were — and remain — divided and were unable to reach a final position on these matters.

Not solving these issues became expensive. For a period of time, a truly perverse economic system existed. Each and every one of the former republics, while remaining within the rouble zone, had the free rider's incentive to maximize budget deficits. Benefits would concentrate on one's own state, while the inflationary costs would be distributed throughout the rouble zone. First, an attempt was made to agree upon common monetary and fiscal policies. Not surprisingly, given the differences in resource endowments, productive structures, policies and goals among the participants, this attempt failed.

Lately Russia has attempted to force the other countries to choose between staying within the rouble zone and following Russian rules of the game or leaving the rouble zone, establishing national currencies, and bearing one's own policy responsibility. Still, these fundamentally clear alternatives remain blurred by the fact that a strengthening Russian opinion — also within the government — sees the abrupt dissolution of the USSR as a mistake. In this view, Russia should take a leading role in a future (con)federation of states encompassing some of the former Soviet republics. These options have a direct impact on current economic policies, particularly in monetary and price matters.

The Argentina of Eurasia?

It has been evident since the beginning of Russian transition that the real alternative to IMF orthodoxy is not a Southeast Asian path, but at best a kind of corporatism of weak governments such as has been seen in some of the large Latin American countries after the Second World War. As Argentina was in 1945 among the ten richest countries of the world, the question has arisen whether Russia is at risk of becoming the 'Argentina' of Eurasia.

The first thing to remember is that contrary to many impressions the Russian state has typically been a weak one. The current state is particularly weak, as the government lingers on without a political base of its own, as the building of Russian institutions to substitute for the Soviet ones has not been particularly successful in a situation of diminishing resources and severe problems in commanding them. The current Russian state is also peculiarly weak as the relations to other former Soviet republics remain unresolved. What is even more important, is the continuing *de facto* decentralization of powers, not only geographically to republics and regions within Russia, but also to enterprise insiders. Often regions and enterprise insiders amount to the same people. A conflict between Moscow and Tyumen does not involve the minority nationalities living in Tyumen, but a dispute of power and resources between Russian leaders in Moscow and the insiders of industries geographically concentrated in Tyumen.

Recent years have shown that the weak government is unable to implement its policies against vested interests in society. But interest group organisation also remain badly organised, incompetent and deeply divided. No proper parties exist. If the government, which after all has at least had a programme, is not able to pursue consistent policies, how could one expect that from insider organisations?

A particularly detrimental problem here is that too many of the relevant interest groups have mainly defensive interests. They stand for protecting existing privileges, existing jobs and existing production through soft loans, foreign trade controls, devaluation and inflation. Unfortunately, there is no reason to suppose that future Russian relative advantages would be even close to the current lack of specialization of the country. Therefore, if structural changes were to be blocked by existing vested interests, Russia will have great problems in maintaining even current income levels. Furthermore, as the Latin American countries also demonstrate, perhaps even recurring lapses into hyperinflation might be unavoidable. In Russian circumstances, that might not simply spell dollarization but perhaps even more the emergence of regional monies and the collapse of Russia as an economic space. The political and military consequences of that cannot be forecast, but they would be bound to be dramatic.

Still, the time may not be too late to regain a degree of control over Russian economic processes. It would seem that two primary conditions are necessary to substantiate such optimism. Russia needs to regulate its relations with the other former Soviet republics and it needs to prevent the Russian economic space from dissolving. Here is the ground for fruitful — if also frightening — speculation.

References

Clague, C. & Rausser, G.C. (eds.) (1992), *The Emergence of Market Economies in Eastern Europe*, Blackwell, London.

Kornai, Janos (1990), *The Road to a Free Economy: Shifting from a Socialist System*, Norton, New York, N.Y.

Russian Economic Reform (1992), The World Bank, Geneva.

Sutela, Pekka (ed.) (1993), *The Russian Economy in Crisis and Transition*, The Bank of Finland, Helsinki.

5 The Cultural and Moral Upheaval in Russia

Timo Vihavainen

The optimistic *homo sovieticus*

In the not too distant past quite a lot was written and spoken about the Soviet man — *homo sovieticus* — whose values and way of life were considered to be quite different from the Western — or any other — model. Books upon the topic abounded. Of authors that published books on the topic after WW II one could point out Klaus Mehnert (1958) Hedrick Smith (1976), Robert Kaiser (1976), Alexander Zinoviev (1981) and Mikhail Geller (1986), for instance.

Most foreign scholars were unanimous about the stability and deep originality of the Soviet culture. Certainly it was admitted that the machinery of the Soviet state greatly influenced the psychology and self-understanding of the Soviet man. However, it was common knowledge that the state was not omnipotent. Not only was there social engineering, the outlook of the Soviet man seemed to rely also on some basic common elements of human psychology. The characteristics of the Soviet man included loyalty to the state, pride in Soviet citizenship, a relatively high level of optimism, satisfaction and a sense of security, plus a well-developed taste for a collective way of life (cf. the works mentioned above, especially Zinoviev).

The so-called dissidents were commonly not considered representative of the great masses. When there was dissatisfaction, it very seldom was directed against the foundations of the system (e.g. Chuchward, 1973, pp. 145-49). The standard of living — vastly superior to the wartime standards and steadily improving — was generally appreciated. In society at large, there were hardly any basic conflicts on values, the generation gap was trifling when compared with the West. Among the students there was curiosity about western values, yes, but no fawning; there was rather a certain latent hostility towards things western, the Soviet system was commonly considered to be in some way superior. Even when one wanted to reform the system, this did not amount to its outright rejection, not to speak of substituting it for its capitalist rival (see Burg, 1961).

It was commonly believed that the Soviet man was a born collectivist. Alexander Zinoviev went as far as to maintain that the collectivism of *homo sovieticus* was nothing else than a common innate human propensity for 'human communality', which the Soviet system had only emancipated and whereupon it could safely rest. Zinoviev mistrusted the possibility of reforming the Soviet system at all — for this very reason. In his view only indefatigable and continuous struggle with the Old Adam (or Oblomov) could possibly raise Soviet man — the natural man — from his inertia (Zinoviev, op. cit.).

The widely held view about the political loyalty of the Soviet man and the stability of his culture was no doubt well-grounded. It was further strenghened by the findings of an American survey of emigrant opinion (Millar, 1987). True, some sovietologists also were of the opinion that the Soviet system had built-in defects that would lead to its eventual collapse. Some even believed that this would happen within a short time. Such forecasts were voiced especially in the 60's, but in the period of détente they were clearly losing in popularity (see Brzezinski, 1969; Cornell, 1970). At any rate, as recently as in the beginning of the 80's it was widely held that the Soviet man was relatively content and well-adapted, not willing to shake the foundations of his society.

Signs of change in the psychology of the common man were, however, taking place. In 1980 John Bushnell published an article which maintained that 'the New Soviet Man' was turning pessimist. Bushnell considered that whereas an unshakable optimism had prevailed in the

Soviet Union in the beginning of the 60's, the tide was turning by the middle of the 70's.

At the beginning of the 60's it still had been believed that the USSR would surpass the west in economic competition within a few years. This was not just what the new party programme said, it was also a source for grave concern in the west. The statistics gave ample ground for uneasiness up to the end of the 70's. If the US economy had grown 3.5 per cent in the years between 1951-1970, the figure for the USSR was as high as 8.7 per cent. Worse still, the dynamism of the Soviet economy could not be explained away by the low starting level. At the beginning of the 60's the US economy had been at the same level, but had grown less than 5 per cent annually on the average (Yeremin, 1972).

The economic optimism of the Soviet man could not be shaken even by the bad harvests at the beginning of the 60's. Even when it became evident by the end of that decade that the promises of the XII Party Congress needed thorough reconsideration, it was only a small group of intellectuals which began to protest. This was the beginning of the dissident movement (see Bushnell, op. cit.).

If we are to believe Bushnell, optimism reigned in the Soviet middle class up to the middle of the 70's. In any case a fatal blow was given by the food shortages of 1975-76. Thereafter the Soviet middle class no longer expected that the living standard of their country would surpass the western level in the foreseeable future. However, some degree of historic optimism was left, and almost all accepted the Soviet system in principle. If this be so, the time of the change is all the more striking, because the west for its part was enduring the consequences of the oil crisis at the same time.

What we must not forget today is that very many people — quite possibly the majority of Russians — believed in communism just one or two decades ago. Communism was also an all-embracing system of thought and belief which explained everything and — very much like a religion — gave meaning to life. Writing in 1980 Bushnell believed that, along with the food shortages, it was especially the increase in foreign contacts — both with the west and with Eastern Europe — which contributed to the growth of pessimism.

Bushnell's analysis and timing may or may not be correct. At any rate some further proof for his basic tenets may be obtained from the history of the Soviet intelligentsia. It has been pointed out that in the 50's and to a certain extent in the 60's even critical intellectuals were still mostly communists. They did not struggle against communism, but attempted to restore its original purity, which spelt a return to the original Leninist norms (see Slapentokh, 1990).

The case for a liberal socialism — but still socialism— was made only at the beginning of the 60's and, for instance, the academician Sakharov still stood for a liberal socialism as late as in the late 60's. However, since the last years of the 60's and, especially, in the following decade the dissidents began to reject socialism as such, and ideas as diverse as monarchism, russophilism, religiousness and human rights came in its stead (see Shlapentokh, op. cit.).

The pace of progress of the intelligentsia's outlook certainly was much ahead of the masses. Shlapentokh also notes that before the 80's the intellectuals did not even bother to think of the masses as a political entity. To try to create a mass movement in the Brezhnevian USSR would, of course, have been a suicidal task, given the omnipresent system of political surveillance. One thinks, however, that the mentality of the Soviet man helped to make the task extremely difficult.

The view that the dissidents were isolated from the masses was further confirmed by the results of a poll in 1991 which showed that 32 per cent of Russians recalled that they had never heard about the dissidents. Fifteen per cent believed that the dissidents had helped the masses to realize the necessity of reforms and also 15 per cent believed that they had not had much effect (Moscow News, 17-24 May 1992). The food shortages of the middle of the 70's probably affected the optimism of the Soviet citizen, as Bushnell believed, but not necessarily his loyalty to the regime and the ideas which it represented. The Russian intelligentsia which a hundred years earlier had 'gone to the people' had also been obliged to realize that the oppressed did not want to rise against their oppressors.

The social contract dissolves

The quietism of the Soviet society during the Brezhnev years has been explained by what has been called the 'Brezhnevite social contract'. The regime had bought — so the argument goes — loyalty and support by guaranteeing for everybody a safety of jobs and a constant, albeit modest, rise in living standards (see Sutela, 1987).

At the beginning of the 80's Victor Zaslavsky, who had much inside first-hand information about the Soviet system, explained the stability of the 'neo-stalinist state' by means of an organized consensus, which exploited both a state-manipulated upward social mobility and an inertia of fear (cf. Zaslavsky, 1982).

The cornerstones of the consensus were, however, tottering by the beginning of the 80's. The curves of economic growth could not be forced upwards and the great 'food programme' merely showed the impossibility of improving the situation even with a drastic rise of inputs. When Gorbachev, at the beginning of the perestroika era, said that the economy had reached a 'nearly critical point' *(predkrizisnaia situatsia)*, it was readily understood that there was a deep crisis which could not be solved by the old methods. Now the whole Brezhnev period was labelled as 'the years of stagnation' and a real campaign of 'debrezhnevization' was launched (cf. Sakwa, 1990, pp. 82-90).

As we remember, Gorbachev introduced new measures which could hardly be popular as such but which evidently more or less shook the foundations of the old consensus. Stressing the 'human factor' implied also a 'fight against unearned income' — it was directed both against those who speculated and against those who did not work hard enough. The even distribution of income was castigated as an unsound 'levelling' *(uravnilovka)*. The much-acclaimed 'acceleration' *(uskorenie)* implied also increasing the amount of shift work, and the ban on alcoholic beverages was directed against quite an essential feature of the Brezhnevist way of life.

Gorbachev brought to the society not peace, but a sword. In literature the Soviet worker — once the sacrosanct hegemon of the state — began to be depicted as an indolent drunkard, envious of those who worked hard and who honestly tried to make their living better, e.g. as in Chingiz Aitmatov's novel *Plakha*, and in Valentin Rasputin's novel *Pozhar* (in English *The Fire*). Such traits had formerly been attached only to the 'petty bourgeois' elements, which should have vanished from the socialist society.

For the masses Gorbachev promised not only sweat and tears, but also a continued rise in living standards just after 'the next two or three years, which will be the most difficult ones'. As we know, a rise in the Soviet GNP during a couple of the first years of perestroika was announced. However, there hardly was any rise in the living standard.

Such nuisances as the disappearance of sugar and the unavailability of liquor could not add to the sense of security and well-being of the Soviet citizens.

The policy of glasnost and the filling of the 'blank pages' of history were, in the beginning, pursued with remarkable delicacy. The great story of Soviet history was still left intact in the report of the 27th Party Congress in 1986, and most of it survived even in Gorbachev's speech on the occasion of the 70th anniversary of the October Revolution in 1987. By and by, especially in 1988 — the *'annus mirabilis* of Soviet history' — and thereafter so much new information about the history of the CPSU was made public that it amounted to saying that a 'genuine' socialist policy had been pursued only during very brief periods during the whole Soviet period (cf. e.g. Keep, 1989, pp. 117-145). The whole story was full of repression, crime, deception, stagnation, and even treacherous foreign policy. The Gorbachev regime tried to present itself as the true heir of the Leninist (as represented in Lenin's last writings) line, which Bukharin in his turn had tried to pursue. The Gorbachev regime disavowed its affiliation to both Stalin and Brezhnev. Perestroika was depicted as a revolution, but a revolution means battle against the powers that be. A revolution in order to restore old political ideas was an awkward concept indeed. The net effect of the 'revolutionary' policy of the Gorbachev regime evidently was the destruction of trust in the CPSU and even in socialism in general.

As has been pointed out above, it had been generally believed that the mass of the Soviet people — even if it had lost its optimism — still was relatively content with and at least loyal to the regime at the beginning of the 80's. To what extent this really was so has not been reliably proven, but at any event, at the end of the decade the tables were turned.

Reasonably reliable information about the attitudes of the Soviet public became available only with the years of perestroika. At the end of 1989 an all-union poll revealed the formidable fact that no more than 4 per cent of the Soviet people declared that they fully trusted the CPSU as the champion of the interests of the people. As late as in September 1989 the figure had been as high as 22 per cent (Moscow News, 18 March 1990). The result may have meant a denunciation of the present leadership of the party rather than an outright dismissal of the communist — or 'socialist' — ideals as such. Rather, the people had lost their faith in Gorbachev and his policy, but not in the socialist ideals. This seems to get confirmation from a poll which surveyed the Moscow region — hardly the most conservative part of the country — and which was made at about the same time. As many as 31 per cent still wanted to have some kind of communist regime in the future and no more than 18 per cent believed that it would have been better if Russia had been governed by a liberal, capitalist government for the last 40 years (Moskovskie Novosti, 4 March 1990).

Endurance without illusions

If the Soviet man was becoming pessimistic already in the last half of the 70's, pessimism was already deep at the end of the perestroika era, nevertheless there hardly was despair. At the end of 1990 15 per cent believed that the crisis would be overcome in 5-6 years, 16 per cent believed that this would happen by the year 2000 and 32 per cent thought that this would happen still later. Anyway, only 12 per cent thought that it would never happen (Moscow News, 16-23 December 1990). In the same year, the polls showed that the majority of the people believed that it was necessary to establish a market economy, although this would spell difficulties for the majority of the people (Moskovskie Novosti, 6 May 1990).

Both polls and the results of the 1993 referendum seem likely to point to one direction: the Russians see the inevitability of change, but are not expecting a sudden improvement of their lot (see also Pipes, 1993). The extraordinary promises made in turn by Lenin, Khrushchev and Gorbachev had failed and the wonders proclaimed to have been realized by Stalin and Brezhnev had been exposed during perestroika. Grown sick with promises, the majority of the Russians seem to be able to stomach the prospect of low or even declining living standards for the majority of the people and a prolonged struggle just to regain the standard of living which had been attained during the Brezhnev era.

The tranquility of the masses is, indeed, striking: inflation has destroyed the savings of the people, which at the beginning of perestroika amounted on the average to about one year's salary per capita. Drastic price inreases caused no disturbances, even though the stability of prices was once regarded as one of the pillars of the Brezhnevite consensus. An analogous phenomenon took place in Germany in 1923 and has been considered as one of the main reasons why the German middle classes withdrew their loyalty to the Weimar regime and gave their vote instead to Hitler. The reaction of the Russians seems, so far, much more modest.

The Russians seem to have also met the disruption of the empire with remarkable stoicism. When, in the beginning of the perestroika era it still — with good grounds — seemed that the Soviet Union could not possibly consent even to a 'finlandization' of Eastern Europe (cf. Burks, 1988), not only Eastern Europe has been totally liberated from the Soviet yoke, but even the Ukraine, Belorussia and Kazakhstan have been dissociated from Russia — not to speak of the Baltic, Caucasian and Central Asian republics.

The dissolution of the Soviet empire may be considered the greatest event of its kind in all of European history. Russia has lost not only its East European empire, but also vast territories which it always considered its 'own'. 25 million Russians have been left outside the Russian borders and millions have fled to Russia proper — evidently facing much material and emotional hardship.

From the point of view of national sentiment one could compare the situation of Russia today with that faced by Germany after the Versailles peace — however the fate of the Russian empire has been much more severe. It may be remembered that Russian national consciousness always had a strong imperial — as distinguished from a purely Russian national — hue. Given the great importance which once was attached to Soviet nationalism in the mental structure of the Soviet man (e.g. McNeill, 1988), the popularity of the 'national patriots' has been surprisingly small.

All this notwithstanding, in a poll made in the summer of 1992, no less than 69 per cent of Moscovites considered that Russia should remain a great power, even though this might harm the relations with the rest of the world (Moscow News, 26 July 1992). Those who believe that nationalism will fill the gap left by the collapse of the Soviet ideology have good grounds for their fears (cf. e.g. Carter, 1990).

The entire cultural atmosphere in Russia has also undergone a thoroughgoing revolution. Western literature, pop-culture, soap operas and other forms of popular TV programming have invaded the Russian information space with incredible vehemence.

Still in the beginning of the perestroika era even Soviet young people were quite critical of Western radio broadcasts (Manaev, 1991.) Whereas the conservative leadership of the Writers' Unions at that time still spoke with horror about the prospect of the western junk culture invading the Soviet Union, now it is the Russian writers — once the intellectual leaders of the nation — who have been left without an audience. The Russian people, which once were thought to be the most literate in the world and whose taste for high culture was famous, now revels in Angelica, Tarzan, Rambo and James Bond. Good literature, including the famous 'thick journals' and even the works of Solzhenitsyn, has ceased to sell (see Lakshin, 1993). The renowned Soviet prudery in things sexual seems to have been swept away overnight. Porn films and magazines, erotic theatre and prostitution abound and even homosexuals have publicly pleaded for their rights. It may, however, be doubted whether the attitudes of the older generations have really changed very much in this respect.

Remnants of the past

Soviet ideology once complained that despite the new social order, some psychological remnants of the past survived for decades, hindering the proper functioning of society. Now, in 1993, just a little more than ten years since the death of Brezhnev and only six years since Gorbachev was still singing the praises of the past, present and future of the Soviet system from the high podium of the 70th anniversary celebration of the Great October Revolution, the once acclaimed socialist society itself seems to be in ruins. Common sense tells us, however, that the mental basis of what once was the Soviet man cannot have changed totally. Remnants of the not-so-distant past must linger on. Evidently, many of what were deemed to be primary characteristics of the Soviet man must have disappeared along with the regime.

The loss of optimism seems to be a natural result of the decaying economy and falling living standard. It is, indeed, hard to be content with a drastic loss of purchasing power, even if there are more goods to buy than ever. Still, with a more consumption-orientated political culture the reaction might have been violent. The fact that Russia has remained relatively calm by any standards can perhaps be at least partly explained by the relative preservation of job security, which has been a characteristic feature of Russian society.

As regards loyalty towards the regime, it can no longer be reinforced by a constant rise in the living standard. This was evident already in Gorbachev's time. The relative loyalty towards the regime seems, however — at least for the moment — to have been under Yeltsin (see e.g. the poll in Moscow News, 26 March 1993). It seems that with him at the helm the Russian people are readier to face hardship than they were with Gorbachev, who up to the end of his regime had the nerve to dangle carrots which few people any more believed to be real.

Endurance, though maybe not a Soviet product, has always been hailed as an old Russian virtue. Another one, hailed both in the writings of the Slavophiles and the communists, was a non-chauvinist attitude towards other nations. If the degree of national sentiment can be measured by the popularity of nationalist parties, its effect on post-communist Russia has not been very great so far.

Now that the faith in a great future has vanished, economical safety has been destroyed and national pride and great-power chauvinist sentiments have been given a formidable blow, what remains of the basic psychology of the erstwhile 'New Soviet Man'?

On this level a certain tough-mindedness has evidently been preserved. At the end of 1989, anyway, no more than 21 per cent of an all-union sample were against capital punishment. 70 per cent were for 'liquidating' assassins, 27-33 per cent wanted to eliminate also prostitutes, drug addicts and homosexuals, 16-22 per cent wanted to include also rockers, those with AIDS contamination and those disabled at birth, and 3-9 per cent listed also alcoholics and beggars in this category (Moscow News, 18 March 1990).

A taste for authoritarian rule was also rather strong in 1989: while 50 per cent were against concentrating power in the hands of one person, 25 per cent stood for it and 15 per cent believed that it could sometimes be needed. In the summer of 1992, when asked whether dictatorship would provide the only relief from the current crisis, 27 per cent of those questioned answered positively, less than half answered negatively and 32 per cent did not respond (Moscow News, 33/1992). The polls hint that there is a substantial contingent supporting strong rule, although most Russians are against one-man rule. By the way, it may be recalled that, at least officially, one-man rule was emphatically denounced already shortly after Stalin's death.

Another trait of the Soviet man was believed to be an inclination to equality — even levelling. In the 1989 poll only 11 per cent of those responding had nothing against the existence of millionaires in Russia. 39 per cent were favourably disposed to millionaires, on the condition that the money was honestly earned. 40 per cent were negative on the grounds that so much money could not be honestly earned and 8 per cent were against such riches, even if they were honestly earned (Moscow News, 18 March 1990).

In 1989, at least, the Soviet man still had clear sympathies for the traditional, not too hard-working Soviet way of life. Only 37 per cent would have liked to earn more by working their hardest, while 55 per cent agreed to have less income in exchange for easier work or a guarantee of their condition's stability (ibid.).

At the same time, there were still many who did not like the idea of totally free speech. 26 per cent were of the opinion that there should be no subjects closed for discussion, but 11 per cent did not want discussions about replacing the Soviet system with a capitalist one and 9 per cent did not want the 'correctness of Lenin's political course' to be doubted (ibid.).

Certainly, the years that have passed must have already changed the picture. Anyway, the polls show that the mental makeup of the erstwhile Soviet man has not changed as quickly as that of the persons in power. We must keep in mind that the Soviet system was not just a straitjacket forced upon an inert people. It produced a psychology which contributed to its perpetuation and it certainly was able to satisfy some basic needs of the people. Not only imperial dreams can reawaken among the Russian people. Alexander Solzhenitsyn, who doubtless has a deep understanding of the psychology of his countrymen, has noted that the 'wild and unproductive' variety of capitalism which has commenced in Russia has given rise to a craving for the past 'equality in misery' (Russkaia mysl, 23-29 September 1993).

The Soviet system also developed and used certain ways and methods of thinking. Its manichean world-view would always find and point out scapegoats for any failings of the supposedly perfect society. In the last instance it was always the foreign imperialists, the capitalists and militarists, who were to blame for all shortages and shortcomings.

True, during some periods their agents would also be found within the borders of the Soviet Union, but in principle the Russians themselves, let alone the Russian working class, were not blamed for anything. By the way, the idea that a scapegoat must always be found, is an old Russian tradition. 'Who is to blame?' *(Kto vinovat?)* was the classical question of the pre-revolutionary Russian intelligentsia.

It would be quite natural to suppose that such patterns of thought, which had been inculcated upon the people for decades, would not lose their appeal just in a few years. Fortunately, the evidence suggests the opposite. At the end of 1989 only 4 per cent of the population thought that the current crisis was caused by external enemies and as many as 44 per cent believed that the Russians' own mistakes were to blame. True, as many as 22 per cent of those polled blamed 'internal enemies', which might be an indication of the influence of Soviet thought patterns (see Moscow News, 18 March 1990; Pipes, op. cit.).

The 'remnants of the past' in the psychological makeup of the new Russian post-communist man have not, so far at least, caused major revolts against the westernizing policies of the government. On other levels they may well have hindered the processes of privatization and marketization, for instance. At any rate, all this still seems to be far from the kind of national resentment and reactionary pathos which once contributed to the rise to power of Adolf Hitler in the Weimar republic. But we have been witnessing just the beginning of a long march. At this moment, the basic social, economical and political problems in Russia are still very far from being solved. Should the policies aimed at their solution further weaken the economic and social situation, the nostalgia for the old values may grow stronger and become a factor which may make it impossible for the process of westernization to survive beyond its first few steps.

References

Brzezinski, Zbigniew (ed.) (1969), *Dilemmas of Change in Soviet Politics*, Columbia University Press, New York and London.

Burg, David (1961), 'Observations on Soviet University Students' in Pipes, Richard (ed.), *The Russian Intelligentsia*, Columbia University Press, New York.

Burks, R.V. (1988), 'How the End of the Soviet System May Come About' in A. Sthromas and M.A. Kaplan (eds.), *The Soviet Union and the Challenge of the Future*, vol. 1, Paragon House, New York.

Bushnell, John (1980), '"The New Soviet Man" Turns Pessimist' in S. Cohen, A. Rabinowitch & Robert Sharlet (eds.) *The Soviet Union Since Stalin*, Indiana University Press, Bloomington, Indiana.

Carter, Stephen K. (1990), *Russian Nationalism: Yesterday, Today, Tomorrow*, Macmillan, London.

Cornell, Robert (ed.) (1970), *The Soviet Political System*, Prentice-Hall, Englewood Cliffs, N.J.

Geller, Mikhail (1986), *Mashina i vintiki*, OPI, London.

Chuchward, L.G. (1973), *The Soviet Intelligentsia*, Routledge & Kegan Paul, London and Boston.

Kaiser, Robert (1976), *Russia: The People and the Power*, Praeger, New York.

Keep, J. (1989), 'Reconstructing Soviet History: A New "Great Turn?"', *Studies of Soviet Thought*, 38, pp. 117-145.

Lakshin, V. (1993), 'Berega kultury', *Svobodnaya mysl*, 9:1993.

Manaev, Oleg (1991), 'The Influence of Western Radio on the Democratization of Soviet Youth' in *Mass Culture and Perestroika in the Soviet Union*, Oxford University Press, New York.

McNeill, Terry (1988), 'The Western Scholarly Debate' in A. Sthromas and M.A. Kaplan (eds.), *The Soviet Union and the Challenge of the Future*, vol. 1, Paragon House, New York.

Mehnert, Klaus (1958), *Der Sowjetmensch*, Fisher Bücherei, Stuttgart.

Millar, James (ed.) (1987), *Politics, Work, and Daily Life in the USSR*, Cambridge University Press, New York.

Pipes, Richard (1993), 'Yeltsin's Move', *The Times Literary Supplement*, 8 October 1993.

Sakwa, Richard (1990), *Gorbachev and his Reforms, 1985-1990*, Philip Allan, Cambridge.

Shlapentokh, Vladimir (1990), *Soviet Intellectuals and Political Power*, Oxford University Press, London and New York.

Smith, Hedrick (1976), *The Russians*, Meridian Books, New York.

Yeremin, A. (1972), *The Economic Advantages of Socialism*, Progress, Moscow.

Zaslavsky, V. (1982), *The Neo-Stalinist State. Class, Ethnicity & Consensus in Soviet Society*, The Harvester Press, New York.

Zinoviev, Alexander (1981), *The Reality of Communism*, Victor Gollancz Ltd.,London.

6 Survival Strategies in a Transition Economy: Everyday Life, Subsistence and New Inequalities in Russia

Timo Piirainen

10 October 1992 the St. Petersburg newspaper *Chas pik* published a small article, from which the following passage is quoted:

> Last week an extraordinary experiment — at least from the point of view of an ordinary townsman — was conducted in our city. A group of American survivalists with Mr Tadeus Malkowski from Poland as their leader completed here 'a survival course in conditions that resemble the war-time circumstances as closely as possible'. Five American young men and women were awarded the first-grade diploma of Mr Malkovski's survival institute with the inscription: 'adept to survive with only the most minimal material protection necessary for the human subsistence'.
>
> Russia is, according to Mr Malkovski, a country where survival skills are of utmost necessity. In a training booklet printed by him, Russia is classified as 'a country of the highest risk degree', and on the basis of the hazardousness of life there it can be grouped together with such countries as Honduras or Chad. The Pole refers to St. Petersburg as a city that is 'most suitable for the training of beginners'. A participant of the survival expedition, Charles Numett, a 21-year-old archaeology student from Oklahoma, describes his experiences:
>
> 'It was not necessary to be armed with M-16 rifles to be able to walk around in the streets of St. Petersburg. When we arrived here Mr Malkovski gave each of us an average Russian monthly salary — 10,000 roubles — confiscated all our dollars and furnished us with traditional Russian clothing, fur hats and heavy boots. For the following month we then had to find our lodgings ourselves, buy our food from your stores and have our meals in your lunchrooms, use the

public transportation and so forth. And at the same time, we had to encounter your culture — visit the theatres, museums, expositions.'

And so forth. The story continues and the writer of the article makes fun of the Americans having so little acquaintance with the Russian society and culture. At the same time, an air of bitterness is clearly visible: the western survivalists did not, after all, learn to know how tough everyday life can be in a country, such as Russia, which is struggling to achieve a market economy and to develop the survival skills an ordinary Russian wage-earner needs in order to manage his or her living. The 'average Russian monthly salary' in October 1992 was not, moreover, 10,000 roubles — i.e. the sum the 'survivalists' received — but only a little more than a half of it, nearly 6,000 roubles. According to the exchange rates then prevailing this sum equalled 15 US dollars. Conversion into dollars does not, of course, portray the purchasing power of the salary in Russia; to give a rough estimate, it was equivalent to the purchasing power of approximately 200 dollars in the United States. Securing daily food, clothing and other basic necessities may thus be an almost overwhelmingly difficult task for an ordinary wage earner. Using the overcrowded public transportation system, carrying on business with administration and local authorities and managing other aspects of daily life can often bring exceptional difficulties, too.

The patience of the Russian people and its ability to endure hardships are virtually legendary notions. A pivotal question is, however, what would happen, if the legendary persistence of Russia's 150 million people came to an end some time. Is the overall standard of living going to keep on sinking while Russia struggles towards a market economy, and if this happens, what might the consequences of such proletarization be? Is a social explosion to be expected, will the vast nation be torn to pieces when the population has had enough of poverty and humiliation? Or are we going to see the rise of a totalitarian and imperialist superpower as the people become tired of the experiment with political democracy, wanting a strong hand that would feed the hungry? It was, after all, an impoverished and humiliated middle class that lifted the National Socialist Party to power in the Germany of the 1930's.

This chapter attempts to provide background material for the evaluation of these questions. In the beginning section, the dynamics of living conditions in Russia are briefly examined. In the following section, the analysis is focused on the activities of Russian households

— on the 'survival skills' — in a situation in which the standard of living is, at least measured by standards common in the industrial countries of Western Europe and America, very low and in which rapid social change is a constant source of uncertainty. The concluding part of this chapter is devoted to a study of the new inequalities and new social stratification in post-communist Russia: a reallocation of resources is taking place, and sharp differences in life chances are now forming. The traditionally egalitarian society is rapidly being transformed into a society of rich and poor; an essential question concerns the nature of this new division and the political processes the new class structure can bring forth.

Below the poverty line

In May 1993 the official estimate of the average monthly salary in the state-owned sector of the Russian economy was 37,600 roubles (approximately 37 US dollars) — during the winter 1992-93 Russia stood on the brink of hyperinflation, and the nominal wages were 12.5 times higher than a year before (Soloviev, 1993).

In May 1993, the average household in St. Petersburg spent 67 per cent of its income on food. During the period from December 1991 to February 1993 the share of monthly household incomes allocated to the purchase of foodstuffs was even higher, varying between 74-84 per cent in St. Petersburg (Protasenko, 1993; cf. Gontmakher, 1993). Purchases other than basic necessities, for example clothing or furniture, are apparent impossibilities if the sole source of income is the salary from employment in the public sector of the economy. In the highly industrialized countries of western Europe, the share of foodstuffs in the household budget comes to approximately 20 per cent. (See Kultygin, 1993; Kutsar and Trumm, 1993.)

We can continue to examine the standard of living in Russia in the light of monetary incomes and expenses. Table 6.1 shows the differentiation of income per household member between households in St. Petersburg in May 1993 (Protasenko, 1993). The figures in Table 6.2 indicate the development of the average income per household member during the period from December 1991 to May 1993 and thus reflect the tempo of the inflation.

Table 6.1. The income of St. Petersburg households per household member in May 1993. The bottom row indicates the development of the average income per household member. *Source:* Protasenko, 1993.

12,000 roubles or less	25 %
12,001-20,000 roubles	38 %
20,001-35,000 roubles	21 %
35,001-50,000 roubles	8 %
50,001-75,000 roubles	2 %
more than 75,000 roubles	2 %
no answer	4 %
	100 %

Table 6.2. The development of the average income per household member during the period December 1991 - May 1993 in St. Petersburg. The rouble values are converted to US dollars at the exchange rate prevailing at each point of time. *Source:* Protasenko, 1993.

	Dec. 1991	Jan. 1992	Feb. 1992	April 1992	Nov. 1992	Jan. 1993	Feb. 1993	March 1993	May 1993
roubles	365	551	862	1,207	4,277	6,781	9,900	10,980	23,885
US $		5.6	8.6	12.0	9.6	11.8	14.8	16.5	21.4

The officially estimated minimum level of subsistence *(prozhitochnii minimum)*, a level of absolute poverty calculated from the price of a basket of basic foodstuffs, was in May 1993 on average 13,507 roubles (13 US dollars) per person. Table 6.1 shows that approximately 28 per cent (Protasenko, 1993) of the St. Petersburg households did not reach even this level of subsistence, if the standard of living is measured solely on the basis of self-reported monetary income.

The respondents in St. Petersburg were also asked to give an estimate of the poverty threshold, i.e. the level of income per household member that would allow the household to lift itself from the poverty level. The mean estimate was 20,970 roubles (19 US dollars) per person in the household. 64 per cent of the households in St. Petersburg had incomes lower than 20,000 roubles per person, as is seen from Table 6.1, and thus fell below this self-estimated poverty line.

Moreover, the respondents in this same survey were asked to approximate the income sufficient for a 'normal life'. The mean of these estimates was 78,532 roubles (70 US dollars) in May 1993. Table 6.1

shows that only a very small minority — less than two per cent of the inhabitants of St. Petersburg — had enough income to reach the standard of living considered as normal by the majority of respondents.

The most important problem for ordinary people in Russia is the acquisition of daily commodities. There are two basic reasons for this problem: first, the insufficiency of income and second, the weaknesses in the production and distribution system that make the commodities unavailable, even if the households had the money to buy them. Table 6.3 shows the relative importance of these two reasons. The data used in the table was gathered in September 1992 in St. Petersburg (Protasenko, 1992); the question was: 'Some claim that they do not have enough money, others that there are no products available. Which is the case for you?'

Table 6.3 shows clearly that the shortage of commodities in the Russian economy soon changed to a shortage of money after price controls were lifted in January 1992. The queues traditionally so typical in Russian cities soon disappeared — or at least became shorter. The products do not disappear any more from the delivery chain to the black market, where they were sold at multiple prices; in most cases, they nowadays succeed in being brought all the way to the grocery store counters. Commodities are on sale, but the prices are often very

Table 6.3. The lack of money and the shortage of goods as the sources of problems in daily life in St. Petersburg (%). *Source:* Protasenko, 1992.

Year 1991	March	April	June	September	December
Not enough goods	26	20	22	21	23
Not enough money	10	19	25	19	11
Not enough of both	53	57	49	55	61
No problems	5	3	3	3	3
Difficult to say	6	1	1	2	2

Year 1992	January	February	March	April	September
Not enough goods	16	10	8	5	10
Not enough money	22	33	47	55	52
Not enough of both	58	50	38	30	30
No problems	2	4	3	7	7
Difficult to say	2	3	4	3	1

high for the ordinary consumer. The structures of distribution and commerce are often quite monopolistic, and the producers and merchants can set the prices high.

A crucial question is, of course, who are the well-off in the post-communist society and whose situation is the most critical. The Soviet Union portrayed itself as a classless and egalitarian society, where the wealth — or the poverty — of the nation was evenly distributed among the population and where the basic needs of everyone were satisfied. It is very difficult to estimate to what extent this equality and protection of the basic necessities was actually achieved. Throughout the entire Soviet period it was extremely difficult for a foreign observer to get reliable information. It was not permitted to openly publish research reports or statistics concerning social problems — for example infant mortality, deficiencies in nutrition, poverty or criminality — in the Soviet Union; the scarce statistical data available was, as a rule, falsified (cf. e.g. Ruutsoo, 1991).

While an accurate appraisal of the equality or inequality of the resource allocation in the Soviet Union cannot be given, it seems, however, very apparent that in Russia, the most important descendant of the Soviet empire, the resources are distributed on uneven terms — and even those resources that can be regarded as daily necessities. The differences in income are continuously growing. In December 1991 — i.e. shortly before the liberation of consumer prices in Russia — the ratio between the average income per household member in the 10 per cent of the St. Petersburg households with the lowest income and the 10 per cent with the highest income was 1:4.1. A year later, in November 1992, this ratio between the incomes of the poorest and richest 10 per cent had widened to 1:8.8, and in May 1993 the highest-income 10 per cent received an average 10.5 times more than the 10 per cent with the lowest income in St. Petersburg. (Protasenko, 1993.) A significant group among the poor was the elderly: 28 per cent of the Russian pensioner households were calculated to receive less than the amount sufficient for minimum subsistence (Khudiakova, 1993). Families with children were, however, found out to be in the most serious situation: in May 1993 45 per cent of the Russian families having children did not have enough income even to reach this level of absolute poverty. For Russian families with three or more children the situation was, if possible, even more dismal: 72 per cent fell below the subsistence minimum! (Gont-makher, 1993.)

The incomes are lowest in the service occupations in the public sector of the economy. The Russian government is forced to squeeze the salaries in the so-called 'budgetary branches' *(biudzhetnie otrasly)* — e.g. education, culture, sciences and health — in order to support the old industry and to prevent the massive unemployment which would be the consequence of the collapse of the giant industrial organizations. The labour force employed in these budgetary branches is predominantly female. Thus the one-parent families with the mother as the sole bread-winner fall in most cases into the category of the households with lowest income.

A look at the survival skills: the activities and options of Russian households

28 per cent of the households in St. Petersburg have an income so low that they do not even reach the absolute minimum required for sub-sistence. 64 per cent of the households fall below the poverty line. Only 2 per cent feel that their income is sufficient enough to permit them to lead a normal life.

What does this indeed dismal account based on the statistics imply? Do these figures indicating a deep and widespread poverty have, in fact, any meaning at all? Daily life in post-communist Russia is certainly not devoid of hardships, but even a quick look at the ordinary people in the streets of Moscow or St. Petersburg — the two big cities where the prices are the highest and the level of consumption for an ordinary citizen according to the statistics lowest (Illarionov, 1993) — seems to bring evidence which contradicts this picture of all-embracing poverty.

The survey results presented above imply, in any case, that the income received from employment in the state-managed sector of the economy is usually not sufficient to guarantee the basic necessities of life. The results suggest, too, that a survey concentrating solely on the amount of money received from official employment may not be the most meaningful approach when studying the standard of living of Russian households. Russian salaries in the state-financed branches of the economy are hopelessly small compared to the price levels in the commodity market. The income from the regular job is thus not likely to be the sole — and maybe not even the most important — source of livelihood and material well-being.

Richard Rose (1991) describes the economic activity of households operating in a planned or transition economy to be composed basically of six types of activity. This composition of the total household activity can expressed as follows:

$$TEA = OE + 2ndE + H + FR + P + FC,$$

where

TEA = Total economic activity of the household;
OE = Work and consumption in the official economy;
2ndE = Work and consumption in the second economy;
FR = Exchange among friends and relatives;
P = Patronage and clientelism with bribes;
FC = Dealing in foreign currency.

According to Rose, a household in a planned — or command — economy thus manages a sort of 'portofolio of economies', i.e. it may invest its resources in various sectors of economic activity in order to maximize its well-being. In a manner similar to that of an investor in the stock market, a household strives to maximize the returns on its investments and, at the same time, minimize the risks of the investments through diversification. Below follows a brief description of the risks and advantages related to each of the six components of the household portofolio.

Work and consumption in the official economy is, naturally, the most commonplace target for investment. The salary from a job in the official economy, or pensions and other compensations received from the state, quite obviously provide the basis of subsistence for the overwhelming majority of Russians. A salary from the official economy is, however, seldom sufficient for the maintenence of living, as the statistics presented above indicate. Hence it is not rational for a household to invest all its resources in the activities of the official economy. 'We pretend to work and they pretend to pay us', as the popular saying went in the socialist countries of Eastern Europe. The low productivity of labour and the often dubious quality of Russian commodities have been often explained by referring vaguely to national character or to the erosion of labour discipline under the communist regime. An explanation based on the behaviour of the economic subjects would emphasize the fact that, in a situation where the salary is insufficient and incentives in the form of rises in wages are missing, the most rational strategy is for a worker to spend only the minimum amount of time and energy on work in the official economy and invest the resources thus saved in other useful purposes, e.g. in being active in social networks or in work in the second economy.

The activities in the area of the second economy or shadow economy are based on payments in money, but this exchange of goods and services is 'unofficial' in the sense that no official records on the transactions are being kept and the activities are not subject to taxation. Usually these second-economy jobs and occupations have the character of part-time employment. In the developed market economies this sector of the economy belongs to the domain of the official labour market and commodity and service markets — as long as the activities are considered legal — but in the real socialism these second-economy activities remained outside the scope of the centrally designated system of production and distribution.

Having a second occupation *(promysl)* has traditionally been customary in Russia; peasants as well as rank-and-file civil servants have practised, among other activities, handicraft and small commerce in order to make ends meet (cf. e.g. Pipes, 1974). The custom — and the need for additional income from sources other than the principal occupation — has persisted from the days of the tsarist regime. An employee in a budgetary organization or a state-owned enterprise may repair cars or TV sets, give piano lessons, drive a taxi without a licence or sell home-sewed clothing as a *promysl*.

The jobs in the second economy may typically be described as service work or commerce. Officially there has either been no need for this work, or the centrally planned system of production and distribution has already produced a sufficient quantity of these goods and services. In practice, the demand has, however, often been far greater than what the official system of distribution has been able to supply, and this excess demand has speeded up the growth of a large unofficial economy. According to even the most cautious estimates, the size of the shadow economy has been estimated to be approximately 20 per cent of the size of the official economy in Russia (e.g. Bystrova and Yeremicheva, 1991, pp. 8-9), while in the more daring appraisals, figures up to 50 per cent are mentioned (e.g. Lõhmus, 1992).

In the course of the transition towards a market economy these formerly illegal activities of the second economy become to a certain degree integrated within the official labour and commodity markets. A part of this formerly hidden economic activity thus becomes subject to taxation. It is very likely, however, that a significant part of the second-economy entrepreneurship will also remain hidden in the future. The criminalization of private economic activity during the Soviet regime created a vigorous and resistant subterranean network economy, and uprooting this tradition of illegal or semi-legal entrepreneurship is likely to prove to be an extremely difficult task. The networks of the shadow economy will hardly become wholly exposed to daylight; to a significant extent they will continue their traditional unofficial existence in order to protect their profits from taxation.

Household production, e.g. growing foodstuffs or do-it-yourself construction and repair work, has been far more widespread in Russia than in the advanced market economies. Household production has most often compensated for the inadequate functioning of the distribution system in the socialist 'deficit economies' (cf. Kornai, 1990). Household production can have the nature of employment in the second economy in cases where the products are made also for sale. The home-made products can be exchanged in the social networks formed between friends and relatives; this exchange of goods happens often as a form of barter without any money being involved.

Social networks have a crucial significance in Russian daily life. Participation in social networks is an important asset: in a problematic situation, far more resources can be mobilized through the network than by a single individual or a nuclear family alone. Some networks can have the character of a functional distribution net, i.e. they are explicitly formed to work as channels of acquisition and distribution of scarce goods. In the deficit economies it has been necessary to stand in line for the goods that are difficult to obtain — and from time to time for most of the goods needed in daily life. These inevitable lines have been organized through the network in such a manner that each individual member has not needed to waste his or her energy on standing in line. The members of a social network can exchange various services and home-made products; job opportunities and career promotions are often arranged through such networks of mutual solidarity and reciprocal favours. The exchange in the networks is based on social obligation, and payment in money is not the predominant type of transaction. The nature of the network may, however, vary from networks held together by close friendship or blood relationship to networks that function solely as systems of commodity provision (cf. e.g. Srubar, 1991; Rose, 1991).

Receiving and giving bribes is, like forming lines, in its typical form a practice associated with the distribution of scarce goods. Richard Pipes (1974), explaining the omnipresence of bribery in imperial Russia, refers to the patrimonial tradition of Russia, i.e. to the fact that political authority and ownership were never clearly distinguishable from each other. For a bureaucrat at the service of the imperial administration his post resembled a private plot of land, granted to him to exploit at will, in order to augment his otherwise meagre salary. The Soviet Union created especially favourable circumstances for the continuation of this tradition: the state apparatus was granted the sole power to make decisions concerning the allocation of resources and, at the same time, all such agencies of civil society that could have effectively controlled the functionaries were abolished. As we can conclude from the income statistics presented above, the salaries in the budgetary organizations are so low that bribe-taking may in many instances be practically a necessity for the subsistence of the public servant.

In the post-communist transition period, marked by political confusion and absence of adequate legislation, the elaborate art of bribery in Russia has assumed new and magnificent proportions. The size of the bribes ranges from the giant payoffs given to functionaries by the new entrepreneurs wishing as soon as possible to receive an official permit for their trade to the bottle of brandy that is given to the doctor at the public hospital in order to ensure a normal child-birth. Virtually every branch of administration has its own special ways to earn additional income: a driver's licence can be obtained without any knowledge of driving at all if the price is agreed, a permission to travel abroad is granted — depending on the size of the payoff — either in two days or after a month, or a burial place for a deceased relative can be found in no time at the otherwise overcrowded cemetery with the help of a present given to the responsible functionary. M.E. Saltykov-Shchedrin, the novelist, noted in the middle of the nineteenth century that in

Russia money was better invested in bribes than in bank deposits (Pipes, 1974, pp. 284-285). This is even more true for an entrepreneur in present-day Russia: the currency is unstable, the banking system unreliable and there are only few sure objects for investments, whereas paying off the local authorities, on the one hand, and criminal racketeers — the *rekety*, as they are popularly called — on the other hand, secures an environment free from harassment from either side (cf. Kryshtanovskaya, 1993, pp. 191-193).

Dealing in hard foreign currency is a special instance of the activities in the second economy. As the value of the rouble has been extremely unstable, foreign currencies have become a more and more popular medium of payment. On the other hand, the significance of the dollar-based black market has decreased, as the prices of the most of the products can now be freely determined and goods can be traded with considerable profits even in the official market. The US dollar seems to have a firm foothold in the economy of the big cities, Moscow and St. Petersburg, but at least up to the the year 1993 'the green' has, however, by no means substituted the rouble as a medium of daily transactions. In the provincial towns the role of the second economy based on the use of foreign currency continues still to be insignificant.

What is the size of the other sectors of economic activity compared to the size of the official economy? Richard Rose (1991) has examined these proportions with the help of large survey data from Bulgaria and the former Czechoslovakia. Table 6.4 (Rose, 1991, p. 28) shows an estimate of household participation in these six spheres of activity based on the data from Bulgaria and Czechoslovakia.

It is doubtful, of course, how reliably we can estimate the size of the shadow economy and the frequency of illegal or semi-legal economic activity with the help of survey questionnaires. The figures presented

Table 6.4. Participation of households in six spheres of economic activity in Bulgaria and Czechoslovakia in 1991. *Source:* Rose, 1991, p. 28.

	Czechoslovakia	Bulgaria
1. Participation in official economy	89 %	79 %
2. Household production	69 %	79 %
3. Networks of mutual aid	47 %	48 %
4. Participation in second economy	34 %	14 %
5. Paid connections, bribes	57 %	40 %
6. Dealing in foreign currency	29 %	18 %

in Table 6.4 are quite likely to underestimate the significance of the activities defined as illegal. Even so, these figures clearly evidence the fact that in 1991 a significant part of the population in these countries manoeuvred, except in the sphere of the official and the inofficial economies, in the shadow economy, too. Comparable estimates based on survey data are not available for Russia. It is likely, however, that the spheres of both the unofficial economy (2 and 3) and the shadow economy (4, 5 and 6) are even more significant in Russia than they were in Czechoslovakia and Bulgaria, given the longer absence of the institutions of the market economy and the strong patrimonial legacy.

According to the study conducted by Rose the vast majority of households had divided their activity to more than one sector of the economy. In Czechoslovakia 66 per cent of the respondent households operated at least in three different spheres of economy and in Bulgaria 57 per cent. Dividing the activity among several different spheres of the economy makes the household, naturally, less vulnerable, especially in times of rapid social change. A good strategy of action, i.e. a good 'portfolio of economies', enables the houshold to manoeuvre simultaneously in several different domains of economic activity. The well-being acquired from several kinds of activities is greater than it would be in the case that the household was dependent solely on the income from the official economy. On the other hand, the household may take disproportionately large risks by concentrating its activities mainly in the domain of the shadow economy, even if the momentary well-being received from these sources would in many instances be the greatest.

Although the income received from employment in the public sector of the Russian economy is usually not sufficient to ensure a decent standard of living — only two per cent of the respondents in the survey data quoted above indicated that they had in May 1993 an income high enough to allow a normal life — the job is still of primary importance. Employment and membership in 'the work collective' *(trudovoi kollektiv)* is important not only because of the salary, but also because of the traditional function of the Russian work place as a channel of distribution of goods and social services. Sometimes this distributive function of employment has been even more important for the daily life of the worker than the salary. In the Soviet deficit economy important factories and administrative departments had their own connections and networks for acquiring the commodities that were difficult to obtain in the official shops; these goods were then distributed at reduced prices exclusively to the members of the work collective. The big employers often arranged the children's day care and the medical services for their employees — and especially the latter have been a considerable privilege, as the public medical services are in many instances of such a low quality that they are usually resorted to only in situations of utmost necessity. Vouchers to the sanatora and vacation centres, as well as many other subsidies and benefits classified as social services, have also traditionally been distributed solely through the work places. A significant part of the resources needed for the well-being of the household may thus be composed of these goods and services provided by the employer. In the Soviet Union the jobs have had — and in Russia they still do have — a clearly distributive function along with their productive function (cf. Heikkilä et al., 1992). Some researchers have even pointed out that it would be more correct to talk about 'distributive collectives' instead of using the standard concept in Russian vocabulary, 'the work collective' (Turuntsev, 1993).

However central the importance of the work place may be, the worst off are usually those who do not have any opportunities to act in any other economic arenas than the official one, i.e. those who are dependent solely on activities officially defined as acceptable in the public sector of the economy. An employee in a budgetary organization, for example a librarian, a schoolteacher or a nurse, who does not have the opportunity to receive bribes in the job, who does not operate in the shadow economy and who has no memberships in social networks formed between friends and relatives, is undoubtedly in a very difficult situation. The old people who do not live in the same household with their children — as is customary in Russia — fall very often below the poverty line, too: their pension is in most cases quite small, they do not have access to the distribution channels connected with employment, and they usually occupy only a marginal position in social networks.

From egalitarianism to class society

Was the Soviet Union in reality such a classless society as it understood itself in the ideological level? Some inequality certainly seemed to prevail: members of the party elite often enjoyed considerable privileges, and, on the other hand, the groups that did not adjust themselves to the above-defined structure of division of work could from time to time become subject to severe repression and discrimination. Thematizing this kind of inequality as class relations is, however, quite problematic: the differences in wealth and authority were not created by social forces such as for example the market forces, but the privileges of the party elite were, on the contrary, granted to it by the means of central planning as privileges corresponding the status of the estate of the 'revolutionary avant garde'.

Russian sociologists have described the Soviet society as stratified into three distinct levels (cf. Lvov, 1993). The top stratum, a rather thin one, was composed of the party elite having economic and ideological power. To this elite stratum were co-opted representatives of various important groupings, organizations, corporate interest groups and minority nationalities. The mirror image of the power elite was the residue, the bottom level of the Soviet society. To this very heterogeneous category belonged those who did not quite fit in the categories of the officially determined division of labour, for example the people living on 'income not from labour' (*netrudovie dohody*), private entrepreneurs, prostitutes, black marketeers, currency dealers, persons 'without a defined place of residence' (*bomzhy*), criminals, chronic alcoholics etc. From time to time, campaigns were launched by the elite against these 'parasitic' groups not having an official status in the Soviet society. (Cf. Lvov, 1993.)

Between these two opposite levels, the elite using the power to make definitions and the residue escaping all these established definitions, were situated 'the middle strata', the vast majority of Soviet people. Among this majority, not belonging either to the elite or to the residue, welfare resources and life chances seemed officially to be relatively evenly distributed. The statistics did not show any remarkable differences in income or wealth between various occupational groups. The income level of skilled manual workers — especially of those employed in the military-industrial complex (*voenno-promyshlennyi kompleks*) — was the highest in the Soviet Union, the nation of workers, whereas white collar groups, among them even highly educated professionals, for example teachers, medical doctors and scientists, were discriminated to some extent (cf. e.g. Kivinen, 1993).

If the conclusions are solely based on the observation of the activity and returns from the official economy, the resources were distributed quite evenly among the great majority of Soviet people. The income received from employment was calculated to cover the basic needs of a household. The problem was the system of distribution: due to its deficiencies the needed services and commodities were not always available. The organizations employing the workforce strived, as was already noted above, to compensate for these inadequacies by creating their own channels of provision and distribution intended exclusively for the members of the work collective. In organizing these alternative channels of provision the work collectives — quite like the individual households — often had to operate in the sphere of the shadow economy. A factory could for example engage itself, outside the official bookkeeping procedures, in barter with other production units, and then distribute the commodities thus obtained to the members of the work collective. The prospects for engagement in profitable activities of the kind varied, however, between work collectives: the workers in a factory producing scarce consumer goods were, of course, better off than employees in administration.

Inequality in the Soviet society was then, above all, inequality regarding the access to the distribution of goods and services. The one who had access to a well-functioning network of distribution could enjoy a considerably higher standard of living than his or her comrade who had to rely solely on the official state-provided shops and services, even if their nominal incomes in roubles had been exactly equal. The privileged groups, for example the party elite and the workers in the most important military production units, had their own and exclusive systems of distribution, e.g. special shops intended for the top functionaries of the CPSU; but among the middle strata, too, there existed considerable inequality related to the distribution of goods.

The varying chances of work collectives to organize the distribution of goods was not, however, the only source of inequality in the Soviet society. A significant part of the households operated, as was pointed out in the previous section, in the areas of the unofficial economy and the shadow economy in order to maximize their well-being. The deficiencies in the distribution of goods could be compensated for by household production. Social networks were built for the purposes of acquiring scarce goods; one member of the network could line up for the desired commodity for all the members of the network. The products virtually never seen in state shops could be purchased on the black market at a price many times the official one; especially with hard currency everything was available. In conditions of constant overdemand it was tempting to steal commodities from the workplace and sell them on the black market at a high price. The functionary distributing the services of the state, who did not enjoy the same privileges as did his or her comrade working in the production, could compensate for this disadvantage by receiving money and presents from clients.

The residue in the Soviet Union was, in fact, not a separate social stratum composed of some 'anti-social' individuals, but, on the contrary, a significant part of the people constantly had the other foot in this sphere of residual and officially non-existent activities while the other was firmly in the official economy. It is possible that the privileged elite usually did not have to operate in this residual sphere, in spite of the widespread accounts of corruption at the upper echelons of the Soviet power, whereas for the majority of the population the ability to manoeuvre smoothly in the residual sphere, the efficient allocation of activity between the official, unofficial and shadow economies, belonged to the basic arsenal of survival skills. Far from being a separate domain of outcasts and drop-outs, the residue in the Brezhnev era pervaded virtually the entire Soviet society. Only relatively few shifted, however, their both feet to marginal ground, even though the short-term economic advantages would often have been considerable. It was far more safe to invest at least a part of the resources in the official economy and thus maintain an officially acknowledged status in the society.

It is difficult to make visible the hidden inequality that prevailed in the Soviet Union with the help of a class analysis similar to those applied to the study of societies in advanced capitalism. It is hard to distinguish any clear-cut classes or strata among the vast majority of the Soviet people, but when networks and households' economic strategies are examined, the differences become distinct. It was, indeed, possible for people to subsist and satisfy basic needs on their salaries alone in the Soviet Union, even if it may have seemed to be out of place to talk about the quality of life or the standard of living in the western sense of these concepts. The deficiencies in the distribution of goods and services were not so large, except during the year 1991, the last year of the existence of the Soviet empire, that they had threatened basic subsistence. A household that had managed to build a good portofolio of economies enjoyed, furthermore, a standard of living that was considerably above this minimum.

What is the situation in the present-day Russia, and how do the conditions differ from the ones that prevailed during the Soviet era? How are the resources and well-being distributed in a post-socialist society? The change and transition, the formation of new social divisions, can be illustrated with the help of a schematic comparison between the planned economy and the market economy. Table 6.5 compares the basic mechanisms that create and reduce inequality and social stratification in planned economies and market economies.

Table 6.5. Some basic differences between the planned economy and the market economy.

	PLANNED ECONOMY	MARKET ECONOMY
The basic principle of resource allocation	Central planning	Market
The domain of the market mechanism	Shadow economy	Official economy
The nature of social stratification	Estates	Classes
The source of inequalities	Estate privileges The mechanisms of the shadow economy and unofficial economy	The mechanisms of the official economy
The compensation of inequalities	Central planning	Social policy
Minimum standard of living	In principle secured	Not necessarily secured

Central planning was the basic principle of resource allocation in the Soviet Union. The elite held the economic and ideological power and determined which goods and services, and how much, were produced. The state apparatus determined as well what kinds of labour force were needed as the size of the various occupational groups. The state decided also about the allocation of the resources intended for consumption: how much was needed to cover the needs of the population, and which groups of the population were to be given priority. The demands of the military-industrial complex, traditionally the most powerful lobby inside the Russian and Soviet state apparatus, were taken into consideration first; the investment needs of the non-military heavy industry were also of primary importance. The remaining share of the national wealth was to be distributed evenly. Equal distribution of wealth and consumption — with the exception of the privileges granted to the elite — was a major aim in a society understanding itself as classless. In an ideal-typical market economy all these allocation tasks are performed not by the firm hand of the state, but instead by the invisible hand of the market.

The market mechanism operates in a planned economy only in the shadow economy that evolves to compensate for the deficiencies and bottlenecks of official production and distribution. As it is likely that even the most wise and considerate planner never has enough information to anticipate all the needs of every consumer, a black market or a large unofficial economy develops to satisfy these unanticipated wants and needs. Terror is likely to be the only recourse for the planner determined enough to uproot the market mechanisms, but if the terror ceases, as in the post-Stalin period, the market mechanisms are revived again. In an economy that is classified as a market economy the market mechanism should, obviously, be the foremost principle of resource allocation, and if the markets function properly, the shadow economy should shrink to concern only the supply and demand of some few criminalized goods, for example narcotics.

In the Soviet Union, as well as in any other centrally planned economy, the division of labour and the compensation received from work at each of the positions of this division, i.e. the share of each member of the society in the total wealth of the nation, were in principle determined by the state. The social stratification of the Soviet society was, in principle, produced by the state. The Soviet Union can thus be defined as a society of estates as distinguished from a 'genuine' class society. There existed primarily two estates in the sense of Max Weber's *Stände* in the Soviet Union: the elite and the people. Outside these determinations remained still a third stratum, the residue, the casteless of the Soviet society.

In a 'pure' market economy the division of labour and social inequality is, in the last instance, determined by market forces. A society based on the market economy has the nature of a class society, and class antagonism, at least to some degree, is an inevitable characteristic of all market economies.

The basis of inequality in an estate society, as the Soviet Union was classified above, is the various privileges and obligations attributed officially to each estate. The dominant estate has its specific and defined tasks in the society, its own code of honour, its own virtues, its own style of life and also its own privileges when the resources of the society are distributed among its members. Inequalities and differences in the standard of living in the Soviet Union were, however, determined not only in terms of these official privileges granted to the dominant estate, but also by the mechanisms of the unofficial and the shadow economy, through which the resources were re-allocated past the official channels of distribution. The market mechanisms operating in the shadow economy worked against the officially acknowledged aims, bringing certain features of a class society also to the Soviet Union.

Class conflict or antagonism between social classes was above identified as a feature typical to market economies. Various structures for the regulation of this conflict and for the compensation of the inequalities that are the basic cause of the antagonism are built into advanced market economies. Structures of this kind are for example the taxation system, social security and incomes policies. The totality of these measures can be called the social policy. In the Soviet Union social policy in this sense — as a kind of regulative superstructure built upon the market mechanisms — did, on the contrary, not exist: if all observable privileges and inequalities were intentionally planned by the state, there naturally was no need to develop any measures aimed to reduce this inequality, either. The centrally planned production of equality or inequality was already social policy as such.

The bottom row in table 6.5 deals with the minimum standard of living in the command economy and market economy. If social policy basically equals simply the official distribution of labour positions and resources intended for consumption, as was the case in the Soviet Union, it is in principle enough to make an official decision to distribute a certain amount of resources to every citizen in order to ensure the satisfaction of the basic needs of everybody — with the precondition, of course, that a sufficient amount of resources is available and the distribution system is working at least to some degree. After the military-industrial complex had first taken its lion's share from the cake there was, indeed, left for every Soviet citizen a slice guaranteeing the minimum standard of living, however meagre this minimum may have been.

In a market economy the situation becomes, however, more complicated. The allocation mechanisms in a market economy do not obey any social principles, and market demand and supply are, quite unlike the central planning commission, wholly unaware of all the calculations concerning the minimum standard of living. A system must be created in which the social risks caused by the market forces are stabilized. A cornerstone of this system is a sufficiently large tax base from which the means for the redistribution can be obtained. It is controversial whether such a revenue base exists in present-day Russia. During the decades of the Soviet Union private entrepreneurship was banned and it existed in principle only as underground activity. It is rather optimistic to expect that all this activity would now at once come to the light of the day, just in order to be taxed. The yields of an income tax taken from the scanty incomes from the official economy are likely to remain small, as well. It is self-evident, too, that a social policy of this kind cannot function adequately without a reliable monetary system; the steep decline of the value of the rouble during the winter 1992-93 left especially those living on income transfers in a particularly vulnerable position.

The bankruptcy of socialism: the survivors and the losers

The outspoken goal of the Soviet state was to achieve a classless and egalitarian society. To realize this ideological aim, the division of labour in the society and the well-being each of the citizens received from his or her labour were, in principle, determined by the planning organs of the state. The reality was, however, different: along with the officially planned mechanisms of resource distribution there existed also unofficial mechanisms that worked in the opposite direction, i.e. towards increased differentiation of the population. For example the occupational groups that have in western industrialized countries been regarded as middle-class undoubtedly had at least some possibility of forming a stratum that was to some extent autonomous from the state. 'The actually existing social structure was far more complex than its official image', as Bystrova and Yeremicheva (1991, p. 8) have put it.

In Russia during this transition period the middle class is widely regarded as the backbone of the new society. The most diverse political parties, movements and groupings address their messages to the middle class. The evolving new middle class is considered to be the most significant stabilizing factor in the Russian society (e.g. Bystrova and Yeremicheva, 1991). In Russia as characteristics of the middle class have been regarded, for example, a level of income allowing a relatively high standard of living, the possession of both professional and cultural qualifications as well as material property, ability to compete in the labour market and a distinct life style differing clearly both from that of the working class and from that of the ruling elite (cf. Lvov, 1993, p. 1). A common characteristic for all the highly industrialized western countries is the high proportion of these middle-class strata within the total population.

But does a middle class thus described actually exist in present-day Russia? Lvov (1993, p. 2) points out pertinently that in the Russia of the year 1993 'the middle class' is predominately an ideological fabrication, much like 'the Soviet people' was for the Soviet Union. The population of the ethnically and culturally diverse Soviet Union was regarded as a monolitic Soviet people that, above all, was patriotic and loyal to its common fatherland and thus also felt solidarity towards other nationalities populating the territory of this common fatherland. The conflicts and hostilities between nationalities that later erupted with destructive force lay well hidden behind this ideological curtain. The widely cherished picture of the middle class as the backbone of the new Russia believing in the market economy camouflages the fact that at this time no such social stratum exists in Russia which could have such a stabilizing impact, and that the social confusion can produce very unexpected political developments. The vast 'middle stratum' of the Soviet society can not transform itself overnight into a middle class that could act as a guarantor of political democracy based on the market economy.

The differences in income in Russia are at the moment growing very rapidly (e.g. Turuntsev, 1993). A new elite consisting of the *nouveaux riches* has already developed, a thin social stratum with an income and standard of living that are remarkably higher than that of the vast majority of the population. This elite — 'the new Russians' — lifted to the wealth by the dawning capitalism, is mainly composed of entrepreneurs of various sorts. Where do these new Russians come from? A significant part of the members of this new economic elite operated in the residual sphere during the Soviet regime; among them are trades-men from the shadow economy, co-operative entrepreneurs, black market dealers and sheer criminals. Another important group com-prises the members of the former *nomenklatura*, the political and econ-omic elite, who have managed to increase their power and privileges in the course of the privatization of state property. A third group consists of highly qualified professionals who previously worked in the state enterprises and who have been able to start a business of their own. The stratum of these new Russians is quite narrow. It is difficult to define clearly its outlines, and thus precise estimates of its size cannot be given. Its share of the total population is, however, by no means more than five per cent. (Travin, 1993.)

Thus elements from the elite and the residue of the old Soviet society are coming together to form the economic elite of the new society. But what about the middle class? Parts of the middle stratum are mobile upwards, and these groups are likely to form a western-type middle class in the future. Another part of this vast stratum is sinking towards the status of a proletariat. According to income statistics the majority of the households belonging to the old middle stratum are at the moment living on the edge of poverty. 'Survival skills', i.e. a good portofolio of economies, the ability to be engaged in various activities of an 'unofficial' kind, are crucially important in determining whether the household is mobile upwards, towards the middle class, or down-wards, towards the proletariat. In the circumstances of flux and inse-curity the ability to gain resources from several different areas of economy is especially important.

Along with the economic elite there can thus be distinguished still two separate strata. These strata can be named 'the survivors' and 'the proletariat'. The relative size of these strata is, inevitably, going to be a decisive factor influencing the development of the political life in Russia. The larger the share is of those striving toward a middle-class way of life, with all the attributes which have characterized it in the western industrial countries, the more probable is the growth of the forces supporting the market economy and parliamentary democracy. And the greater the share is of those sinking ever deeper into poverty and humiliation, the more widespread is the longing for the old life, in which a strong hand of the state provided at least the meagre basics of living, military parades as pastimes and, as a source of self-esteem, the awareness of being the servant of a mighty and expansive empire.

References

Bystrova, A. & Yeremicheva, G.V. (1991), *Prerequisites for Formation of the Middle Class in the Soviet Society*, Institute of Sociology, St. Petersburg branch, Russian Academy of Sciences, St. Petersburg.

Gontmakher, E. (1993), 'Ne do zhiru, byt by zhivu...', *Argumenti i fakti*, no. 33/1993.

Deacon, Bob (1992), 'East European Welfare: Past, Present and Future in Comparative Context' in Deacon, Bob (ed.), *The New Eastern Europe*, Sage, London.

Heikkilä, Matti et al. (1992), 'Iskulauseista taikasanoihin: Markkinasuhteisiin siirtyminen ja sosiaalipolitiikka entisessä Neuvostoliitossa', *Sosiaaliturva*, no. 3-4/1992.

Illarionov, A. (1993), 'Nash uroven zhizni', *Argumenti i fakti*, 25 June 1993.

Khudiakova, Tatiana (1993), 'Samie nuzhdaiushchiesia — semi s detmi', *Izvestiia*, 1 June 1993.

Kivinen, Markku (1993), *Yhteiskuntaluokat Venäjällä — alustavia huomautuksia*, a paper presented at the Seminar of Comparative Sociology, 16 February 1993, University of Helsinki, Department of Sociology

Kornai, Janos (1990), *The Road to a Free Economy: Shifting from a Socialist System*, Norton Press, New York.

Kryshtanovskaya, Olga (1993), 'The New Business Elite' in Lane, David (ed.), *Russia in Flux. The Political and Social Consequences of Reform*, Edward Elgar, Aldershot.

Kultygin, V.P. (1993), 'Poverty and Social Trends in Russia', *Scandinavian Journal of Social Welfare*, vol. 2, no. 3/1993.

Kutsar, Dagmar & Trumm, Avo (1993), 'Poverty among Households in Estonia', *Scandinavian Journal of Social Welfare*, vol. 2, no. 3/1993.

Lvov, Nikolai (1993), *Konseptsiia 'srednego klassa' v Rossii perioda modernisatsii sotsialnoi struktury*, a paper presented in the Seminar of Eastern European Research, 22 February 1993, University of Helsinki, Department of Social Policy.

Lõhmus, Aivo (1992), 'Varjotalous hajoitti Neuvostoliiton', *ARG*, no. 4/1992.

Pipes, Richard (1974), *Russia under the Old Regime*, Penguin Books, Harmondsworth.

Protasenko, Tatiana (1992), 'Uroven bednosti — 2,500 rublei, uroven normalnoi zhizni — 10,000 rublei', *Nevskoe vremia*, 13 October 1992.

Protasenko, Tatiana (1993), 'Kak my zhili v dni Konstitutsionnogo soveshchaniia', *Nevskoe vremia*, 9 July 1993.

Rose, Richard (1991), *Between State and Market. Key Indicators of Transition in Eastern Europe*, University of Strathclyde, Centre for the Study of Public Policy, Glasgow.

Ruutsoo, Rein (1991), 'Miten neuvostotilastoja on luettava?', *Tiede & edistys*, no. 2/1991.

Soloviev, A. (1993), 'A nashi rebiata za ty zhe zarplatu...', *Argumenti i fakti*, no. 32/1993.

Srubar, Ilja (1991), 'War der reale Sozialismus modern? Versuch einer strukturellen Bestimmung', *Kölner Zeitschrift für Soziologie und Sozialpsychologie*, vol. 43, no. 3/1991.

Travin, Igor (1993), *Tendentsii ismeneniia sotsialnoi struktury sovremennogo rossiiskogo obshchestva*, a paper presented in the Seminar of Eastern European Research, 1 March 1993, University of Helsinki, Department of Social Policy.

Turuntsev, Evgeni (1993), *The Fall of Paternalism?*, Institute of Socio-economic Studies of Population, Moscow (mimeo).

7 Class Relations in Russia

Markku Kivinen

Introduction

How to examine the social structure of a society that apparently seems to be in a state of flux? If 'all that is solid melts into air', how can these fluid relations be grasped for the purposes of a sociological analysis? As the title of this book suggests, however, even in Eastern Europe strong continuities do exist along with the flux and change. In order to grasp these underlying continuities, the processes of social differentiation that took place under Soviet socialism must first be examined.

In the previous chapter an attempt was made to analyze the formation of social classes in post-communist Russia by referring to the distribution of life chances among the population. Life chances and the possibilities of maintaining middle-class life styles are, however, but only one aspect of the question concerning the formation and re-formation of social classes. The redistribution of life chances during the current transition is a highly relevant issue, especially in a situation where a significant part of the people appear to be deprived of even the most basic necessities. But if we are to study the more persistent tendencies and continuities of social differentiation, the analysis must be based on the examination of some other spheres of social activity, too.

From the point of view of the tradition of class research, production and the labour process provide the most adequate basis for such an analysis. A class theory based on the analysis of the politics of production and its changes can also shed some additional light on the reasons for the collapse of Soviet socialism. In the previous chapter, it was argued that Soviet society was basically a society of estates and not a class society, in the sense that all officially recognized social differentation and stratification was produced by the state and not by market forces, i.e. the movement of the capital. According to this view, only the mechanisms of the shadow economy and the unofficial economy produced social differentation resembling class division. But there was an additional, and perhaps even more important, source of differentiation of a similar kind, namely the increasing autonomy gained by various professional groups as Russia was industrialized and the labour positions diverged.

The formation of civil society in Russia has been an important subject of debate during the recent years (see e.g. Cohen, 1982; Alapuro, 1993). Was it the autonomy gained by the professional groups resembling in many respects western middle-class groups that created pressure towards the formation of a civil society, i.e. of a sphere of public activity separate from the state apparatus? And was it this pressure that decisively contributed to the launching of perestroika and finally to the dissolution of Soviet socialism? The question about the civil society can not, of course, be reduced to class theory, but an elaborate class analysis can nevertheless make these inherent tensions of Soviet socialism more visible.

This chapter consists basically of four parts. The first part deals with the previous theoretical attempts to analyze Soviet socialism in class terms. Thereafter, various characteristics of class relations are identified in Soviet socialism, especially in the area of labour processes and division of labour; this examination is largely based on the class theory developed by Kivinen (1989). Thirdly, empirical theses are presented concerning the specific nature of classes during the last years of the Soviet regime; these remarks are based on the material collected by the International Comparative Project on Class Structure and Class Consciousness. The fourth and concluding part presents a brief discussion about the future development of the class structure in Eastern Europe.

The Soviet self-understanding

Existing theories of the class structure that prevailed during Soviet socialism can be divided into three broad categories:

1. The standard Soviet view, which said and says (some scholars still adhere to this theory) that class relations in socialist society are essentially non-antagonistic and that all class differences are gradually withering away.

2. The power-theoretical view on the class relations of socialist society, which describes it as a society ruled by bureaucrats, the intelligentsia, or managers. In this category we have such theorists as Trotsky, Djilas and Burnham. More recently, there are also many Russian bureaucracy analysts who represent this line of theorizing.

3. The attempts by analytical Marxism to define socialism and 'state-bureaucratic socialism' as specific forms of exploitation.

As class antagonisms are based on private ownership of the means of production, there could be no irreconcilable conflicts of this type in socialism: this was the fundamental premise of Soviet social theory. This did not mean to say that there were no classes. Traditionally, Soviet sociologists made a distinction between workers and collective peasants on the basis of form of ownership. In addition, they identified the intelligentsia as a separate social stratum which belonged to neither of these classes. Within the working class, a distinction was traditionally made between skilled and unskilled labourers. According to this standard view, unskilled labourers were supposed to be disappearing altogether, as indeed were all differences within and between social classes (cf. Glezerman, 1949 and 1962; Semjenov, 1962; Kugel, 1968; Rutkevich, 1968; Shkaratan, 1973; Rutkevich, 1978).

Although class relations are thus defined as relations of functional cooperation, this does not imply a complete denial of inequality in work and reproduction situations. In fact, in the history of socialist countries different ideological (and practical and political) stages in attitudes towards egalitarianism can be detected (see e.g. Parkin 1971, pp. 137-159).

Wage differentials between blue-collar and white-collar workers in the Soviet Union decreased considerably immediately after the revolution. Many countries pursuing a policy of people's democracy followed suit and introduced a similar radical policy of income distribution after the Second World War. At the same time, there were some serious efforts to eliminate or at least reduce educational inequality by introducing separate quotas for workers' and peasants' children.

On the other hand, Stalin attacked the ideology of excessive equality (*uranilovka*) as early as the 1930's. He insisted that skilled labourers and the new 'cadres of management and technology' had to be guaranteed better material incentives and privileges. This led to the development in the Soviet Union of a highly complex income distribution system and the growth of privileges.

After the Stalinist era, a number of measures were introduced that reversed this development. Minimum wage levels were raised and workers engaged in routine tasks were also paid more than earlier.

During the 1980s, Soviet sociology called into question many previous truths and certainties in two different ways. Although it was still maintained that the basic course of development was towards increasing social homogeneity, it was now gradually admitted that socialism produces new forms of social differentiation and that it is equally important to have concrete research in this area (Igitkhanyan and Kirkh, 1982, and Titma, 1986). In addition, there was also increasing criticism of the existing system of income distribution: do the differences in consumption level, the critics asked, really reflect differences in work performance in the case of company management, for instance (Ovsiannikov, 1986)?

There was also growing scepticism of the theory that technological progress automatically leads to the elimination of unskilled labour. This, it was now argued, required the involvement of workers in decision making and increased autonomy at all levels of the work organization (Gordon and Nazimova, 1985). At the same time, Soviet sociologists such as Leonid Gordon began to refer to the necessity of a middle class.

Researchers in socialist countries often argued that the absence of distinct class boundaries in their societies was due in large part to the high level of social mobility. However, in the light of the latest empirical research results, this can be disputed. Although it is true that opportunities for upward social mobility were greatly improved in people's democracies after World War II with the reform of the educational system, the situation has in fact been increasingly similar to that in advanced capitalist countries ever since the 1960's. Recent results from the Soviet Union (e.g. Blom and Filippov, 1988; see also Aitov, 1986), for instance, show that opportunities for upward mobility declined quite significantly between the 1950's and 1970's.

Up until very recently it has been more or less impossible to utilize the results of Soviet structural research from any other than the standard perspective; this is because the material has been organized and analysed within large class groups (workers, collective peasants, intelligentsia). However, more recent studies also include far more detailed analyses of differences between occupational groups. At the same time, researchers have been outlining new classifications that no longer fit into the old class model (Ivanov et al., 1985; Shkaratan and Rukavishnikov, 1986). During the past three years these efforts have provided a solid basis for elaborating more complex stratification models — but only at the expense of completely discarding the analysis of class structure.

A more interesting line of theorizing, at least from a power and structural point of view, is represented by the efforts that have been made to analyse interest conflicts within the structures of socialist bureaucracy — a concept that began to gain currency in Soviet sociology only towards the end of the 1980's (see Zaslavskaya, 1986 and esp. Hasbulatov, 1991).

As yet the theorizing that has been done in the Soviet Union on the question of power has been fairly crude and unsophisticated. There has been no theoretical analysis of the mutual relationships between different forms of power; for example, the important issue of whether and how power resources differ within the 'politics of production' is completely open, nor has there been any serious work to analyse mental labour as a power issue. Only the first dimension of power identified by Lukes (1974) — i.e. power related to decision making — has been thematized in reasonable detail. By contrast, the approach that emphasizes 'non-decision-making power' is still absent. Similarly, Soviet theorizing on interests has produced no theoretically justified conception of latent interests. This same criticism applies in large part to the power-theoretical class conception, which in one way or another is based on 'the power of the new class'.

The power of the New Class

The theory of socialism as a new form of class domination is older than the socialism which has really existed. One of the earliest writers to realize that white-collar workers could use socialism to take over from capitalists and to start exploiting the workers directly was the Polish revolutionary Jan Waclaw Machajski (1937, quoted in Bruce-Briggs, 1979):

> By attacking the factory-owner the socialist does not touch in the slightest the salary of his managers and engineers. The socialism of the past century leaves inviolate all the incomes of the 'white-hands', as the 'labour wage of the intellectual worker', and, in the words of Kautsky, it declares that 'the intellectuals are not interested in exploitation and are not taking part in it'.

In the 1930's a student of Machajski's, Max Nomad, identified the Soviet system with the supremacy of the intellectual class, and in the 1940's the American Trotskyite Max Schachtman crystallized this view on the Communist Party as a representative of the new class as follows:

> The new bureaucracy emerged, grew up and seized power in response to the organic needs of a backward and isolated country in a unique and unexpected world situation. The new class satisfied those needs (more or less) in accordance with its own nature, the conditions of its own existence. At the same time it changed backward Russia into modern Russia, made it a powerful, industrially advanced country (Max Schachtman, 1943, quoted in Bruce-Briggs, 1979).

Another American Trotskyite, James Burnham, took critical distance from Marxism, arguing in his book *The Managerial Revolution* that the capitalist class is not succeeded by the proletariat but by salaried managers. For him, managerial states were represented by the Soviet Union, fascist Germany and (to a lesser extent) the United States of the 'New Deal' (Burnham, 1941).

In the 1950's Milovan Djilas developed his famous analysis of socialism in which there had emerged a new ruling and exploiting class. This class consists of people who have specific privileges and economic preferences because of the administrative monopoly. In the last instance this administrative monopoly is based on the dominant position of the Communist Party in both economic and political life. It is a 'bureaucratic class' which is created by the parties' monopoly position but which constantly undermines the position of the party itself:

> As the new class gathers momentum and establishes a form of its own, the meaning of the party will decline. The hard core of the new class takes shape within the party and at the top of the party, in the same way as in the state's political organs. A unified party that was once full of initiative will disappear and transform into traditional oligarchy of the new class, which will irresistibly recruit into its ranks those who want to join a new party and rejects those who have ideals. (Djilas 1957, p. 55.)

The concept of a New Class — whether that is defined as consisting of intellectuals, managers, or party bureaucrats — is problematic in more than just one sense.

First of all, the theory is essentially a political one; analysis of the economic aspects of class relations is not given sufficient attention. Although Djilas speaks of a ruling and exploiting class, his theory contains no systematic analysis of the mechanisms of exploitation. This shortcoming has been one of the main concerns in the work of analytical marxism, which I shall discuss later.

Second, different forms of power do not necessarily coincide in socialism. Conservative versions of this argument, such as that of Raymond Aron, call into question the whole notion of the class nature of socialist society. According to Aron (and contrary to the assumptions of Burnham) no coherent managerial group can develop in socialism because the party prevents the promotion of the specific interests of these occupational groups. On the other hand, as far as I can see, it would be a gross simplification to regard all other actors as being excluded from power except the party (see however Faber, 1991). Rather than trying to reduce all power to one single source, certainly it makes more sense to analyse different power resources that are related to a managerial position, to mental work or to a position in the party hierarchy.

Giddens (1973) and Parkin (1971), for example, have drawn attention to the differences in forms of power for the very reason that the party seemed to recruit its cadres primarily from amongst the working class, who will then work to curtail the privileges of managerial or professional groups. The latest research evidence, however, suggests that the communist parties of socialist countries were increasingly being taken over by white-collar groups. Top party management in particular was generally very well-educated. In other words, this argument would appear to be losing its plausibility.

Third, privileges are not inherited in socialism in the same way as in capitalism: a hierarchic position cannot be inherited in the same way as capital. This counterargument, however, can also be modified in two ways:

— While economic capital cannot be inherited, that does not necessarily apply to cultural capital. In fact, one might assume that in socialist society the importance of distinctions related to way of life and culture is even more pronounced than in capitalism.

— As we already pointed out earlier, social mobility decreased significantly in socialism during the last two decades. This may provide a new basis for the formation of a demographic identity for the New Class. This is particularly likely in the event that different political and cultural power resources begin increasingly to coincide.

Socialist exploitation

One of the main intentions of John E. Roemer (1981 and 1982) and Erik Olin Wright in their recent theorizing has been to develop new concepts for the analysis of social classes in existing socialist societies. That effort has been largely informed by Roemer's new theory of exploitation (see also Wright, 1985).

Roemer defines exploitation as a particular kind of causal relationship between the incomes of different actors. If it can be established that the welfare of the rich is related to the deprivation of the poor in a causal fashion, then it can be argued that the rich exploit the poor. Roemer applies a game theory approach to comparing different forms of exploitation; in other words, he approaches the organization of production as a game. There prevails a relationship of exploitation between a coalition of two social actors (S and S') if the following conditions hold:

1) There is an alternative, which we may conceive as hypothetically feasible, in which S would be better off than in its present situation.

2) Under this alternative, the complement of S, the coalition S', would be worse off than at present.

Different forms of exploitation can be extracted from a set of rules of withdrawal: these will indicate in what circumstances a certain agent is better off. According to Roemer the material basis for exploitation is formed by the unequal distribution of productive assets. He proposes a distinction between three types of exploitation relations: feudal, capitalist and socialist.

The assigning of alternative games to each mode of production represents an essential condition for the conceptualization of exploitation. Under capitalism workers own no 'physical assets' (means of production) and they must sell their labour power to the capitalist for a wage. In the game-theoretical sense, workers are exploited insofar as it can be demonstrated that there exists an alternative game to capitalism in which both conditions hold. Roemer and Wright say that such a game is one in which each worker would receive his or her per capita share of the total productive assets of society. In this alternative game the workers would be better off and the capitalists worse off.

In the alternative game for socialist exploitation, each player would receive his or her per capita share of inalienable assets (occupational skills). A certain coalition of players could be characterized as socialistically exploited if it could improve its position by withdrawing from the game with its per capita share of skills, leaving its complement worse off. (See Roemer, 1982, pp. 238-263.) This is a form of exploitation which is based on control over scarce skills. Here the income of skilled workers is in excess of the cost of producing those skills, and therefore they have a vested interest in maintaining skill differentials.

Wright, however, argues that these categories do not help us to understand the nature of existing socialist societies. In Roemer's scheme socialist society can be characterized as some sort of non-bureaucratic technocracy. Experts or the intellectual class have complete control over their own skill or knowledge assets and by virtue of that position they are able to appropriate part of the surplus product. However, Wright says that experts do not seem to represent a dominant class in those societies and their internal dynamics does not seem to be related to skill differentials. There is, according to Wright, one important type of productive asset missing from Roemer's analysis, and that is the organization.

In capitalist society organization assets are usually controlled by managers and capitalists. Within individual business firms those assets are controlled by managers, under constraints imposed by capitalists through their ownership of capital assets. In 'state-bureaucratic social- ism' the control of organization assets acquires much greater signifi- cance: it is no longer the task simply of company-level managers but of the state's central planning organs. So the statement that exploitation in this type of society is based on bureaucratic power means that the control of organization assets determines the material basis of class relations and exploitation.

The argument that control over organization assets is a basis for exploitation means, firstly, that non-managers would be better off and managers and bureaucrats worse off if the former withdrew from the game with their per capita share of organization assets (i.e., if organiz- ational control were democratized). Secondly, it means that through their control of organization assets managers or bureaucrats also con- trol part of the produced surplus value. Wright emphasizes that better off here refers not to the amount personally consumed but to the amount of income managers effectively control.

The main difficulty with Wright's and Roemer's theorizing is that they operate with the concept of exploitation at the market level, thus abstracting from the relations of the production process (Blom and Kivinen, 1990). For example the results from a comparative analysis of different occupational groups in Finland and Soviet Estonia suggested, paradoxically, that Soviet socialism was not in fact a class society at all in the sense that Wright understands it, since income differentials between those individual groups were significantly smaller than in capitalism (Blom et al., 1991). Nevertheless there are very clear differen- ces to be observed in terms of overall work and reproduction situation.

Processes of class relations

In analyzing capitalist class relations, various processes of class rela- tions can be identified behind different forms of mental labour (Ki- vinen, 1989):

— professionalization;

— the emergence of managerial hierarchies;

— the emergence of scientific-technical professions;

— the separation of clerical work from management and the degradation of its content;

— the development of caring as a specific form of wage labour, its professionalization and hierarchization;

— changes occurring in the position of skilled workers and in their qualification requirements;

— the changing place of small companies in the economic structure and the development of specific forms of work organization (e.g. paternalism) within those companies.

In order to draw an adequate picture of class relations in Soviet socialism, it is necessary first of all to ask how these processes differ between socialist and capitalist societies. That question must be settled both at the theoretical and empirical level; only then can one proceed to discuss class groups in socialism and their boundaries. The following comments should not be read as results; they are primarily intended as guidelines for the investigation.

(1) The power resources of different professions would seem to have been more restricted in socialism than they are in capitalism in at least two important respects:

— professional organizations in socialism do not have the same kind of power as professional organizations in capitalism to fend off external interventions in the definition of job tasks;

— in socialism labour markets serve not only as pure market mechanisms, but they are also subjected to the political allocation of labour power.

Many writers have insisted that a clear distinction should be made between the intelligentsia, which consists of professional groups on the one hand, and the political elite, which operated within the party apparatus, on the other. This would mean a replacement of the relationship of professions to capital in capitalism by a relationship to apparatshniks (see e.g. Davis and Scase, 1985). However, it is of crucial importance to ask how this so-called intelligentsia tried to maintain its own specific nature by means of its way of life and cultural capital, for in socialism that group did not have access to the harder 'politics of production' power resources possessed by its counterpart in capitalism.

(2) It is a false premise to regard Soviet socialist and capitalist societies as similar systems where managers represent the dominant class; this view overlooks some important differences in property relations and in the goals of the capital accumulation process. In socialism managers were responsible not for the functions of global capital (cf. Carchedi, 1977; Kivinen 1987, pp. 63-64) but for the functions of state planning (Davis and Scase 1985, p. 90). This means that their position in the social hierarchy was different. The company manager in the socialist state was subject to the orders issued by the system and to political control, which also means that he or she had less autonomy and less responsibility.

(3) In the United States and Germany the engineering profession began to emerge as a significant force during the last decades of the nineteenth century; in the Soviet Union the scientific-technical intelligentsia was essentially a product of the much later process of Stalinist industrialization. In Soviet socialism engineers traditionally enjoyed an ideologically stronger position than other professions, representing as they do the 'development of the forces of production'. In recent years, however, the proportion of women in this category has increased substantially and wages do not seem to differ to any significant extent from those of skilled workers. Besides, many engineers are nowadays engaged in other than scientific-technical jobs, such as clerical work.

(4) The relative position of lower white-collar employees in Soviet socialism was clearly poorer than that of their colleagues in capitalism, some of whom still carry features of a middle-class situation (Shernovolenko, 1984; Russkikh, 1983; Lane, 1987):

— Their salaries were lower than those in any other urban wage-earner group.

— They had no real opportunities for career advancement — although this does not apply to the few men in these positions.

— Their level of job satisfaction was exceptionally low.

— They enjoyed far less social prestige in their occupations than skilled workers.

— Unlike skilled craftsmen, white-collar employees in Soviet socialism received no training on the job. Their job tasks were considered highly routine and easy to learn. Even with the introduction of computer technology the relevant debate has not raised the
issue of changing qualification requirements in clerical work.

(5) In comparison with white-collar employees, craftsmen and skilled
workers were held in fairly high regard in socialism, for both ideological and cultural reasons. This was reflected in wage levels and the
amount of on-the-job training, for instance. However, there remains
some disagreement as to how the cultural difference between factory
and office developed in Soviet socialism (e.g. Parkin, 1971; Lane, 1987;
Davis and Scase, 1985).

Work organization

In a comparative analysis of the structuration of the work situation in
Finland, a market economy country, and Soviet socialist Estonia (Blom,
Kivinen, Melin and Rannik, 1991), the following basic differences were
identified:

1) Income differentials between occupational groups were larger in
   Finland than in Estonia. On the other hand, income differentials
   between genders were somewhat more noticeable in Estonia than
   in Finland. In Estonia relative incomes were highest among industrial workers, whereas in Finland pay levels were highest among
   managers.

2) In all occupational groups Estonian workers had a higher educational level than their colleagues in Finland.

3) There were very clear differences between the two countries in
   experiences of physical and mental stress at work; these were
   much more common in Finland than in Estonia.

4) Finnish managers had more decision-making authority than their
   Estonian colleagues, whereas Estonian workers had supervisory
   power and task authority more often than Finnish workers.

If the comparative analysis of the work situation in these two countries were restricted simply to an empiricist comparison of individual
dimensions, the picture emerging of the Estonian work organization

would be overly positive. People in Estonia had less strenuous jobs than people in Finland, greater autonomy on the job, decision making was decentralized and educational levels were high throughout. However, this sort of empiricist analysis completely ignores the mutual relationships between the relevant variables as well as the situational contradictions. It is for this reason that priority must be given to the analysis of the structuration of the work situation and to its contradictions (cf. Luokkaprojekti, 1984; Kivinen, 1987; Kivinen, 1989; Blom et al., 1992).

The high level of job autonomy in the Estonian work situation and the low level of strenuosity were not due to the rejection of capitalist sweating doctrines, such as Taylorism. In fact, in view of the management strategies at Estonian work places, they should be strictly Taylorized. The reasons for the high level of autonomy and the low level of strenuosity were indeed to be found in the low level of technological sophistication at workplaces and to the dictates of the shortage economy. In this situation one may speak of 'forced autonomy' and an inefficient work process which were causing porosity and low work intensity. This forced autonomy emerges in situations where it is necessary to adapt to inadequate materials and technology (Burawoy and Lukacs, 1989, p. 314).

The structuration of the work situation of Estonian wage earners clearly reveals the central contradictions in the work organization of planned economies, i.e. the contradictions between

1) Taylorist management strategy and the actual structure of labour control;

2) the power represented by company management and the control exercised by the party apparatus and the state;

3) job security and the high mobility of labour power, a problem that has been tackled by attempting to develop internal labour markets; and

4) traditional 'administrative' methods of management and the increasing educational level of the labour force (Zaslavskaya, 1989), a problem leading to Estonian workers, who have a higher educational level than their Finnish colleagues, feeling more often that they are unable in their jobs to fully utilize their knowledge and skills.

The uncertainties in a planned economy created a situation where wage earners had the 'right not to work hard' — which, according to some critics, was the only true right of the Soviet worker. The problem was clearly visible in the reluctance of managers to impose stricter, 'technically justified' performance norms, because management must always take into consideration the uncertainty factors of production (late delivery of raw materials, unexpected changes of plan, substandard components, etc.). Indeed, with the beginning of perestroika, there was more and more talk in the Soviet Union about bad discrepancies between pay and performance.

The research evidence from the early 1990's indicates that at least at the company level, the forms of work organization typical of Soviet socialism are still very much in place.

Civil society

The upheavals in Eastern Europe and in the Soviet Union during the past few years can be interpreted, both theoretically and politically, as an attempt to create a specific sphere of civil society (cf. Rupnik, 1988; Szücs, 1988; Vajda, 1988; Havel, 1988; Zaslavskaya, 1989; Pelczynski, 1988). Although the concept of civil society is very difficult and complex, the basic argumentation is simple and straightforward. The basic problem of Marxist theory of the state is its class reductionism, which precludes a thematization of the level of civil society that is irreducible to the state or the economy (Kivinen, 1989).

Marxist theory of the state has always criticized the legal state as an illusory reality of either the class state or commodity exchange (cf. Kivinen, 1977). This critique was thrown overboard with perestroika. The project now was to construct a specific socialist legal state in which no bodies would be beyond the reach of law. At the same time, it was recognized that it is necessary to have a certain degree of plurality as well as the institutional machinery for mediating specific interests. Similarly, in the constitution of the public sphere, the class perspective was discarded in favour of the principle of openness (*glasnost*). The intention was to create a civil society based on legality, publicity and plurality (cf. Cohen, 1982). One of the most disputed issues today is how far the political organization is actually founded on civil society.

However, civil society is not only about certain ethical and political principles, but also about dimensions of the social structure that cannot be conceptually reduced to social classes. According to John Urry (1982, p. 70) the dimensions of the structuration of civil society can be outlined, in order of importance, as follows:

1) spatial organization of labour and of residence into nations, regions, cities, towns, countryside, neighbourhoods;

2) sexual division of labour, i.e. the differential allocation of gender into spheres of production and reproduction, and the organization of gender relations;

3) religious, ethnic and racial allocation of subjects;

4) differentiation of subjects on the basis of trade union and professional association; with this is intertwined also the role of political organization, publicity and culture;

5) generational allocation of subjects.

A challenging task for empirical research would be to examine the composition of social classes by looking at the interaction between these levels of civil society in the context of an analysis of class relations (which in turn is based on an analysis at the level of the labour process).

Social classes in Russia — preliminary empirical theses

In this section are presented some empirical results on the Russian class structure from the period prior to the beginning of the privatization process. The analysis is based on the survey material collected by Erik Olin Wright in connection with the International Comparative Project on Class Structure and Class Consciousness. This material is based on a representative standard population sample from the European part of Russia. The data was collected during the spring 1991 — the last year of the existence of the Soviet Union. Even though the effects of privatization and marketization are not yet reflected on the survey results, the basic patterns of class formation in Russia are nevertheless portrayed in the material.

The Russian class groups in the following examination are operationalized on the basis of the class theory of Kivinen (1989), using the criteria of profession and managerial position (see Appendix). The intention has been to create an operationalization that corresponds to the thesis of the composition of the new middle classes in advanced capitalist countries presented earlier in this chapter, i.e. that the core of the new middle classes comprises all wage earners representing professional, capital-adequate and scientific-technical types of autonomy, irrespective of their managerial functions, and those who have managerial functions in clerical work. Those in performance-level clerical work with some degree of autonomy, as well as craftsmen, care-workers, and workers in small enterprises who do have autonomy, form a group of contradictory class locations which fall in the middle ground between the core of the new middle classes and the working class. In the class situation of these groups we can detect features which are characteristic of both the core of the new middle classes and the working class. Finally, within these types of autonomy, those in managerial positions come closer to the core of the new middle class.

It is clear that this kind of operationalization involves many problems. An adequate operationalization of such historical class criteria would have to be based on extensive comparative analysis of professionalization, work organization, management strategies, etc. However, since this is clearly impossible within the confines of one empirical project, we will have to content ourselves with much more preliminary tools.

On the other hand, there is reason to suspect that in many cases the results and conclusions would hardly be very different if we started out from one or the other of Wright's class theories or from John Goldthorpe's scheme. The differences between these theories will only become apparent when we move on to a discussion of interests, strategies and processes. The empirical material used here is cross-sectional and can therefore shed no light on the processes of class relations. On the other hand, it does provide a good opportunity to analyse the total structures, the profiles and structuration of class situation and consciousness. Ultimately this kind of analysis may also call into question that particular class theory which is taken as a starting-point (cf. Kivinen, 1989, p. 55-57).

1. Although there were clear differences between the class structures of Russia in 1991 and those of advanced capitalist countries (most notably the absence in the former of an entrepreneurial popula-

Table 7.1. Class position of wage earners in different countries by gender in 1991 (%). NMC = New middle classes.

	USA	Sweden	Norway	Canada	Finland	Russia
Core of NMC	25	20	27	27	23	27
Men	33	24	35	32	29	32
Women	18	14	16	20	16	24
Margin of NMC	23	30	25	24	31	25
Men	24	28	23	24	31	23
Women	23	33	28	24	32	27
Working class	51	50	48	49	46	48
Men	44	48	42	44	40	45
Women	59	53	56	56	52	50
Total	100 %	100 %	100 %	100 %	100 %	100 %
N	(1504)	(1037)	(1491)	(1467)	(790)	(1458)

tion), the relative sizes of the working class and middle-class groups do not necessarily differ very much.

Table 7.1 compares the Russian class structure with the internal differentiation of wage earners in certain advanced capitalist countries. Although the operationalizations are not fully comparable (cf. Kivinen 1989, p. 131-134), they are based on similar premises. According to these results middle-class groups occupy an equally important place in Russia as they do in advanced capitalist countries. However, in Russia there are various forms of 'mental work' which are specific products of the country's planning system and bureaucracy. The proportion of this bureaucratic-administrative type of autonomy of the total economically active population is 3 percentage points and of all those belonging to the core of the new middle classes 11 percentage points. Another noteworthy difference is the predominance of women in the professional type of autonomy in Russia. While in all advanced capitalist countries at least half of all professionals are men, Russian women account for two thirds of this group. Similarly, women are overrepresented among both managers and engineers in Russia. The core of the new middle classes in Russia is indeed more female-dominated than in advanced capitalist countries.

2. Class situations are in many ways structured differently in Russia than in advanced capitalist countries. On a number of dimensions the core of the Russian new middle classes comes closer to the working class than in advanced capitalist countries.

This thesis is based on a fundamentally new approach to class analysis (Blom and Kivinen, 1987). Class analysis is a complex process involving numerous different levels. A basic distinction which has to be made is the one between class position and class situation. Class position has to do with the structural relations of domination within production. The concept of class situation, then, refers to more concrete phenomena: reproduction situation (income, education, position on labour market) and working conditions. Any adequate analysis of class consciousness, organization and the action of class subjects must be preceded by an analysis of the links between class positions and class situations.

In any international comparison it is important to look precisely at the structuration of class situation. Similar structures may have very different impacts at the level of class situation. The purpose of the following theses is to provide some empirical depth and content to the above generalizations of the structuration of the class situation of the new middle classes.

3. Income differentials between social classes were less marked in Russia than in advanced capitalist countries; also, the relative position of craftsmen in comparison with the core of the middle classes was essentially better.

The income differentials between the core of the new middle classes and the working class were according to the survey material gathered in 1991 substantially smaller in Russia than in the advanced capitalist countries. Especially the position of Russian craftsmen was found to be very different in comparison with their colleagues in advanced capitalist countries. Another distinctive feature of the situation in Russia is the low income level of professionals. Income differences between genders were at least as great as in western countries. The development during the last three years in Russia has, however, dramatically increased the differences in income.

Table 7.2. Some characteristics of class situation and class consciousness in Russian social classes (%). NMC = New middle classes.

	Core of NMC	Margin of NMC	Working class
Vocational training	80	77	67
Willingness to be further educated	50	41	25
Work controlled daily	12	28	45
Work difficult to control	29	25	13
Satisfied with job	72	66	61
Has not taken part in interest struggles	89	85	94
Willingness to take action in the event of lay-offs	73	70	63
Would hardly report a theft	44	50	55
Religious	22	28	35
Favours worker involvement in the introduction of new technology	48	45	27
Favours worker involvement in decision making on products	48	40	30
Favours management election by voting	53	60	62
Believes that family's welfare will decline during next 5 years	51	59	48
Considers division between specialists and performance level inevitable	72	74	70
Feels that government policy is responsible for poverty	81	88	86

4. The majority of Russian wage earners have a vocational training. However, paths of training and educational interests vary across different class groups.

Table 7.2 describes the proportion of people with a vocational training in different class groups. This reveals no differences. However, a closer analysis of training paths suggests that educational networks within companies and vocational schools are clearly working-class institutions, whereas the majority of university graduates are likely to end up in a middle-class position. The role of technical colleges in this system is least clear. The keen interest in education among the core of the middle classes is most clearly visible in the question concerning willingness to improve one's qualifications (Table 7.2). All in all, the differences between social classes in educational levels are largely similar to those in advanced capitalist countries. In Soviet sociology the problem of meritocracy has been debated since the 1960's (Yanowich, 1977, p. 55-99; Aitov, 1986).

5. Differences in the control of work were very similar to those found in advanced capitalist countries. The working class was subjected to direct and usually daily control, whereas the middle class had more autonomy on the job. However, career opportunities were clearly poorer among middle-class wage earners in Russia than in capitalist countries and career advancement also had lesser significance.

Attention was earlier drawn to the wide differences here between capitalist countries. In particular, the work organization in the United States seems to be essentially more flexible in this respect than the Nordic model. Russia would seem to fall somewhere between these two extremes. However, the differences in Russia between class groups are less outstanding than in capitalist countries (cf. also Blom et al., 1991). The questions on job control (see Table 7.2) also point to class differences in work control. Working-class jobs are easier to control and they are controlled on a daily basis.

There were also clear differences in terms of career opportunities. Russian wage earners belonging to the core of the new middle classes seemed to have less career opportunities than the middle-class groups in any capitalist country. In the former Soviet Union career building did not necessarily bring even economic benefits because the highest wages were paid to skilled craftsmen. Indeed, the feeling among middle-class groups is that there was no point in sweating. In this respect the difference with the capitalist countries was very clear.

6. Social classes have no organizations of their own and consciousness is not structured on a class basis in the same way as in advanced capitalist countries.

There seemed to be in 1991 no significant differences concerning the ambitions of self-employment among wage earners in advanced capitalist countries and Russia. It is noteworthy that there were no differences here between the working class and the middle-class groups. Similarly, attitudes towards privatization revealed no class differences; this also lends support to the conclusion that class consciousness and class culture are undifferentiated. In stark contrast to the situation in advanced capitalist countries, there seemed to be no major differences between Russian wage-earner groups in work orientation, although working-class women tend to adopt a more instrumental attitude than other groups.

7. All groups in Russia have very little experience of defending their interests. However, the middle class shows a somewhat higher willingness to take action than the working class.

As we can see from Table 7.2, the participation of Russian wage earners in interest struggles is at a very low level. While in advanced capitalist countries the working class has traditionally been more willing to take action than the middle-class groups, the atomization of Russian society has prevented the evolution of any class-based action cultures. This is clearly visible in the absence of any distinct, coherent set of working-class interests. However, some studies point to clear differences in the attitudes of social classes to market economy (Yadov, 1992). For instance, middle-class groups seem to be more interested in social participation than the working class. Following the collapse of the traditional form of administration, the whole society seems to be marred by a serious legitimacy crisis, which is reflected, for example, in attitudes towards theft (Table 7.2) or future hopes.

All in all, there is a clear absence in Russia of distinct profiles of class consciousness and action of the kind we are accustomed to seeing in advanced capitalist countries. However, at the level of class situation and habitus the middle class is clearly distinguished from the working class.

The future of the Russian class structure

Although Russia is currently in a state of profound social disorganization, there remains one objective in Russian society that shows no signs of weakening: the attainment of market economy. However, market economy and capitalism come in many different shapes and forms; there is more than one possible path of development towards capitalism:

> We were promised capitalism and that's what we got. Not only the popular masses but also managers of all descriptions had these fancy ideas of chic Parisians shops, while they forgot all about the hungry and unemployed people of Lima and Sao Paulo, which are much closer to us. The airplane has taken off and some of the passengers still think that they will be landing in Paris or Stockholm. But in actual fact the plane is headed for Burkina Faso, because this

airline and planes constructed like this do not fly west. Someone may eventually
reach their destination and live in Moscow just like in Paris. But that is at the
expense of those who live as if they were in Burkina Faso. (Kagarlitsky, 1992, p.
14.)

Nonetheless capitalism remains the ultimate goal, and sooner or later
the privatization of the economy is bound to lead to the growth of an
entrepreneurial population. There are also many social movements
today that would like to see a middle class flourish (Kivinen, 1993).
Indeed it would seem reasonable to assume that the wage-earning
middle class in Russia will eventually break loose from the working
class in terms of both organization and activity. The important thing
here is that in the absence of the old mechanisms of political control,
the middle class will be free to develop its market capacities through
the strategy of professionalization. In this process we will see the same
sort of career and educational structures grow up as we have in
advanced capitalist countries. However, it is important to bear in mind
that the professional classes in Russia are heavily female-dominated
and that the type of political-bureaucratic autonomy here has its own
distinctive characteristics. It remains very much an open question what
sort of professionalization will develop on the basis of these premises.

A central factor with regard to the professionalization of the middle
class is the future course of development of the private sector and its
relationship to the state sector, which at least for the time being remains
predominant. The different forms of privatization involve various
mutually contradictory interests. Throughout the whole of Eastern
Europe it remains unclear what kind of bourgeoisie or entrepreneurial
population will develop out of the post-socialist revolutions. At least
the following trends of privatization and related interests can be identified (cf. Cox, 1992):

1) Spontaneous or 'nomenklatura' privatization, which is most force-
   fully advocated by the old economic elite or dominant class. This
   refers to all such processes in which former company managers in
   one way or another take over ownership of the company or parts
   thereof. This form of privatization is in fact very common
   throughout Eastern Europe, and it is perhaps still the most significant form of privatization. It often involves 'pathological privatization' as well, which is based on outright corruption. Managers
   who used to be part of the nomenklatura apparatus often pocket

quite phenomenal profits by using for their own private purposes the machinery and labour of state-owned companies.

2) Privatization by the state acts as a counterbalance to spontaneous privatization in Eastern Europe. It is paradoxical that the new political elite which is strongly in favour of privatization and market economy needs to turn to the state in order to have restrictions imposed on the spontaneous privatization carried out by the former nomenklatura and in order to offer a serious alternative. State privatization may be controlled and coordinated either directly by ministries (as is the case in Poland) or by special state organizations or companies (as in Hungary or in what used to be the GDR).

3) International capital has its own interests in the process of privatization. In many cases it seems that the only option available to major corporations is to sell the whole company to foreign investors because the necessary capital simply does not exist within the country.

4) The founding of new companies also contributes to the growth of the private sector. For the time being most domestic entrepreneurs are engaged in the fields of trade or services.

5) Another group with special interests to defend are the former owners and their descendants whose land and property has been nationalized.

6) In some cases company workers and employees are given a shareholding in the company. This is closely related to the project of creating forms of privatization that are ideologically acceptable to the working class. However, there is always the risk that the workers are left with the least profitable shares or with companies that are virtually bankrupt to start with, while the nomenklatura are left with the best bits (cf. e.g. Bomsel, 1990).

7) The distribution or sale of government bonds or shares in state companies to the people. In Russia Yeltsin's administration has already attempted this strategy.

The Russian policy so far has been to combine different strategies of privatization (Frydman et al., 1993). It is not possible in this connection to go into the details of privatization practices, but it seems quite obvious that the Russian situation is a case apart with its own distinctive characteristics. First of all there is no movement in Russia to restore properties to former owners. Secondly, there is much less resistance among the political elite to nomenklatura privatization than is the case in other Eastern European countries. Thirdly, 'insiders' in Russia (both managers and company employees) occupy a very strong position in Russian privatization.

An important role in the growth of new entrepreneurial groups is played by the 'second economy' of socialist countries, the structures of which overlap with the traditional state sector and with the emerging new capitalist sector. If we further bear in mind that both the state sector and the private sector have their own hierarchic structure (on the one hand from nomenklatura managers to the state working class, on the other from the new owners of privatized companies to their workers), the picture that unfolds is complex indeed. Terry Cox has observed that in this kind of situation the entire class structure is more or less fluid: people move across from one sector to another and often act simultaneously in different sectors. Consequently numerous contradictory or ambivalent class positions develop as people try to ensure their own fair share of economic, social or cultural capital.

Ivan Szelenyi may well be right in arguing that the question of the relationship between the state and private sector in post-socialist societies may constitute a key issue with regard to the formation of hegemonic projects (Szelenyi and Szelenyi, 1991). However, this sort of structural speculation is necessarily rather abstract as long as we do not know how the exercise of establishing some sort of balance in the economy is going to succeed. The transitional crisis may turn out to be far more serious than just a minor interlude on the road to a new capitalist class structure.

Although it is impossible at this point to say exactly how the privatization process and the ongoing economic changes are going to affect the class structure in Russia, a crude typology of possible trends in development can nevertheless be presented (Figure 7.1).

A social class is in a strong position when it has achieved stability in terms of ownership or power resources and class situation and when it has powerful organizations to lean back on. This, of course, is an ideal-type situation; not all of these conditions will necessarily apply at the same time. Nonetheless this perspective provides a useful pre-

Figure 7.1. A typology of alternative patterns of class relations.

		Bourgeoisie			
		strong		weak	
		Middle class			
		strong	weak	strong	weak
Working class	strong	1	2	3	4
	weak	5	6	7	8

liminary basis for comparing Russia with other societies and at the same time for a discussion of its future development.

Figure 7.1 classifies societies according to whether the bourgeoisie, the wage-earning middle class and the working class in those societies are strong or weak on the criteria outlined above. The figure provides only a crude outline in that it does not include the petty bourgeoisie at all; a more detailed analysis would require the inclusion of urban self-employed groups as well as the peasantry.

In this sort of analysis the countries of Western Europe are mainly located in cell 1. In these countries ownership based on capital is well-established, and professional and managerial groups have definite and undisputed privileges over and above the working class. On the other hand, the working class has its own powerful organizations and in this sense forms an important part of civil society. In these societies only a minor part of surplus value goes towards the consumption of the capitalist class. Therefore they cannot be described as exploitation societies proper.

Russia, on the other hand, would appear to be setting out to play its game from cell number 8. Here, ownership structures are still in the process of taking shape, and in terms of its class situation the middle class does not differ from the working class (although it is important not to forget the role of educational structures and educational interests). The working class also lacks its own organizations through which it would have become incorporated into civil society. Nevertheless in the present situation the bourgeoisie is taking shape with the process of privatization, the middle classes are seeking to use their own power resources in order to create managerial and professional structures, and even the working class is beginning to organize itself. These processes are still in their early stages, and the success or failure of different classes in implementing their respective strategies will largely determine their future course of development.

The process of privatization is advancing all the time among others in the form of nomenklatura privatization, in which the former power machinery is trying to convert its 'organizational capital' into ownership of economic capital. However, it remains unclear how the privatization of major corporations is going to happen. It is indeed quite possible that privatization will lead, not to the formation of a strong bourgeoisie, but rather to a weak bourgeoisie that is dependent on foreign ownership and foreign capital. In this case the options open to Russia would be 7, 3 and 4.

Alternative 7 might involve a long transitional stage during which old structures remain in place for a long time at the corporate level (Clarke, 1993). Managers would be in power in companies and professionals would begin to attain a privileged position as producers of modernization, for example (cf. Kivinen, 1993). The working class, by contrast, would be hit by increasing unemployment and in organizational terms it would remain disunited. In alternative 3 the working class would begin to organize and succeed (e.g. through ownership by the workers) in maintaining old structures that are aimed at the reproduction of the labour collective at the company level. Alternative 4 might be related to a situation where privatization fails, where old educational structures collapse, managerial strategies are vague and unspecific, but where the working class succeeds in maintaining its current position through industrial action, for example. In political terms all of these alternatives would probably involve different kinds of restoration projects or endeavours in some way to uphold left-wing projects.

If a strong bourgeoisie emerges with the privatization process, either on the basis of the former nomenklatura or otherwise, then options 1 and 2 or 5 and 6 will be possible. Alternative 2 resembles Germany during the Weimar Republic. This kind of situation might develop, for example, as powerful egalitarian projects frustrate the attempts of professionals and managers to break loose from the working class. This alternative also involves the possibility of extremist movements.

Alternative 5 resembles the kind of society currently represented by the United States, where there is a strong bourgeoisie and middle class but where the working class is quite weak in terms of both its consciousness and organization (Ahrne and Wright, 1983). This alternative is not a very likely scenario, since the working class in Russia is quite strong in the traditional reproduction type; it is the middle class that has to create new structures and positions.

If alternative 6 were to materialize, then the class structure of Russia would begin to resemble the situation in those developing countries where the bourgeoisie is so strong that the bulk of surplus value produced in society is spent in private consumption (which is the case most notably in the countries of Latin America). In this kind of society it is legitimate to speak of exploitation in the proper sense of the word. One factor that clearly supports this line of development in Russia is the absence there of the rationality of capitalism. If the current form of doing business — in which the aim is to make short-term profits by means of trading and speculation — were to remain dominant, then there would be a real risk of the country beginning to move towards the Third World. On the other hand, there are good reasons to doubt whether the educated middle class of Russia will accept this sort of system and whether the strong egalitarian endeavours of the working class can be completely undone.

Within the sociology of politics it has long been a matter of controversy whether the development of democracy requires primarily a strong middle class or a strong working class (Burris, 1986). Closely related to this are other, more specific problemizations in which a distinction is made between the liberal, upper middle class and the more authoritarian-minded lower middle class. However, it remains doubtful whether such generalizations are of any real value since the consciousness of different social classes is in any case contradictorily determined and since different discourses struggling for hegemonic power can become attached to different sides of consciousness.

Thus the Stalinist discourse, for example, defined the working class, on the one hand, as a modern and disciplined group in relation to the carnivalistic and reactionary masses. On the other hand, it also used the anti-intellectualism of the working class as a weapon: prejudices against mental labour, xenophobia and anti-semitism (Fitzpatrick, 1982, p. 132; cf. also Willis, 1979). Given the fact that social classes occupy contradictory habitus in this way and that they are unconscious, it is very difficult to make any relevant inferences from the class structure as to what kind of chances democracy has of succeeding.

In Russia today, where there exists no mature civil society, many potential lines of development involve obvious risks of populistic and authoritarian tendencies. However, it would be too simplistic and straightforward to suggest that a strong working class or middle class would automatically be able to prevent their realization.

Appendix: operationalization of the Russian class structure

The class structure variable has been operationalized in the Russian material as follows:

1. The starting point is provided by the combination of mental work and authority/decision-making in the processes of class structure. This helps to avoid the anomalies in Wright's scheme. In the present solution authority (which here means the same thing as managerial position in Wright's class scheme) specifies and complements the factor of mental work (for a more detailed discussion of this solution, see Kivinen, 1989, esp. p. 43).

2. The operationalization starts out from the different types of autonomy, which are defined on the basis of occupations. Position in managerial hierarchy is used as an additional criterion. The important thing is that these additional criteria are taken into account in different ways in different types of autonomy. On the basis of a detailed description of the occupational classification, the following presents the ground rules for the exercise of operationalization. New types of autonomy are also constructed.

Scientific-technical autonomy
— Engineers and closely related occupations
— Technicians and closely related occupations

These are included in the core of the new middle classes if they have a position in the managerial hierarchy. If not, they are included in marginal groups.

Professional autonomy
— Scholars and academic researchers
— Medical doctors
— Humanists
— Teachers
— Clerical staff within the arts, mass communication, etc.

The same rule is applied as above.

Saleswork autonomy
— Shop assistants etc.

— Buffet salespeople
— Waiters/waitresses
— Barbers/hairdressers

Those occupying a position in the managerial hierarchy are included in marginal groups, others in the working class.

Clerical autonomy
— Clerical employees engaged in routine work in offices and warehouses
— Hotel administrators

Those with managerial functions are included in marginal groups, others in the working class.

Caring autonomy
— Nurses
— Kindergarten nurses
— Housemaids
— Ward nurses
— Auxiliary nurses, children's nurses
— Childminders, maids

All included in marginal groups.

Craftsman's autonomy
— Workers engaged in qualified handicraft

All included in marginal groups. This type of autonomy also includes the following occupational groups insofar as they occupy a position in the managerial hierarchy:
— Operators
— Machine workers
— Traffic workers
— Drivers
— Physical labourers
— Agrarian workers
— Cooks
— Dishwashers
— Porters, messengers
— Lift operators
— Cleaning workers

Otherwise these groups belong to the working class.

Bureaucratic-administrative autonomy
— Managers within bureaucracies
— Officials in state party organs
— Officers of the militia etc.

These are included in the core of the new middle classes. Those occupying a managerial position in the following occupations are included in the marginal groups:
— Doormen, watchmen, ticket inspectors, private detectives

— Rank-and-file in the militia
— Soldiers
— Firemen
— Social workers
— Employees at employment agencies
— Customs officials
— Sailors

Managerial autonomy
— Company managers
— Department etc. heads

All included in the core of new middle classes.

Small enterprise autonomy
— Small enterprise managers

All included in the marginal groups of of the new middle classes.

This is the operationalization that provides the basis for the crude distinction of wage earners into core and marginal groups of the new middle classes and into the working class.

References

Aitov, N.A. (1986), 'The Dynamics of Social Mobility in the USSR' in Yanowich, Murray (ed.), *The Social Structure of the USSR. Recent Soviet Studies*, M.E. Sharpe, New York.

Alapuro, R. (1993), 'Civil Society in Russia' in Iivonen, Jyrki (ed.), *The Future of the Nation State in Europe*, Edward Elgar, Aldershot.

Blom, R. & Filippov, F.R. (1988), 'Razvitie sotsialnoi struktury obshchestva v SSSR i Finlandii' in Filippov, F.R. (ed.), *Sotsiologiia i sotsialnaia praktika. Sovetsko-finlandskie sotsiologicheskie issledovaniia*, Institut sotsiologicheskih issledovaniia AN SSSR, Moskva.

Blom, R. & Kivinen, M. (1990), 'Analytical Marxism and Class Theory' in Clegg, Stewart (ed.), *Organization Theory and Class Analysis. New Approaches and New Issues*, De Gruyter, Berlin and New York.

Blom, R. & Kivinen, M. & Melin, H. & Rannik, E. (1991), 'Structuration of Work Situation in Finland and Soviet Estonia', *International Sociology*, 3/1991.

Blom, R. & Kivinen, M. & Melin, H. & Rantalaiho, L. (1992),*The Scope Logic Approach to Class Analysis*, Avebury, Aldershot.

Bomsel, O. (1991), *From socialist norms and sanctions to the market economy*, paper presented at the 10th EGOS Colloquium in Vienna, Austria, July 15-17, 1991.

Bruce-Briggs, S. (1979), 'An Introduction to the Idea of the New Class' in Bruce-Briggs, B. (ed.), *The New Class?* Transaction Books, New Brunswick.

Burawoy, M. (1990), *Painting Socialism: Working Class Formation in Hungary and Poland*, paper presented at the 8th Annual Aston/Umist Conference, Birmingham, March 28-30, 1990.

Burawoy, M. & Lukacs, J. (1986), 'Mythologies of Work. A Comparison of Firms in State Socialism and Advanced Capitalism', *American Sociological Review*,6/1986.

Burnham, J. (1941), *The Managerial Revolution*, New York.

Burris, V. (1986), 'The Discovery of the New Middle Class', *Theory and Society*, 1986, Vol. 15, no. 3.

Carchedi, G. (1977), *The Economic Identification of Social Classes*, Routledge and Kegan Paul, London.

Clarke, S. & Fairbrother, P. & Burawoy, M. & Krotov, P. (1993), *What About the Workers? Workers and the Transition to Capitalism in Russia*, Verso, London and New York.

Cohen, J. (1982), *Class and Civil Society. The Limits of Marxian Critical Theory*, The University of Massachusetts Press, Amherst.

Cox, T., (1992), *Structural Barriers to Market Reform in Eastern Europe*, Paper presented at the Annual Conference of the British Sociological Association, University of Kent, April 6-9, 1992.

Davis, H. & Scase, R. (1985), *Western Capitalism and State Socialism*, Verso, London.

Djilas, M. (1957), *Uusi luokka. Kommunismin todelliset kasvot*, Gummerus, Jyväskylä.

Faber, D. (1991), *Before Stalinism*, Polity Press, London.

Filtzer, D. (1990), *Economic Reform and Production Relations in Soviet Industry*, paper presented at the 8th Annual Aston/UMIST Conference, Birmingham, March 28-30, 1990.

Fitzpatrick, S. (1982), *The Russian Revolution*, Oxford University Press, Oxford.

Frydman, R. (et al.) (1993), 'The Privatisation Process in Russia, Ukraine and the Baltic States', *CEU Privatisation Reports*, Vol. 2, Budapest, London, New York.

Garnsey, E. (1975), 'Occupational Structure in Industrialized Societies: Some Notes on the Convergence Thesis in the Light of Soviet Experience', *Sociology*, 3/1975.

Giddens, A. (1973), *The Class Structure of the Advanced Societies*, Hutchinson, London.

Glezerman, G.E. (1949), *Likvidatsiia ekspluatatorskih klassov i preodolenie klassovyh razlitshii v SSSR*, Moskva.

Glezerman, G.E. (1962), *Perehod ot sotsializma k kommunizmu i stiranie klassovyh granei, Ot sotsializma k kommunizmu*, Moskva.

Gordon, L.A. & Nazimova A. (1985), *Sovetskii rabochii klass*, Nauka, Moskva.

Hankiss, E. (1990), *East European Alternatives*, Oxford University Press, Oxford.

Hasbulatov, R.I. (1990), *Biurokraticheskoe gosudarstvo*, Moskva.

Havel, V. (1988), 'Anti-Political Politics' in J. Keane (ed.), *Civil Society and the State. New European Perspectives*, Verso, London.

Igitkhanyan, E.D. & Kirkh, A.V. (1982), 'Vazhnie problemy v razvitie sotsialnogo struktura sovetskogo obshchestva', *Sotsiologicheskie issledovaniia*, 1/1982.

Kagarlitski, B. (1992), *Hajonnut monoliitti*, Orient Express, Helsinki.

Kivinen, M. (1977), 'Oikeusmuoto ja valtio — muotogeneettisen johtamisen rajoista', *Sosiologia*, 4/1977.

Kivinen, M. (1987), *Parempien piirien ihmisiä*, Tutkijaliitto, Jyväskylä.

Kivinen, M. (1987), *The New Middle Classes and the Labour Process — Class Criteria Revisited*, Department of Sociology, Research Reports 223, University of Helsinki.

Kivinen, M. (1993), *The Prospects of the Professional-Managerial Project in Russia*, paper presented at the 11th EGOS Colloquium, Paris, 6-8 July 1993.

Kivinen, M. & Melin, H. (1991), *The Soviet Class Structure — Some Preliminary Remarks*, paper presented at the VIth International Meeting of Comparative Project on Class Structure and Class Consciousness, Grenada, Spain, July 23-26, 1991.

Kugel. S.A. (1963), *Zakonomernosti izmeneniia sotsialnoi strurktury obshchestva pri perehode k kommunizmu*, Nauka, Moskva.

Lane, Ch. (1987), 'The Impact of the Economic and Political System on Social Stratification and Social Mobility: Soviet Lower Whitecollar Workers in Comparative Perspective', *Sociology*, 1/1987.

Lukes, S. (1974), *Power: a Radical View*, Macmillan, London.

Luokkaprojekti (1984), *Suomalaiset luokkakuvassa*, Vastapaino, Jyväskylä.

Nove, A. (1983), *The Economics of Feasible Socialism*, George Allen & Unwin, London.

Parkin, F. (1971), *Class Inequality and Political Order. Social Stratification in Capitalist and Communist Societies*, Macgibbon and Kee, London.

Pelczynski, Z.A. (1988), 'Solidarity and "the Rebirth of Civil Society"' in J. Keane (ed.), *Civil Society and the State. New European Perspectives.*, Verso, London.

Razvitie sotsialnoj strukturi obshchestva v SSSR (Pod.red. Ivanov, V.N.) (1985), Moskva.

Roemer, J.E. (1981), *A General Theory of Exploitation and Class*, Cambridge University Press, Cambridge, Mass.

Roemer, J.E. (1981), *Foundations of Marxian Economic Theory*, Cambridge University Press, Cambridge, Mass.

Rupnik, J. (1988), 'Totalitarianism Revisited' in J. Keane (ed.), *Civil Society and the State. New European Perspectives*, Verso, London.

Russkikh, B.G. (1983), *Prestizh professii slushashih — nespetsialistov kak odin iz faktorov upravleniia razvitiem sotsialnoi struktury obshchestva. Upravlenie sotsialnymi protsessami*, Nauka, Moskva.

Rutkevitsh, M.N. (1968), *Problemy izmeneniia sotsialnoi struktury sovetskogo obshchestva*, Moskva.

Rutkevitsh, M.N. (1978), 'O ponjatii sotsialnoj struktury', *Sotsiologicheskie issledovaniia*, 4/1978.

Semjonov, V.S. (1962), *Preobrazovanija v rabotshem klasse i intelligentsii v protsesse perehoda k kommunizmu. Iz istorii rabochego klassa SSSR*, Leningrad.

Shernovolenko, V.F. (et al.) (1984), *Semia i vozproizvodstvo struktury trudovoi zaniatosti*, Kiev.

Shkaratan, O.I. (1970), *Problemy sotsialnoi struktury rabochego klassa SSSR*, Moskva.

Shkaratan, O.I. & Rukavishnikov, V.O. (1986), 'Social Strata in the Class Structure of Socialist Society. (An attempt at Theoretical Construction and Empirical Investigation)' in Yanowich, M. (ed.), *The Social Structure of the USSR. Recent Soviet Studies*, M.E. Sharpe, New York.

Szelenyi, I. (1988), *Socialist Entrepreneurs: Embourgeoisement in Rural Hungary*, University of Wisconsin Press, Madison.

Szelenyi, I. & Szelenyi, S. (1991), 'The Vacuum in Hungarian Politics: Classes and Parties', *New Left Review*, 187/1991.

Szücs, J. (1988), 'Three Historical Regions of Europe' in J. Keane (ed.), *Civil Society and the State. New European Perspectives*, Verso, London.

Titma, M.K. (1986), 'On the Question of Social Differentiation in Developed Socialist Society', in Yanowich, M. (ed.), *The Social Structure of the USSR. Recent Soviet Studies*, New York.

Urry, J. (1982), *The Anatomy of Capitalist Societies. The Economy, Civil Society and the State*, Verso, London.

Vajda, M. (1988), 'East-Central European Perspectives' in J. Keane (ed.), *Civil Society and the State. New European Perspectives*, Verso, London.

Willis, P. (1979), *Learning to Labour. How Working Class Kids Get Working Class Jobs*, Gower, Aldershot.

Wright, E. O. (1985), *Classes*, Verso, London.

Yanowitch, M. (1986), 'Introduction' in Yanowich, M. (ed.), *The Social Structure of the USSR. Recent Soviet Studies*, M.E. Sharpe, New York.

Zaslavskaya, T.I. (1985), 'Economic Structure Through the Prism of Sociology', *EKO*, 7/1985.

Zaslavskaya, T.I. (1985), *A Voice of Reform*, M.E. Sharpe, New York.

8 Social Problems and Social Policy in Russia and the Baltic Countries

Jussi Simpura

In the eyes of their closest western neighbours, Russia and the Baltic countries easily appear as threats today. This is not because of expansionist trends but because of internal developments in the former socialist countries. Deterioration of living conditions and sharpening of social problems in those countries are suspected of leading to uncontrolled tensions, which would be felt as a migration pressure and increasing disorder in the neighbouring countries. In particular, drugs and crime from the east and from the south are a constant worry for Finland, their closest neighbour, situated only two hours away from St. Petersburg and within sight across the sea from Estonia. These worries are felt and shared by Sweden and Germany as well, although to a lesser extent, thanks to the longer distance. In the Scandinavian countries, the strong welfare traditions makes one ask what might be the role of social policy in ameliorating the conditions in Russia and the Baltic countries. For western observers from other countries, the idea of turning to social policies when considering social problems might sound odd. It will turn out, however, that the issue of social policy is crucial in understanding what is happening in Russia today.

To begin with, we shall briefly describe the developments of living conditions in the Soviet Union and in Russia. Thereafter, a review of a number of social problems will be given, including some information on the Baltic countries. Finally, the development of social policy and its future prospects will be discussed. In the concluding chapter, a proposal will be made to see the developments in Russia and the Baltic countries as a parallel to the transition which is taking place in the Nordic countries and their welfare systems. The focus of the description is on Russia. The Baltic countries will be touched on only in passing. This article is not a systematic review of various sectors of social policy. Such reviews are available elsewhere for Russia (see e.g. Deacon et al.,1992), but are still forthcoming for the Baltic countries.

The continuous and unforeseeable process of change makes all studies outdated even as they are being published already. In a way, it is premature to present any prognoses yet. While the wave of reforms all over Eastern Europe has raised interest also in social policies, it is becoming increasingly difficult to document all the changes taking place now, (cf. e.g. Manning's, 1992, critique on a book about housing policy in Eastern Europe). The effects of the ongoing processes will not become visible until the possible stabilization of the situation, perhaps several years from now. Even then, in order to be able to evaluate those effects, one needs research and descriptive data on the unstable conditions of today. Presently, it is of utmost importance to pose questions on the development of social policy. The researchers task would be to be certain that the information and research needed to answer such questions will be available.

In the domain of social policy, research and the production of data are still enormous problems in Russia and in the Baltic countries. A UN Expert Mission on social policy, having visited Moscow in spring 1992, quotes the phrase 'the tyranny of misleading information', as an illustration of the quality of the available information (Hay and Peacock 1992a, 62-63). Equally, Rein Ruutsoo (1991) has presented a colourful description of problems in statistical data production in Estonia in an article with the title *How to Read Soviet Statistics*. Ruutsoo provides examples of the numerous tricks, besides direct falsification and concealing of information, that were used to camouflage the real contents and quality of the statistics. Most of the data concerning living conditions and social problems were regarded as highly confidential information. A good example is provided by studies on the prevalence of crime in St. Petersburg in the 1970's. The results of those studies were declared secret and research reports were distributed in numbered copies only to selected trustees of the power elite. As a consequence, the tradition of empirical and descriptive social research was only weakly developed. Another fresh example confirms this observation. In 1992 the Institute of Sociological Research of the Russian Academy of Sciences published a collection of articles about changes in the way of life during perestroika (*Obraz zhizhni v usloviiakh perstroiki*, 1992). In the two hundred pages of the book there are long discussions about the concept of the way of life in the turmoil of social change, but only very little empirical evidence is provided about changes in the way of life in various sub-groups of population since the mid-1980's.

What do 'social policy' and 'social problems' mean?

In the former socialist countries, a discussion about basic concepts is unavoidable. Even such expressions as 'social policy' and 'social problems' are far from being self-evident in Russia and in the Baltic countries. Under the old regime, social policy was almost an empty concept, as all policies were 'social' by definition. The term 'social policy' was rarely used in itself. In the present conditions, social policy has become more useful as an expression, but at the same time it carries many of its pejorative connotations from old times. For many, one of the major sins of the old system was that things 'social' were given too strong a role in society. Therefore, the concept of social policy is still associated with the old rule and past conditions.

Social policy is, however, gaining new contents. In 1986 at the beginning of perestroika, the influential academician Tatyana Zaslavskaya questioned the ideology of equality as a basis for social policy. In her view, social policy should not be a policy of equality. Rather, it should be a policy of distinctions, favouring those working for the common development and disfavouring those who prevent the improvement of living conditions. 'It is this approach of distinctions that makes *policy* out of social policy' (emphasis by Zaslavskaya, quoted by Murarka, 1987).

The thoughts presented by Zaslavskaya evidently were aimed at a new role for social policy as a stimulus for those who were ready to promote the growth of welfare. Social policy, then, should also be harnessed together with economy and administration to promote the general welfare.

The politics of distinction were actually realized before perestroika, although in a quite different sense than that proposed by Zaslavskaya. Today, it is openly admitted that the former Soviet Union was a class society, where the ruling elite, the *nomenklatura*, had secured special privileges for itself (cf. e.g. Yarigina and Yavlinsky, 1993, p. 1-2). One of the major tasks in developing social policy today is to tear down this system of privileges.

The recent development of living conditions has produced new distinctions, some of them completely purposeless by any standards. A large new class of impoverished and deprived people is emerging. The meagre public resources for the implementation of social policy may prove insufficient even to save those marginalized groups. Social policy, then, will itself be marginalized by mere economic necessity. On the other hand, this very process of mass marginalization has called more attention to the issues of social policy. Thus, in a recent study conducted among the members of the city council of St. Petersburg (Aarrevaara, 1992), it turned out that the councillors regarded questions related to social policy as the most important in their work.

In Russia, the idea of social policy as an activity focused only on the most marginalized groups has gained support from the prevailing political ideology since 1991. The liberation of the economy and other domains of social life from dependency on the patronizing state was seen as an essential goal. While Gorbachev still dared to present the Scandinavian 'social democratic' welfare regime as a model for Russia, later leaders have tended rather to be guided by the liberalistic patterns from the US. Privatization and independence from the state support have come to the fore. State-centred social policy is needed only to maintain the extremely marginalized groups. Further support for such a political line has been provided by organizations coordinating international economic aid for Russia. The World Bank has adopted a leading ideological role here. In the most recent months, however, the spokesmen of the assistance organizations have also joined with those who warn about the excessive speed of reforms, leading to an increasing risk of social catastrophes (cf. Hay and Peacock, 1992).

In the Baltic countries, the concept of social policy has been subjected to similar reformulation as in Russia. The cultural ties of these countries with the west have influenced the search for models for social policy. In Estonia and to some extent also in Latvia some proposals have been made that the countries should develop themselves in the direction of the Nordic welfare states. The acute difficulties in the Nordic countries of continuing with the Scandinavian welfare regime have pushed down such proposals. In addition, the recent right-wing turn in Estonian politics has further alienated the government from Scandinavian models. In Lithuania, the Catholic religion, the ethnic homogeneity of the population and the return of former communists into power in the latest elections make the situation there different from that in the other Baltic countries. Otherwise, too, Lithuania is more closely connected with Central European countries. In the present difficult material conditions there are, however, very few major proposals for the development of social policy.

The concept of 'social problems' is also far from being self-evidently and collectively understood in these countries. Under the old regime, the existence of social problems was officially hardly admitted. Thereafter sensational news on various difficulties both during perestroika and later have filled the media. It is customary to divide social problems into categories such as housing, health, family, education etc. Such a typology has been applied for instance in *Soviet Social Problems* by Jones et al. (1989) describing the last years of the Soviet Union. Endless lists of social problems are available, but most of the lists are based on random selection or administrative distinctions, paying little attention to the substance of the issues and their interrelations.

In the introductory chapter to that anthology Hollander points out that difficulties in resource allocation were immediately connected with the emergence of serious social problems. He listed a number of such social problems, linked with the chronic lack of resources. The low level of public health, the backwardness of the rural areas and the consequent internal migration, insufficient and obsolete housing, the miserable conditions of the elderly, diminished birth rates due to material scarcity, environmental deterioration and the ineffective and insufficient treatment of substance abusers were all mentioned as examples. The inflexibility of administrative and political structures only made many of the problems worse.

A more systematic classification of social problems might appear helpful in understanding the changes in Russia and in the Baltic countries. In a study of social problems in the countries around the Baltic Sea (see Simpura and Tigerstedt, 1992), the following tripartite classification was suggested. First, closest to the surface, are the problems of deviant behaviour, such as crime and drug problems. Second, there are a number of problems related to structures of production, such as unemployment and poverty, and also environmental issues and housing problems. On the third level, there are the problems related to power and identity. Ethnic issues, which are important not only in the Baltic countries but also in Russia, are located on this level.

Following these categorizations we shall now turn first to discuss the general development of living conditions, then to have a look at deeper structural problems in society and finally to turn to the problems of deviant behavior.

The development of living conditions

Two main lines of thought have appeared in evaluations of the development of living conditions. The first one is the catastrophe line, while the second line firmly believes in a breakthrough of the ongoing reforms. The catastrophe line pours down descriptions of misery, misfortune and hopelessness, ranging since the years of stagnation through perestroika till the present day and even further ahead far into the future. Also the more optimistic line provides reports on catastrophes, but mostly as testimonials of the inabilities of the old regime and its remnants. At the same time the optimistic line emphasizes the irreversible nature of the ongoing reforms, which also have already led to a number of positive changes. Thus the discussion on the future of former socialist countries is full of contradictions. For instance, the Swedish economist Anders Åslund, a former adviser of the ex-Prime Minister Jegor Gaidar, declared in January 1993 that shock therapy had brought a final victory for capitalism, with concomitant material welfare throughout Eastern Europe (Dagens Nyheter, 22 January 1993). He also mercilessly criticized those specialists who dared to doubt the views of a rosy future. In Sweden, Åslund's writings raised a debate in which the most vigorous reactions came from two esteemed experts in Eastern European issues, Kristian Gerner and Stefan Hedlund (Dagens

Nyheter, 28 January 1993). Among other things they pointed out that there is certainly no unanimity among experts on the future of Eastern Europe.

Evidently, there are contradictions between the reports presented in the media and observations made of everyday life. On the surface, many things work still or work already, depending on the perspective of the speaker. The Swedish disputants mentioned above are no exceptions. The reform optimist Åslund keeps saying that the availability of commodities is basically good throughout Russia, although the market is not yet completely satisfied. His critics Gerner and Hedlund remind him of the invisible prices of these commodities. For instance, to secure the supply of meat in 1992, one third of the cattle was to be slaughtered. This of course may be detrimental from the point of view of the coming anti-famine measures. Anyway, it is obvious that large masses of population have lost the basic security provided by the old system, and there does not yet exist any new system that would be able to compensate for these losses.

Trends in the development of living conditions were discussed also in Chapter 6 in this book. The unreliability and unavailability of the information makes it very difficult to evaluate the trends in living conditions. The GNP statistics do not make sense, studies on consumption are focused on the problems of determining and attaining the minimum subsistence levels, the housing situation is very poorly described in available documents, and the health statistics contain plenty of inexplicable fluctuations and inconsistencies.

Using only one very crude indicator, the life expectancy of the population, it would appear that living conditions have worsened since the 1970's (on the population's health in general see Mezencheva and Rimashevskaya, 1990). In particular, the life expectancy of men has begun to decline. A temporary improvement was brought by the infamous anti-alcohol campaign in 1985, but its effects were soon negated by the inventive solutions of the population to the problems of alcohol availability. The data on the most recent trends seem contradictory. Leading public health officers emphasize the fact that all real catastrophes have been avoided, and there are no signs of a dramatic deterioration of health conditions. This was the view of the Russian Minister of Health in an interview published in *Izvestiya* in the last days of 1992. Everyday life observations are also contradictory. For instance, there are divided opinions on whether there are people who would have starved to death because of insufficient or delayed assistance for those living in deprivation.

The sensational events of recent years have hidden the long-term development from many observerers. There is, however, an exceptional series of studies on changes in living conditions from the city of Taganrog on the shore of the Asov Sea (see *People's Well-being...*, 1989; Rimashevskaya, 1992). This longitudinal study was made in the years 1968, 1978 and 1989, covering a period of more than 20 years. The results show that there was a general improvement of living conditions till the early 1980's. Better incomes, more opportunities for consumption and better housing were a fact, although the progress was slow. Only one of the many indicators in the study reported a negative development. That was the subjective evaluation of the citizens in Taganrog of their personal health. Even then, the changes took place in the better-off end of the health distribution, so that the share of those who regarded their health to be good went down a bit, whereas the share of those with only satisfactory health increased. There were hardly any changes in the shares of those who classified their health as bad. One explanation for this slight worsening of the situation was environmental pollution. In this industrial town in Southern Russia, the incidence of respiratory infections was constantly increasing.

From the point of view of the population at large, an important factor is the ongoing demographic change increasing the percentage of the elderly in the population. The declining birth rates have been a constant worry for a long time already, in particular as the regional variation of birth rates has been large. In the former Soviet Union, the lowest birth rates were reported in the Northeast, i.e. in the Baltic states and in the Leningrad region, while the highest rates were met in Central Asia. In the western parts of present-day Russia and also in the independent Baltic countries the demographic situation is similar to that in Western Europe, with a very large share of the elderly in the population. As many of the problems of livelihood and health are most acute among the elderly, the demographic change is an important factor in social policy.

The problems of income insufficiency have become more visible during recent years. The rise of prices, the instability of the monetary system and rapid inflation have worsened the position of that part of the population in particular which is dependent on a so-called 'fixed income'. This income category consists of all kinds of payments from the state budget, such as pensions, subsidies and even public wages. The retired and the elderly, families with small children and some public employees belong to this 'fixed income' group. Those groups of the population whose income is earned in relation to the emerging markets, both production and services, will do better. Still, there are whole branches of industry where the survival of the employees is endangered by the decline in the demand for their products by the state. Of course, the military industry is the most striking example. The difficulties are most serious in those hundreds of towns which are completely dependent on military industries. For instance, in St. Petersburg it has been estimated that as much as 70 or 80 per cent of the industrial production in the city is in the military industry. The actively discussed conversion of old production facilities into new forms suited for the market economy proceeds very slowly. Evidently, these processes may lead to the worsening of the living conditions of large groups of people employed in the old industries.

Social structure and social problems in Russia

A three-part categorization of social problems was suggested above: 1) the problems related to power and identity, 2) those concerning the organisation and structure of production, and 3) the problems of deviant behaviour. Of course, a large number of other categorizations could be presented. For instance, Hollander (1991, p. 11) distinguishes between 'asocial behaviour', 'escapist behaviour' and 'conditions related to structures and situations'. He also presents three major causes for social problems in the Soviet Union, or Russia. The first was the general development of modernization, which produces social tension and various problems everywhere, not only in Russia. The second was the limitations of the political and ideological system with regard to modernization, leading to the inflexibility of the system. And third, Hollander mentioned those political and ideological concepts that made it possible, for instance, to consider phenomena related to religion and ethnicity as social problems.

In the following, three broad issues will be discussed, each of which is of crucial importance for the emergence of social problems in Russia today. Unemployment and the organization of labour, the role of women and family, and ethnic issues are all central questions to be answered.

Unemployment in the western sense of the world is still largely unknown in Russia. The official unemployment rate is low, although the reported figures have varied greatly. Examples of the various estimates have been given by Hay and Peacock (1992a, p. 67). In the entire region of the former Soviet Union there were in 1992 about 500,000 unemployed persons, i.e. less than one per cent of the labour force. Still, as early as in 1990, the state planning organization Gosplan had estimated that the number of the unemployed would have been as high as 5.9 million. Later, one of the Russian deputy prime ministers had presented for the Russian federation alone the figure of 6 million unemployed. The International Labour Organization, again, presented a forecast that up to 11 million persons would be unemployed by the end of the year 1992. As an example of what might come the 15 per cent unemployment rate of Poland has often been mentioned.

Open unemployment, which is measured by the number of active job seekers, is still a relatively insignificant problem in Russia, although many believe that the situation might rapidly turn worse. More important is the hidden unemployment and the phenomenon called 'joblessness' (Hay and Peacock, 1992a, p. 68). This notion refers to that group which is neither looking for employment nor economically active in any other way. There are, of course, highly variable estimates on the rate of hidden unemployment.

Another problem is related to the low productivity of labour. A study made in Siberia (Jelovikov, 1992) showed that the number of employees belonging to the category of 'skilled workers' could be reduced by 13 to 15 per cent without any significant effect on the output of the local enterprises. The respective rate of hidden unemployment among the less educated workers was between 30 and 40 per cent. Although the problem is well-known, nothing very much can be done. In Russia, the workplace has been and still is more than merely a unit of production or a place for earning wages. The workplace has provided many of the commodities and services, including health care and social security. The workplace was also an important channel for acquiring goods otherwise inaccessible. Becoming unemployed would mean exclusion from this circle of distribution, the benefits from which may be much more valuable than the cash salary in itself. Even in the not so rare cases where the employer has not been able to pay wages any longer, totally or to a large extent, the workers have often continued coming to work just for the sake of these additional benefits. True, many of these benefits have also disappeared in recent years, but still those employed are better off also in terms of opportunities of acquisition of commodities than are the marginalized groups.

The second problematic area, which may become quite crucial in the near future, is the status of women and the prospects for action to improve the quality of everyday family life (see Chapter 9). Although gender has been a central ideological issue for decades, and the high labour force participation of women was celebrated as a victory of equality, the realities of everyday life are another story. Single-parent families are common, and the divorce rate has been one of the highest in Europe. In a study made in the late 1980's it turned out that one third of Russian marriages ended up in a divorce by the fourth wedding anniversary (Sanjian, 1991). The reported causes of divorce provide a dismal picture of the women's position. In the western parts of Russia, excessive drinking by the husband was the number one cause, further to the east intergenerational conflicts within the household became dominant. It appears that among the male population of Russia a strong attitude prevails requiring that women bear the family and household responsibilities alone. It is no surprise, then, that in many cases women think the quality of their and their children's life improved thanks to the departure of the spouse.

The position of women is changing, and the changes may become substantial with the ongoing social revolution. Mass unemployment is threatening the labour force participation of women in particular, although they are not the only victims. Men belonging to the unskilled labour force will certainly get their share, too. Facing such threats, the Russians may have to raise the question of gender roles once again. Russia in 1993 was a promised land for a multitude of different organizations, some of which are strongly engaged in the battle between the sexes. In January 1993, the author of this chapter happened to be present in St.Petersburg when a new anti-female organization for men was established. This organization had a quite aggressive tone in its programmes, starting with the view that women are responsible for the present misery by neglecting their domestic duties, whatever they were, and by occupying jobs belonging to men. That particular organization has remained unpopular but similar ideas may emerge elsewhere. Evidently, the tension between men and women regarding their respective social roles is increasing, and the most likely outcome of such processes is that the already almost unbearable burden of the women will only become heavier.

The third important phenomenon is the ethnic issues. Both in Russia and in the Baltic countries ethnic conflicts arise in connection with other social problems, where they appear to be quite irrelevant. In the Baltic countries it is not uncommon to hear that many of the present difficulties are but consequences of the post-war Russian occupation (for more detail see Simpura and Tigerstedt, 1992). Examples of such issues are environmental pollution, the disruption of the production system, drunkenness and crime. In Russia stories about the Caucasian mafia have been well-known for decades. Within the present Russian federation there are dozens of regions with the potential for outbursts of ethnic conflicts. Often economic interests are involved, as many regions populated by ethnic minorities possess valuable natural resources.

On the other hand, most ethnic minority groups are small indeed (cf. e.g. *Yazikovaia situachia v rossiiskoi federatsii*, 1992) and they seldom have a majority even within their own regions. The minority groups hope that the Russians would understand their efforts for greater autonomy. The Russians, for their part, not infrequently see themselves as benefactors who have rescued the smaller peoples from the wilderness for civilization. Also, the sufferings of the Russians during the war are portrayed as a sacrifice for all the peoples of present-day Russia. Therefore, small ethnic groups striving for more autonomy are simply ungrateful to their Russian protectors. From the point of view of social policy, such ethnic issues produce and increase tensions, which often generate large parts of the field where perceptions on social problems are formulated.

To summarize, the ongoing social transition has rapidly widened the gap between expectations and everyday life realities, and consequently structural tensions are emerging throughout society. Perestroika in itself was a promise never fulfilled, leading only to enormous disappointment. A similar fate may await also the more recent reforms. The much-praised patience of the Russians is really being tested, as the expected improvement of living conditions repeatedly fails to take place.

Problems of deviant behaviour

In the neighbouring countries to the west óf Russia and the Baltic countries much concern has been caused by the threat of the migration of crime and drugs from the east to the west. Also in the former socialist countries themselves, such problems of deviant behaviour have gained increasing attention. It has been, however, very difficult to estimate the extent of the problems. The unreliability of data sources becomes striking when talking about criminality, drunkenness and drug addiction. Evidently, the attention paid to these problems does not necessarily reflect the statistical variations regarding their prevalence.

The analysis by Mikko Lagerspetz (1992; 1993) of press material concerning social problems in Estonia provides an illuminating example. In the early years of perestroika, the publicity in the press was dominated by issues dictated by those in power, i.e. by the official party machinery. Such issues in the late 1980's were, for instance, alcohol problems, lack of discipline at work, or ineffectiveness and bureaucracy. Insufficiences in democratic processes came to the fore, along with emerging nationalistic mobilization, ethnic issues and closely related ecological problems. The analysis by Lagerspetz does not cover the period after Estonia regained independence, but it appears as if the definitional field of social problems has changed again. Economic difficulties and the continued presence of the Red Army in the Baltic countries are major issues now. Although drunkenness, for instance, has disappeared from the front pages and headlines, it is hard to believe that the prevalence of alcohol problems has changed much since the stabilization of the effects of the Gorbachev alcohol reform in 1985.

The data on crime testify to a link between crime and drunkenness. After the 1985 alcohol reform there was a decline in crime rates for some two or three years. After that the trend turned upward. This development has been reported both from Russia and the Baltic countries (see Gilinsky, 1992; Lagerpsetz, 1992; Seps, 1992; Mikalkevicius & Sinkunas, 1992). The increase in the crime rate is visible in all crime categories. The explanation for this rise hardly lies only in the increased private activity in acquiring alcoholic beverages, but there are also signs of a general decline in public order. Again, the problem of data sources becomes most acute here. An authentic anecdote will illustrate the difficulties. In 1990, the author accompanied a western criminologist to an international conference in Russia with a number of prominent Russian experts among the participants. The aim of the criminologist was to find a reliable estimate of the number of prisoners in Russia. The Russian experts represented all the major institutions, both from law enforcement, administration and research, and they were supposedly well-informed indeed. Still, there was a huge variation between their estimates, so that the largest figure presented was tenfold compared to the smallest one. The problem here is, besides the real lack of information, also definitional issues such as the very fluid borders between prisoners, other groups subjected to various forcible measures, and the 'normal' population. Understandably, the results from this round of interviews were never published.

In the text above there are several references to alcohol problems. In Russia and to a lesser extent also in the Baltic countries, alcohol is an important issue, both in culture and everyday life, both as an economic and as a political factor. Again, the information on the prevalence of the problem deviates widely from the public perception. The Gorbachev alcohol reform aimed first and foremost at improved work discipline and thereby at increased productivity (see e.g. Partanen, 1990). It also produced some positive results, such as improved health conditions and decreased criminality. But the negative side was at least equally impressive. Extensive illegal trade and production, often with remarkable ingenuity, was a visible outcome. Another very crucial consequence was a sharp decline in the revenues, where alcohol had the record-high share of some 16 per cent before the reform. For many reasons the reform was gradually abandoned. By the beginning of the 1990's, alcohol consumption had almost reached pre-reform levels, if the consumption that is not reported in official statistics is taken into account (see e.g. Levin and Levin, 1988; Nemtsov and Nechaev, 1991). It is well-known that the level of alcohol consumption is highest in the western parts of Russia and equally high in the Baltic countries, being close to the top Western European levels (see e.g. Simpura, 1992). Accordingly, then, the prevalence of alcohol-related problems is also high today. Irrespective of this, alcohol-related problems have almost disappeared from the public debate in all these countries.

The third issue to be mentioned here concerns drug problems. These problems have attracted much attention in the neighbouring western countries and also more widely further west. It is even more difficult to find any reliable indicators on drugs than was the case with crime and alcohol problems. Some crude estimates can be arrived at by comparing various sources and by accounting for the differences in control and treatment systems. So, for instance in the countries around the Baltic Sea, the overall prevalence of drug problems in the St. Petersburg region was lower than in Germany and Denmark, but higher than the rates in the other countries around the Baltic Sea (Simpura, 1992). Much ado about nothing? Certainly not, although the severity of drug problems in Russia and in the Baltic countries does not look dramatic in comparison with the rates further west. The seriousness of drug problems in the former socialist countries is evidently felt more concretely than in the west, as the control and treatment systems in the east are badly equipped to meet the increasing pressure, even at relatively modest problem rates. As a consequence, drug problems are also more visible to the general public and in the public debate.

Social policy, its development, and its problems

In a recent compilation of articles on social policy in Eastern Europe, Manning (1992, p. 33) distinguished between four major periods of development between the 1917 October revolution and perestroika. The phases are familiar from other contexts, although the names proposed for them by Manning may raise some discussion. He calls the first period (1917-1921) utopian, the second (1921-29) urban, the third (1929-57) industrial, and the last (1957-84) the period of welfare and productivity. In the first period, the task of social policy was straightforward and easily recognized in the conditions of civil war: to support the literacy campaigns, to combat epidemics, to promote hygiene in the collective effort of building the brave new world. In the second period, where the name 'urban' sounds odd in a thoroughly rural country, the grievances to be ameliorated were not any more easily agreed upon. According to Manning, the dominant feature of this period was the rise of sectional interests, leading finally to the search for scapegoats, for instance among private farmers. The third period covers the Stalin era, when a forcible industrialization of the country took place. Manning names the supply and discipline of labour as a perennial concern in that time. Other issues related to social policy were seldom raised. The post-war years till Stalin's death are today the golden era in Soviet history for many in the older generation as far as material well-being was concerned. Finally, Manning's fourth period begins from Khrushchev and ends with Brezhnev and Andropov. It contains the time of optimistic progress in the late 1950's and early 1960's as well as the years of stagnation. It seems as if a firm belief in the stability of political and social conditions made it possible to trust in an inevitable, although slow progress. This belief evidently spilled over into the sphere of social policy as well.

In the Baltic countries the historical development was even more unstable than in Russia. During the brief period of national independence between the two world wars social policy was hardly raised as an issue. Conflicts in domestic politics, attempted *coups d'etat* and dictatorial tendencies pushed social policy aside. It should be remembered, too, that the Baltic countries at that time were predominantly rural countries, and not too badly off, for instance in comparison with their northern neighbour Finland. However, the building of a Nordic welfare state, already started in Sweden, reached Finland during the mid-thirties (cf. Haatanen, 1992) but never really touched the Baltic countries.

One of the features which distinguished the Baltic countries from their Nordic neighbours was the structure of the possession of land. The Baltic countries were more strongly dominated by a large-estate agriculture than were the Nordic countries. Thus, they never became nations of smallholders, such as Finland for instance was till the 1950's. True, a number of land reforms were carried out in the Baltic countries during the time of independence. The most radical reforms took place in Latvia, and the most moderate reforms in Lithuania (see Zetterberg, 1990 and also Niitemaa and Hovi, 1991). All three countries remained relatively unindustrialized. In a recent article Schlau (1990) quotes sources according to which the share of industrial workers in the labour force was in 1934 as high as 21 per cent in Estonia, less than 15 per cent in Latvia and only 6 per cent in Lithuania.

The Second World War and the post-war era brought a total upheaval to the Baltic countries. Besides losing their political independence, the countries suffered immense war-time population losses and material damages that led to a weakened economic structure. The results of the land reforms were abolished for good through the enforced collectivization of agriculture, fully completed at the turn of the 1940's to 1950's. At the same time, forced migration out of the country to other parts of the Soviet empire rose to tens of thousands, or even to one hundred thousand in countries with two to three million inhabitants. Population losses were large indeed in each country, reaching one third of the population in Latvia, and exceeding 10 per cent also in Estonia and Lithuania. To fill the place of those who fled, were killed or sent into internal exile, increased numbers of Russians and other Soviet citizens were imported. Most of them worked for the armed forces, as was the case in Latvia in particular, or for the centralized all-union industrial plants, founded in particular in Estonia in the 1960's and 1970's. The effects of this migration were most strongly felt in Latvia and Estonia. As for social policy, an important fact was that most of the migrants lived in the Baltic countries only for a short time. Those migrants were but a small part of countless millions of Soviet migrant workers. In the course of such processes, with an intensified pace since the 1950's, arrangements of social policy as well as other related conditions became similar to those elsewhere in the Soviet Union.

What kind of social policy system was ultimately established in the Soviet Union? Deacon (1992, p. 5), in a review covering all Eastern European countries, presents a summary of the advantages and disadvantages of the system that emerged. For a large majority of the population, the workplace was practically guaranteed, but for those who needed it the protection against loss of work was almost non-existent. The wages of workers were good in relation to other population groups, but the hidden benefits of the *nomenklatura* effectively eliminated this achievement. The free health service worked well in principle, but lubrication of the system with bribes and presents was constantly required. Mortality and morbidity remained, however, relatively high, and preventive medicine was largely neglected. Child care was tightly organized ever since the first months, but on the other hand the mothers hardly had a choice between going to work and staying at home. In the labour market most sexist divisions prevailed. Housing was heavily subsidized and therefore cheap, but the system of distributing housing could not be characterized as even-handed. The state took responsibility for social security and pensions, but the benefits were strictly tied to the working history, and the system provided only meagre assistance in cases of acute need. The party and the state paternalized the citizens, but did not provide them with any opportunity to make grass-roots proposals to improve social conditions.

It is necessary to understand the socialist welfare regime from the inside in order to evaluate the problems faced and caused by the ongoing reforms. It is evidently essential to understand that production and consumption were, in a way, organized in the same units. Production units, and all other workplaces as well, were not only a source of monetary income but also distributive channels for various commodities and services to the workers. Resources for the production activities were delivered by following rules dictated by the central planning system. The resources, then, trickled down from the top, and similarly the production output was distributed and delivered further according to centralized decisions. The workplaces were responsible for the satisfaction of a large part of the material and social needs of the employees. Commodities and services were distributed through the workplace. The technical management ran the production, trade unions were in charge of the distribution of goods and services, and party organs dealt with control and coordination. All these three functions were intertwined, both on the level of workplaces and of the municipalities. In western terms, the need for services outside the workplaces was relatively limited.

This system has many roots in Russia, both politico-ideological and historical. It bears resemblance with that feudal way of thinking where the serfs were dependent on the landlord, but at the same time it was the landlord's duty to look after his subjects. Possession of wealth and property, care-taking and power were all collective by nature. The late medieval *mir* organization was a realization of this thinking. There are several names for the numerous manifestations of similar ideas, such as the 'Asiatic mode of production', where the most crucial distinction from the European one is the collective but centralized mode of possession (cf. Radaev and Shkaratan, 1992, p. 303). There is a lord over every landlord, and in the centre sit the Czar and God. Good and Evil flow from the centre to the periphery, from top to bottom.

A more modern proposal for the name of such a system is 'etacratism', referring to the penetrating influence of the state throughout society (Radaev and Shkaratan, 1992). In this system, the transmission of information and commodities between two cells at equal distance from the centre but in different sectors has been difficult, and in principle possible only via the centre. Central planning agencies and ministries in Russia even today exercise power which is based on this model. For instance, buildings, land and production machinery belong to these central agencies. Local decision making is difficult, since resources as well as raw materials and infrastructure, are controlled by central bodies. Of course, this centralized structure is gradually withering away, but this certainly will take several years.

Presently the problems of financial and monetary structures in Russia have an important effect also on social policy. The instability of the economy is leading to difficulties both for the financing of social policy and for its clients. As for financing, an important fact is that in the earlier system social policy activities were intertwined with many other activities, all of which had a common financial background and allocation system. Therefore, it is difficult to determine the share of health and social welfare in the GNP, as a major part of health and welfare expenditure was administered via channels quite distinct from those specially designated for these purposes. Now, in the transition period, the old system, which was largely based on benefits in kind, is being replaced by a new system of pecuniary benefits. In order to be successful, the new rule would need an efficient taxation system and funds protected against inflation. Neither of these conditions is presently fulfilled. Inflation cuts down the funds, even though the collection of funds has been intensified. Decisions concerning the level of pensions and other public assistance payments are often delayed and the purchasing power of the benefits is diminished.

The supply of social and health services is scarce for those without any link to the workplaces. If, in addition, such persons do not have that unofficial social network of family, neighbours, friends and colleagues which is indispensable in Russia today, the problems of survival may become serious indeed. A number of the elderly and families with children or with handicapped family members already face such a situation. They are entitled to various forms of public assistance, providing, however, only a minimal assistance reserved to those in utmost need. In addition, the provision of social services is scarce in general, and social work, in any western sense of the word, is still practically unknown in Russia. Instant education of social workers has been started, often in quite surprising forms. For instance, in winter

1993 a whole technical school in St. Petersburg was transformed into an institute of social work, continuing with the same teachers and the same students as before the reform. The army is also a resource. Officers have been recruited and re-educated for positions in the social welfare administration.

Today, Russia is full of examples of increasingly serious difficulties in social policy. The problems of health care and housing are well-known. The privatization of housing is awaited by many with fear, as millions of people cannot afford the new market prices. So far, housing has been cheap, although no luxury is provided, and the houses have deteriorated due to lack of repairs. For instance in St.Petersburg almost half of the population are living in the so-called *kommunalki*, i.e. in apartments shared by two or more households. For them and for many others the emerging market prices of housing are mostly unattainable.

As for health services, one of the major problems is the lack of medicine and equipment, leading among other things to problems of hygiene at hospitals. Domestic production barely functions, and the country cannot afford to buy medicine and materials for hard currency. The consequences may become dramatic for some patients, in particular for those with severe chronic diseases. As an example, in autumn 1992 there were announcements in St. Petersburg newspapers of the distribution of insulin, donated by Denmark in such an amount as to satisfy the demand for a few months. One can only imagine the situation that would have emerged without the Danish donation. Similar conditions are an everyday reality for many other groups.

The question, then, is how to build social policy and how to develop health and social welfare services in such economic and social conditions? The idea that a 'transition to market relations' with maximal privatization could rapidly create effective health and social services and the required insurance system looks unrealistic. Admittedly, there are signs of the emergence of such a system, but evidently it will never cover any larger groups of population. Many of the developers of social policy see a crucial problem in the fact that there are no middle classes in Russia capable of self-organized action. Some others point out that the 'social infrastructure' is weakly developed in Russia (see e.g. Patsiorkovsky, 1989). For still another group, the solution of the problems requires the establishment of the civil society. Were there a sufficient social infrastructure, if the civil society would emerge, or if the middle classes could be developed to adopt their natural role as the engine of social change, any problem could be solved. But the great question remains of how to give birth to these necessary structures. So far, all attempts to create them from above have been in vain.

The idea of insufficient social infrastructure is related to the idea that the citizens, under the old regime, had become incapable of taking the initiative. The *homo sovieticus* is often mentioned as the most detrimental product of the old system, blocking effectively all reforms. One can, however, question this line of thought. To survive in the present-day conditions of the transition economy countries, quite exceptional skills and initiative are certainly required. Evidently, there are also a large number of social networks to support survival in everyday life. Even living in shared apartments — an indication of very poor living conditions for many western observers — can become a resource, as the neighbours may extend the social networks needed for the acquisition of goods and services. So, there may be some basis for optimism that public structures will gradually be created to support social policy, if only disorder can be avoided and economic and material conditions do not totally collapse.

Structural change in east and west

The problems of social policy in Eastern Europe look immense when compared with the conditions in the industrialized countries in the west. However, something similar is going on almost everywhere in Europe, in that social structures are challenged and social policy systems are under the pressures of radical change.

In the Scandinavian countries, the present economic crisis in Sweden and Finland and the possible membership of the European Union may lead to a major re-evaluation of social policy. Differences between the present EC member countries are large, and the strengthening of integration is only beginning. How to share the responsibility between public and private actors, what kind of division of labour to establish between the two genders, what kind of role to give to families and how to solve the problems of financing social policy? Any answer to these questions is likely to lead to radical changes in the social policy system, in some countries at least.

The possibility that industrialized countries outside Europe will also get involved cannot be excluded. In the internal debate in the USA, issues related to social and health policies have already been raised to the fore. The most expensive health care system in the world, which nevertheless leaves tens of millions of people without elementary protection, is finally being revised. Tax increases have been announced, aiming partly at improved assistance for those suffering from mass poverty created in the 1980's. Presently it looks as if also Japan cannot remain unaffected as it struggles with its elderly populations and weakening work motivation.

Still, the outlook for the crisis is different in different countries, although certain fundamental changes are taking place in the former socialist transition economies, in the Scandinavian countries as well as in the EC. In Russia and in the Baltic countries the political instability is of quite a different kind compared to anything going on in Western Europe. An important aspect here is the different status of the concept 'social policy' in different countries. In the Nordic countries, social policy has been commonly regarded as a positive central element in social and political life, even now, notwithstanding the present fiscal crisis, and even despite the fact that the prime ministers of both Sweden and Finland in winter 1993 declared that the Scandinavian model of the welfare state is dead (New York Times, 22 February 1993). In the EC countries, social policy has had a more secondary position. In Russia and in the Baltic countries, social policy is a two-edged sword. On the one hand it carries the burden of the old regime, but on the other hand the acute crisis in living conditions is provoking increasing interest in social policy and its prospects. From the point of view of Russia and the Baltic countries the ongoing battle between welfare regimes in the western world certainly does not help them find their own solutions. Foreign examples are becoming scarce, as no one model looks superior to its competitors.

The famous typology of welfare regimes by Esping-Andersen (1990) serves as a starting point for a temporary evaluation of the prospects of Russian and Baltic social policies. The universalist, corporatist and liberalist regimes, the first two often being called also social democratic and conservative Catholic models, have entered into a battle in Europe. The universalist model is losing ground, but it is still unclear how the other two models will succeed. As for Russia, it seems that the steps taken in the early 1990's combined liberalistic and monetarist economic doctrine with liberalistic welfare ideas. In practice, however, the steps in this direction were few and small. In Estonia, the present political atmosphere is favourable to liberalistic solutions, but the Nordic influence is also strong, and there is still some interest in developing also universalist approaches. The most serious obstacle in Estonia to setting up a universalist social policy is the ethnic division of the population. Large groups face the risk of receiving only a secondary role in the country, including the realm of social policy. In Latvia the situation is somewhat similar to that in Estonia, but the ethnic problems are even more serious and the Scandinavian influence smaller than in Estonia. Lithuania is a Catholic country facing Central Europe. It was the first of the Baltic countries to experience the return to power of communists through democratic processes. Therefore, the country may today be more open to universalist solutions than was the case in the early 1990's, although a corporatist impact from Central Europe cannot be excluded. In Lithuania, the developments in Poland will certainly be reflected in the formation of social policy. And interestingly, former communists have regained political power also in Poland.

In the concluding chapter of his book *New Eastern Europe* (1992) Bob Deacon proposes that the development of social policy in the transforming economy countries does not necessarily have to follow any of the three models proposed by Esping-Andersen. An alternative route would be, for example, to turn to experiences in the east, instead of western models, as soon as the first outbursts of revolutionary changes have calmed somewhat. The authoritarian capitalism applied in the Far East, South East Asia and the Near East, with a decisive role for state interventions, might work in Eastern Europe better than any western model. This prospect of the future bears resemblance to the above-mentioned 'Asiatic mode of production', and the related state-power, or etacratism (Radaev and Shkaratan, 1992). So, the typology by Esping-Andersen must perhaps be augmented in the coming decades through the addition of an etacratist welfare regime.

References

Aarrevaara, Timo (1992a), 'Ukrainan paikalliset päätöksentekijät', *Hallinnon tutkimus*, 1992: 1.

Aarrevaara, Timo (1992b), 'Uusi paikallishallinto Pietarissa', *Helsingin kaupungin tietokeskuksen tutkimuksia* 4/1992, Helsinki.

Deacon, Bob (1992) 'East European Welfare: Past, Present and Future in Comparative Context' in Deacon, Bob (ed.), *The New Eastern Europe. Social Policy: Past, Present and Future*, Sage, London.

Esping-Andersen, Gøsta (1990), *The Three Worlds of Welfare Capitalism*, Polity Press, Oxford.

Gilinskij, Jakov (1992), 'Social problems and deviant behavior in St. Petersburg' in Simpura, J. & Tigerstedt, C. (eds.), *Social Problems around the Baltic Sea*, NAD-Publications, Helsinki.

Haatanen, Pekka (1992), 'Suomalaisen hyvinvointivaltion kehitys' in Riihinen, O. (ed.), *Sosiaalipolitiikka 2017*, WSOY, Helsinki.

Hay, Michael & Peacock, Alan (1992a), 'Giving Advice to Government: The Case of Russia', *Business Strategy Review*, Summer 1992.

Hay, Michael & Peacock, Alan (1992b), *Social Politics in the Transition to a Market Economy*, The David Hume Institute, Edinburgh.

Heikkilä, Matti et al. (1992), 'Iskulauseista taikasanoihin. Markkinasuhteisiin siirtyminen ja sosiaalipolitiikka entisessä Neuvostoliitossa', *Sosiaaliturva* 3/1992 (1992a) and 4/1992 (1992b).

Hollander, Paul (1991), 'Politics and Social Problems' in Jones, A. et al. (eds.), *Soviet Social Problems*, Westview Press, Boulder, Colorado.

Jelovikov, Leonid (1992), 'Rynok truda: vershina aisberga i ego podvodnaia chast', *Chelovek y Trud*, 3:1992.

Jones, Anthony, Walter D. Connor & David E. Powell (eds.) (1991), *Soviet Social Problems*, Westview Press, Boulder, Colorado.

Kangas, Olli (1992), 'Eurooppa, sosiaaliturva ja Suomi. Eurooppalainen sosiaaliturva suomalaisessa valossa', *Sosiaali- ja terveysministeriön monisteita*, 24:1992, Helsinki.

Lagerspetz, Mikko (1992), 'Estonia: Changing Problems in a Re-emerging State' in Simpura, J. & Tigerstedt, C. (eds.), *Social Problems around the Baltic Sea*, NAD-publications, Helsinki.

Levin, B.M. & Levin, M.B. (1988), *Alkogolnaia situatsiia 1988*, Institut Sotsiologii RAN, Moskva.

Manning, Nick (1992a), 'Social Policy in Soviet Union and its Successors' in Deacon, Bob (ed.), *The New Eastern Europe. Social Policy: Past, Present and Future*, Sage, London.

Manning, Nick (1992b), 'The Reform of Housing in Eastern Europe and the Soviet Union', *Journal of European Social Policy*, 4:1992.

Meissner, Boris (1990), *Die baltischen Nationen Estland, Lettland, Litauen*, Markus Verlag, Köln.

Mezentsheva, E & Rimashevskaya, N. (1990), 'Health of the USSR Population in the 70's and the 80's: An Approach to a Comprehensive Analysis', *Social Science and Medicine*, 31:1990.

Mikalkevicius, Algirdas & Sinkunas, Stanislovas (1992), 'Ideology and Alcohol Problems in Lithuania' in Simpura, J. & Tigerstedt, C. (eds.), *Social Problems around the Baltic Sea*, NAD-Publications, Helsinki.

Murarka, Dev (1992), *Gorbatshov*, WSOY, Porvoo.

Nemtsov, A.V. & Netshaev, A.K. (1991), 'Alkogolnaya situatsija v Moskve v 1983–1990 gg.', *Sotsialnaia i klinicheskaia psihiatria* 1:1991.

Niitemaa, Vilho & Hovi, Kalervo (1991), *Baltian historia*, Tammi, Helsinki.

Obraz zhizni v usloviiah perestroiki (1992), Institut Sotsiologii RAN, Moskva.

Partanen, Juha (1987), 'Serious Drinking, Serious Alcohol Policy', *Contemporary Drug Problems*, Winter 1987.

Patsiorkovsky, V. (1989), *Sotsialnaia infrastruktura*, Tsentralnyi ekonomiko-matematicheskii institut AN SSSR, Moskva.

People's Well-being in the USSR: Trends and Prospects (1989), USSR Academy of Sciences, Nauka Publishers, Moscow.

Radaev, Vadim & Shkaratan, Ovsey (1992), 'Etacratism: Power and Property — Evidence from the Soviet Experience', *International Sociology*, 3:1992.

Rimashevskaya, Natalia (1992), *Family, Well-being, Standard of Living and Quality of Life of Russian Population*, Manuscript, Institute for Socio-Economic Studies of Population, Russian Academy of Sciences, Moscow.

Ruutsoo, Rein (1992), 'Miten neuvostotilastoja on luettava?', *Tiede & edistys* 2:1992.

Sanjian, Andrea S. (1991), 'Social Problems, Political Issues: Marriage and Divorce in the USSR', *Soviet Studies*, vol. 43, 4:1991.

Schlau, Wilfried (1990), 'Die Wandel in der sozialen Struktur der baltischen Länder' in Meissner, B. (ed.), *Die baltischen Nationen*, Markus Verlag, Köln.

Seps, Dzidris (1992), 'Alcohol Problems in the Latvian Cultural and Political Context' in Simpura, J. & Tigerstedt, C. (eds.), *Social Problems around the Baltic Sea*, NAD-Publications, Helsinki.

Simpura, Jussi (1992), 'Alkoholiongelmat sosiaalisina ongelmina Itämeren ympärysmaissa. Baltica-tutkimus sosiaalisista ongelmista käynnistynyt', *Alkoholipolitiikka*, vol. 57, 3:1992.

Simpura, Jussi (1992), 'Alcohol, Drugs and Social Problems around the Baltic Sea' in the conference report *Baltic Cities Expert Meeting on Drug Supply and Demand*, Turku 3-5 June 1992, Sosiaali- ja terveysministeriö, Helsinki.

Simpura, Jussi & Tigerstedt, Christoffer (eds.) (1992), *Social Problems around the Baltic Sea*, NAD-Publications, Helsinki.

Valkonen, Martti (1992), *Kirjeitä Moskovasta*, Otava, Helsinki.

Yarigina, Tatyana & Yavlinsky, Grigory (1993), 'Social Policy in the Transition from Centralized to Market Economy' in *International Expert Meeting 'Towards a Competitive Society in Central and Eastern Europe: Social dimensions'*, STAKES, Helsinki.

Zetterberg, Seppo (1989), 'Kansallinen herääminen — Itsenäisyyden aika — Ribbentropista Gorbatshoviin' in *Studia Baltica. Näkökulmia Baltian maiden historiaan ja kulttuuriin*, Arena, Jyväskylä.

9 Changes in the Status of Women in Russia and Estonia

Elina Haavio-Mannila and Kaisa Kauppinen

Introduction

Women's life was greatly influenced by perestroika and glasnost, policies which were proclaimed in the former Soviet Union in 1985. Due to the policy of free expression, public critical discussions took place about women's social status, their heavy double role in the workplace and at home, and the workplace climate that favoured men. In Soviet society, the question of the status of women was considered resolved since, officially, women and men had equal rights, obligations and opportunities for self-realization. Great optimism that quick changes and improvements would be forthcoming was attached to the early phase of perestroika.

There were, however, no rapid improvements in the status of women due to the economic crisis in Russia and the other Soviet countries. There were even changes for the worse: after the quotas guaranteeing equal participation in the political system had been abolished, female participation in the processes of political decision-making declined. In addition, their share of the work load was further increased by economic insecurity and problems of everyday life.

Despite the egalitarian socialist ideology and attempts to further gender equality in education, the Soviet woman was not at any stage in the history of the USSR equal to the man. The female work force was unevenly distributed in the different fields of production; women were underrepresented in politics and positions of authority, and within the family the woman was held responsible for the overall care of the family and its members. Open discussion about the status of women and the relations between the genders is now possible. Women are bringing up issues relating to, among other things, infant mortality, abortion, and problems of health and social welfare.

According to Anastasia Posadskaya (1993b), there was a gender delusion attached to perestroika. Many factors related to the transition process affected the genders differently and were partly disadvantageous to women. Resolving these questions will be a real challenge to post-socialist society. Nowadays, the expressions 'equality', 'women's emancipation', and 'solidarity' have, in common usage, primarily negative connotations. They are associated with the former policy, in which equality prevailed in theory but not in practice. Their use is problematic on account of their politically loaded meaning. The vocabulary must be renewed, according to Posadskaya, or the expressions must get new contents.

This chapter deals with the circumstances and activities of Russian and Estonian women at work, in the family and in politics. In addition to Russian, Estonian and American research, also the results of the research work obtained during the years of bilateral scientific cooperation between Finland and the USSR are used as sources. Besides attitudes toward work and the family, perceptions of women's and men's tasks in society are dealt with, based on attitude surveys carried out in Russia. The status of women is bound up with the political system and women's movements. The transition from communism to the market economy changed the nature of women's political participation and women's organizations. In this chapter, attention is focused on the contradictions which have characterized Soviet policies and culture in connection with the status and roles of men and women. They manifest themselves in the following conflict: on one hand, full-time participation in working life was expected of women, as of men; on the other hand, women were expected to take care of the home, children and themselves according to the traditional female role. Another conflict exists between the tendency to label women as being overemancipated and masculine, on one hand, and on the other, to expect femininity and subservience of her, following the old sexist tradition.

The development of egalitarian views in Soviet society

According to Marxist-Leninist theory, women's participation in production and public life was a key question of socialist society. Women's public role was seen as important. The family was regarded as an outdated institution that obstructed social activities; the family carried on old traditions, it represented backwardness and it was the core of the bourgeois system (Geiger, 1968; Dahlström, 1989; Lapidus, 1993). The Bolshevist revolutionary vision held that the family should be deprived of its economic status and social foundation, and that society as a whole be redirected from the private sphere towards the public. Some of the caring, rearing and moral functions of the family were transferred to public institutions such as day-care centres, schools, central kitchens, public laundries, party youth organizations etc. Through them, the goal was to rationalize and to annihilate the institutions and views considered bourgeois.

The original Soviet approach strived to achieve equality between the genders by transferring functions from the home to the public sector. It did not include the modern feminist strategy that both the male and the female role had to be defined anew (Lapidus, 1993).

In the former Soviet Union, women were well educated and their status was strong compared to their Western sisters. Partly, this was founded on the communist ideology, according to which women's emancipation was based on the conception that through paid work women could free themselves from the slavery and oppression of the patriarchal family and housework (Lenin, 1951, cited by Sacks, 1988). The communist ideology was reflected even in the attitudes to work: work was a means not only of earning money but also of personal development. This ideology of work meant that to be a 'good woman' the woman had to participate in work outside the home and, in so doing, be a good citizen and a role model for the children.

During Stalin's rule official Soviet policies became more family-oriented. The significance of the family was stressed as the creator of social stability, and the formerly condemned family values were rehabilitated. Public attention was attached to population growth, and

attitudes toward abortions were negative. Stalin's strategy of industrialization emphasized the construction of heavy industry while consumer goods and service industries received less attention. Light industry would have produced such commodities, facilities and services
as rearing a family would demand. This industrial policy forced households to function on the basis of an old-fashioned technology. Social
services, such as day-care centres, old-age homes and hospitals, were
not qualitatively developed and so the level of care provided by them
remained low. As women's participation in working life was very
common, the households — and there especially the women — were
hard pressed to satisfy everyday needs. The home was, again, the centre
of social reproduction, contrary to the original Soviet ideology (Lapidus, 1993; Posadskaya, 1993a and 1993b; cf. Dahlström, 1989).

Soviet society was founded on the dual female role: women played
an active role both in production and in the home. Women's participation in working life was encouraged by stressing their equal rights and
responsibilities with men, by widening educational opportunities and
by transferring the additional costs of the female work force to be paid
by the society, for instance, through paid maternity leaves. Women's
participation in industrial production, however, did not change the fact
that women answered for the family responsibilities and the moral
atmosphere in the home (Lapidus, 1993). As an example of this, Russian
wives considered it their duty to monitor their husbands' alcohol
consumption more generally than did wives for example in the neighbouring Finland (Holmila, Matskovsky and Rannik, 1989).

Education

Literacy gives power, especially in the countries where it is hard to gain
and to master. Before the Socialist Revolution in 1917, Russia was a
backward country. Only 21 per cent of the population could somehow
read and write. In the countryside, only 12 per cent of the men and eight
per cent of the women had gone to school for more than three years.
After the revolution, there were programmes carried out to abolish
illiteracy. School was made compulsory, campaigns were held to abolish illiteracy, and also women who had earlier been denied schooling
could take part in it. In 1926, as many as 56 per cent of the population
aged from 15 to 49 years could read and write in the USSR. The

difference between men and women soon diminished and disappeared. As early as at the beginning of the 1930's illiteracy had almost entirely disappeared. (Koval, 1989b.)

The high standard of women's education in the former Soviet Union has been considered one of the best attainments of the socialist system. However, women have not been able to fully utilize their education in working life. Women's average pay level is lower than men's because, very often, women's tasks are not commensurate with their education, for one thing. The results of a study show that one fourth of women believe that their work does not correspond to their competence (Rimachevskaya, 1993).

Women's lower pay levels and positions at work are partly due to the fact that women participate in further occupational training less than men. After entering matrimony two thirds of working women do not improve or add to their occupational or professional skills (Rimashevskaya, 1993). The infrequency of further training among Russian women has been due to the fact that in Russia the workdays are longer than, for instance, in Finland (Niemi et al., 1991). So, especially women who have family responsibilities tend to leave out evening courses. According to Lapidus (1993), most women drop out of evening courses after the birth of their first child. Furthermore, women believe less frequently than men that additional training would promote their careers, which diminishes their motivation.

In the USSR, women's promotion in working life was not considered of much importance to society. Many highly educated women thought that a position of authority would cause more disadvantage and envy in the workplace than real benefit. Many of them perceived that their superior position was in conflict with their femininity. The general atmosphere in working life favoured men as superiors and launched them naturally up the career ladder (Kauppinen-Toropainen, 1991).

Paid work

The original Soviet policy started from the egalitarian vision of women's full-time participation in production. Together with the ideological message, the demand for a female work force was created by strong industrialization during the first five-year plan (1928-1932). It grew still greater during World War II, when women replaced the millions of men who were at war and perished there. In 1945, women's share of the work force was as large as 56 per cent (Lapidus, 1993).

Contrary to the USA, Britain and Germany, women in the USSR remained in the tasks they had been replacing and did not go back home after the war. In 1946, there were only 59 men for each 100 women in the age group from 35 to 59 years in USSR. This demographic imbalance increased the supply of female work force because many women had to manage by themselves: on account of Stalin's terror and the enormous losses during the war numerous wives and widows became the main supporters of households. In 1959, the share of the households supported by women was 30 per cent of all households. In the same year, the women's share of the whole population was 55 per cent, but 63 per cent of all the people over the age of 35 years. By 1985, this demographic imbalance in the numbers of the genders had levelled (Lapidus, 1993). The gradual reversion to demographic balance and the rise in the living standard could have led to a decrease in the supply and demand of the female work force. This did not happen, however. On the contrary, the women's share in the work force increased from 47 per cent to 51 per cent from 1960 to 1970.

During the recent years of reform policy, women's share of the work force remained large; in 1989 it was 51 per cent. In 1989, over 87 per cent of women of working age, that is, aged from 16 to 55 years, were in the work force or were full-time students. The only regions in the USSR where women did not participate in the work force on a large scale were the republics of Central Asia and Trans-Caucasia. (Lapidus, 1993.)

The development of labour legislation

Immediately after the Socialist Revolution, legislation was passed in the USSR for the enforcement of equality between men and women. The equality policy concerned mainly working life, where equal pay was prescribed for equal work. In marriage, the principle of equality abolished inequality between the spouses; marriage was seen as a voluntary contract between free persons. Men and women acquired equal rights to property and parenthood. During Stalin's rule, however, the development towards equality ceased. It was claimed that all matters pertaining to the status of women had already been solved and that they needed no further attention. This view shut out all critical debate and discussion on the issue. (Posadskaya, 1993a, 1993b.)

Despite the declaration of the equality of the genders in Soviet law, women have been regarded as a work force demanding special protection, as the weaker gender (Rimashevskaya, 1993). For instance, paid maternity leaves and support systems for families with many children were prescribed by law. From the middle of the 1950's on, different kinds of special benefits were developed for women which were related to maternity as a social institution rather than to women's physiological role of a child-bearer (Narusk, 1991; Posadskaya, 1993a).

The contradictions in the social views of gender equality can be reduced to the conflict between the equal opportunities of education, culture, politics and work, on one hand, and, on the other hand, the special benefits that women are given for their role in social reproduction. These benefits often led to the discrimination of women in working life (Posadskaya, 1993a).

A decisive step toward the market economy was taken in 1990 when the law pertaining to small enterprises was passed in the Congress of the USSR People's Deputies. Employment exchange centres were opened the following year, in 1991. Attitudes to women's work and to women's participation in working life have changed. Whereas participation in work was earlier considered a duty, it is now considered a right. An unemployed person is defined as a woman aged 16 to 55 years or a man aged 16 to 60 years who is not employed in paid work, who is registered in an unemployment centre, who is seeking work, and is ready to work. In Moscow from 80 to 90 per cent of the unemployed were, according to Posadskaya (1992), women; in the whole of Russia, the share is said to be about two thirds.

Nowadays, if there are any new openings for women, they involve generally manual work: carrying tiles, textile work, sewing, nursing, or child care. As 75 per cent of those looking for employment are specialists with expert technical training, the supply and demand of work do not correspond in quality. It is especially difficult for women nearing retirement age and for mothers of small children to find employment.

Women's working conditions have been prescribed by law. Women are forbidden night work and working in unhealthy conditions, limits have been set for carrying loads and lifting, and women's retirement age is lower than that of men. In spite of this legislation with its restrictions, many women continued to work in unsatisfactory conditions. In 1991, four million women were employed in work which was not in compliance with women's health and safety legislation. In industry, 44 per cent of the women worked in unhealthy conditions (Posadskaya, 1991b).

The road of protective limitations solely for women has come to an end. Researchers maintain that men's working conditions should also be improved. Especially in industry men work in unhealthy conditions; in construction, 83 per cent of those whose work is unhealthy are men. Men's life expectancy in the USSR was noticeably lower (64.5 years in 1989) than women's (74.0 years). Researchers recommend that enterprises should create healthy working conditions for both women and men instead of paying extra for working in unhealthy conditions. Specific regulations directed toward women can be used against the interests of women. (Posadskaya, 1993b.)

The structure of the female work force

Although women have participated in working life in Soviet society on a large scale, considerations of gender still define the social roles as far as skill qualifications and social status are concerned. However mathematical ability has not been labelled as 'male' in the socialist countries in the same way as in the Western countries. It was original and unique in the world that there were so many Soviet women functioning, for instance, as physicians and engineers. According to Natalia Rimashevskaya (1993), in 1989 67 per cent of the physicians and 58 per cent of the engineers were women.

Earlier, female engineers generally took on administrative and specialized tasks. According to the information given by the association of engineers in Tallinn, the capital of Estonia, 45 per cent of the management (managers, chief engineers) of Estonian industry were women, as well 74 per cent of the technical specialists, the majority of whom were engineers (Kandolin, Rannik and Haavio-Mannila, 1991a). During recent years, the engineering professions have become dominated by women in Russia and Estonia, but the salaries do not deviate much from those of skilled workers. Nowadays, many female engineers are employed in other than strictly technological or scientific tasks, for example, in office work (Kivinen, 1993).

Although women in Soviet society have generally been functioning as physicians, their share on top of the professional pyramid of physicians is small. In Moscow, 14 per cent of the surveyed female physicians were chief physicians in 1991; in neighbouring Finland, for a comparison, eight per cent of all the female physicians were chief physicians or medical directors in 1988. In both the countries 25 per cent of all male physicians were holding such positions. (Yasnaya, Kandolin and Kauppinen-Toropainen, 1993.)

Even higher education does not seem to guarantee as many positions of authority to women as it does to men, but women seem to succeed in tasks of expertise. According to a Soviet study, 48 per cent of men with a university or intermediate college education, but only seven per cent of women, were in superior positions (Lapidus, 1993). During the last decades of the Soviet rule, women's participation in such positions increased: in 1956, only one per cent of the managers of enterprises were women; in 1975, they were as many as nine per cent; and, in 1985, no less than eleven per cent (Lapidus, 1993). While women's share of all positions in business management was six per cent, it was 31 per cent in light industry, and 21 per cent in the textile industry and 14 per cent in the food industry (Rimachevskaya, 1993).

During the war many male teachers and scientists died and women were needed to take over these tasks. In 1986 40 per cent of all scientific workers in the Soviet Union were women, as well as 28 per cent of those holding the masters degree and 13 per cent of those holding the doctorate (Koval, 1989a; Rimashevskaya, 1993). In 1988, one third, that is, 22,855 of the 60,000 scientific workers of the Academy of Sciences in the USSR were women. Women's share grew larger towards the lower levels of the hierarchy: 1.6 per cent of the members of the Academy were women, 7 per cent of the full professors, 15 per cent of the other professors, 25 per cent of the senior researchers, but nearly half of the younger researchers. Of the directors of the institutes of the Academy 2.1 per cent were women, 12 per cent of the heads of departments, laboratories and sectors, 10 per cent of the chief researchers, 18 per cent of the research directors, 30 per cent of the senior researchers, and 52 per cent of the younger researchers. (Koval, 1989a.)

International comparisons show that the official gender equality policy of the USSR succeeded, despite its deficient realization, in raising women's social status. According to the results of a study in six countries (the USA, Sweden, Norway, Canada, Finland and Russia) which was conducted by Kivinen (1993), female dominance in the Russian class structure is typical in occupations having 'professional autonomy'. While in all the industrialized countries at least half of the professionals are men, in Russia women's share is two thirds. There are also more women than average among the directors and engineers in Russia. Consequently, the core of the new middle classes — if it is meaningful to talk about the middle classes in the Russian context — includes more women in Russia than in the developed capitalist countries.

Working conditions and the quality of work

In industry, construction and agriculture the working conditions of Soviet women were often poor. Their situation has been especially bad in the timber, paper, food, and graphic industries, where their share varies from 30 to 50 per cent of those who are employed in heavy labour. In industry women are more often employed in manual labour while men work at machines and devices. About one third of the women working in industry receive special benefits for unhealthy working conditions (Rimashevskaya, 1993).

Why have women continued to work in unhealthy and difficult working conditions? There are several reasons for the lack of pressure for change, such as the lack of alternatives, the harsh economic situation of the family, as well as the low retirement age, shorter workday, the fairly high pay and longer leave granted in exchange for the hard work (Kobzeva, 1992).

The glorification of manual labour in the USSR (Treiman, 1977) has diminished class differences. For example Kivinen's study measured attitudes towards work by asking the workers if they considered their work pleasant and if they spent their leisure time or entered into friendly relationships with their workmates. His data showed no significant differences in Russia between the core of the middle class, its edge, and the working class. Men's orientation to work did not vary according to social status, and there were no differences between the genders in white-collar occupations. Working class women's attitudes to work were the most instrumental: they considered the work unpleasant and they did not relate to their fellow workers as much as the other groups (Kivinen, 1993).

It was the aim of the USSR to abolish class differences. This official policy was successful at least in the respect that some qualities of work, such as independence and the climate of the workplace, varied less according to social status in the USSR than in the Nordic countries and the USA (Kandolin et al. 1991a; Haavio-Mannila 1992; 1993). At the end of the 1980's working conditions and the quality of work were in the USSR worse than in the Nordic countries and USA. The workdays of engineers, teachers, technicians and factory workers were longer than in the Nordic countries but shorter than in the USA. The strain caused by the work was greater: the work was pressing and the schedules were tight. The work was less independent: it was not possible for the worker to decide about the pace of the work or the working order; the work was neither interesting nor diversified. Compared to the situation in the Nordic countries, the freedom of movement of the Soviet workers was more limited: they were not allowed to leave their workplace, nor were breaks or discussions with co-workers allowed to the same extent as in the Nordic countries. (Haavio-Mannila, 1992; 1993.)

More often than in the Nordic countries or the USA social relations between co-workers in the workplace in the Soviet Union were warm. In Soviet workplaces co-worker friendship networks helped in solving personal problems. Colette Schulman (1977) has described the work collectives of Russian women. They build up a feeling of belonging together and of mutual support in coping with the problems of everyday life. By this, she does not mean the official collectivistic working units, but the unofficial networks which are formed between women in the workplace and which have their own leaders, behaviour norms and laws of friendship.

From the point of view of gender equality it is problematic that in the former communist countries friendships between men and women in the workplace were more easily labelled as erotic or sexual relationships, and flirting and sexual harassment in the workplace were more common than in the Nordic countries. In the USA, sexual harassment was, however, more common than in the Soviet Union and the Nordic countries. Workplace love affairs were nevertheless not frequently talked about in the former USSR. One reason for the infrequency of love affairs could be that the communist workplace policy actively discouraged romances between fellow workers. It was feared that they would increase the divorce rate, which was high already. It was the task of the party cells and trustees at the workplace to reprimand the lovers and to hinder sexual relationships between co-workers. (Haavio-Mannila, 1992; 1993; 1994; cf. Konecki, 1990.)

The wages and salaries

The disparity in pay between men and women in Russia is at least as dramatic as in the West. The incomes of the women in the core of the new middle classes do not deviate much from the average income of the working class (Kivinen, 1993). Women's incomes in the USSR did not increase with age as much as did those of men. They ranged from 65 to 75 per cent of men's earnings (Rimashevskaya, 1993).

The inequality of the spouses in the family is shown by the fact that the wife's pay was about 60 per cent of the husbands pay, according to recent studies conducted in Estonia and Russia (Haavio-Mannila, 1992; Kauppinen-Toropainen, 1993). One reason for women's low earnings is that in the fields where there is a lot of female labour, such as light industry and services industries, the general pay level is low. Another reason for women's low pay level is that blue-collar occupations dominated by men are, because of the glorification of manual labour, more highly paid than many white-collar occupations dominated by women (Lapidus, 1993). For example, in Estonia in 1988, the pay of teachers requiring higher education was of the same order as that of male workers in industry. Neither did the pay of female engineers differ much from that of skilled workers. (Kandolin et al., 1991a.)

There are differences in pay between the genders also within occupational groups. For instance, in 1991 the earnings of surveyed Muscovite female physicians were reported to be 75 per cent of those of male physicians (Yasnaya et al., 1993). In 1988, according to a survey among Estonian female engineers, three per cent earned more than 320 rubles a month compared to 41 per cent of the male engineers (Kandolin et al., 1991a).

Combining family and work

For a long time low birth rates were a cause of worry to politicians and decision makers in the European regions of the USSR. The first child was born, on average, during the second year of marriage, and the second child 6.6 years from the date of marriage (Rimashevskaya, 1993). This low natality may partly be explained by the low standard of living and the housing shortage. Only ten per cent of the young people entering into matrimony had a dwelling of his or her own. Generally, the family got a separate dwelling ten years after marriage. Three fourths of the families started their life together residing with the parents of one of the spouses (Pankratova, 1989).

The high infant mortality rate, the poor standard of health and the deficient hygiene of the hospitals make maternity problematic (Rimashevskaya, 1993). Since getting contraceptives is difficult, births are mainly controlled by abortions; consequently, Russia is the leader in the statistics of abortions. There were 101 abortions per thousand women aged from 15 to 49 years in Russia in 1992; in France, for example, this figure was 15 in the same year (Garnik, 1993).

Infant mortality has declined although it is still high on the basis of international comparisons. In 1975, 31 children out of a thousand died under the age of one year in the Soviet Union; in 1989 23 out of a thousand (Rimashevskaya, 1993). There were, however, great regional differences in the USSR. In Russia in 1992 the infant mortality was 22 per mil (Garnik, 1993). By way of comparison it may be mentioned that in Finland infant mortality has declined from 33 per mil in the first decade of the 1900's to 23 in 1950 and to 7 in 1992 (Haavio-Mannila and Kari 1980; Garnik, 1993).

In the Soviet economic system, the level of the pay and pensions was based on the assumption that there were two working parents in the family. This system was related to the original communist ideology, according to which everyone had to participate in productive work. The average individual pay provided less than two thirds of what was required for maintaining a family of four. Thus, economic factors required women's participation in paid work also when they were married (Lapidus, 1993).

Being a full-time homemaker has been undervalued in Soviet society. Only few women would have withdrawn from working life even if it had been economically possible. Women had internalized their independent role and did not want to get into a situation in which they would be dependent on the husband's income (Rimashevskaya, 1993). Signs of women's latent opposition to paid work could, nevertheless, be seen under Soviet rule as early as in 1970 and 1979 in attitude surveys carried out among students in the Estonian university town Tartu. It was the ideal of Estonian girls to be less engaged in occupational work than men in order to stay at home as full-time homemakers and to do more daily housework than men do. By way of comparison female students in the neighbouring Finland, more often than those in Estonia, wanted to work like men, to get the same education as men get and to divide the household work equally with men, according to a survey conducted in 1972 (Tiit and Haavio-Mannila, 1981).

In 1990 a law was passed in the Soviet Union to improve women's status as well as to protect children and families. Women were entitled to choose either to stay at home with the child for the first three years or to continue to work for pay (Posadskaya, 1993b). It was a popular argument that day-care centres would be more expensive than paying the mother the minimum wage. The poor hygiene in the day-care centres and the quality of the child care worried the mothers. Maja Pankratova (1989) observed that the attitudes about the care and the food of the day-care institutes were more critical in cities than in the rural areas.

The law guaranteed some benefits for women with families: part-time work, adaptable working hours, and days off for family responsibilities. Earlier, women whose children were under 12 years of age had had the right to move to half-time work. Working part-time was, however, regarded as a deviation during the Soviet period. Full-time work was regarded as the norm. Women were no more interested in part-time work than employers. Not even today are enterprises willing to employ women who want to work part time. On the other hand, part-time work has increased in the service industries and its meaning has changed accordingly. It is no longer considered a special advantage but a form of underemployment (Posadskaya, 1993b).

From the beginning of 1991, fathers have also been able to take parental leave in Russia. What is radical about the parental leave is that it can also be used by grandparents or some other close relative. The change is mainly ideological because, in practice, very few men make use of this right (Posadskaya, 1993b).

Household work

The amount of time spent by women on household work was studied in Russia, Latvia and Finland during the years from 1986 to 1988 (Niemi et al., 1991). In Russia and Latvia, women were engaged in housework for one hour longer daily than women in Finland, while the difference for men was about ten minutes. The time women spent in household work in Russia and Latvia was therefore 66 per cent, but in Finland only 62 per cent, of all the time spent in housework by men and women. In the USA the time spent in household work by women was 67 per cent of all the time spent in it (Robinson, 1988). Russian women were not in that respect in a worse position than women in Western industrial countries like USA. Their greatest problem was the physical demands made by the housework, because there were few household appliances and shopping takes time and is troublesome (Sacks, 1988).

In Estonia household work also accumulated on women more than in Finland. According to surveys among young families carried out in 1984, young married men in Helsinki prepared food, washed dishes, and went shopping, as well as took the children to day-care centres more than did men in Tallinn. Yet, the spouses quarrelled more about household work in Finland than in Tallinn. The pressure for change concerning the division of housework may have been greater in Finland (Haavio-Mannila and Kelam, 1990). In 1993, according to a study based on a representative sample of the whole Estonian population, the division of work in the home was more uneven in Estonia than in Finland (Narusk and Kandolin, 1993).

In Estonia, the attitudes towards the division of labour between the spouses also supported the traditional model. In 1984 about 90 per cent of young Finnish spouses believed that the housework in the family should be equally divided, taking into consideration the amount of work and the interests of the spouses. Half of the Estonian men and 28 per cent of the Estonian women surveyed did not share this opinion. They were either of the opinion that the wife should do women's and the husband men's traditional household tasks, or that household work should be the wife's responsibility and the husband should help her or that the husband should earn the living for the family while the wife stays at home and devotes herself wholly to housekeeping (Haavio-Mannila and Kelam, 1990; unpublished information from the same data).

It has been said that it is the woman's nature to feel that 'her basic task is to be mother', 'to keep the fire burning', 'to be the homemaker' for whom 'the home is her world'. It is the husband's natural lot 'to be the provider for the family', 'the protector', and 'the public figure'. Stereotyped views of this kind have strengthened opinions that housework is a self-evident addition to the paid work conducted by Russian women. Since household technology is scarce, the mother is estimated to use during one home shift energy equivalent to that expended during a 15-20 kilometers' walk (Rimashevskaya, 1993).

In 1989, 40 per cent of household work time was used in preparing food, according to a study on the use of time among female urban residents in the Soviet Union. From 1980 until 1989, the time used in preparing food had increased by 12 per cent because semi-finished food products were no longer available in the shops. Laundering and alterations took 20 per cent of the domestic working hours, cleaning up 13 per cent and shopping 18 per cent. These figures are from the years before the 1991 and 1992 price increases which raised, for instance, laundry prices tenfold and put public laundries out of the ordinary woman's reach. The heaping up of housework on women can be illustrated by the results of a study conducted in the town of Taganrog in southern Russia: of the 14 domestic tasks listed on a questionnaire only one was reported to be a man's task — that of driving the car. The fact that only three per cent of the surveyed families had a car makes the result quite amusing (Posadskaya, 1992).

The Russian and Estonian woman's burden of work was lightened somewhat by the circumstances created by the housing shortage and the deficiency of public care for old people. There were often other people in the household in addition to the members of the nuclear family, for instance, parents or sisters of the spouses. For example, it was shown that 17 per cent of Estonian urban residents lived in extended families in 1978; only seven per cent of their Finnish counterparts lived in this way in 1977 (Haavio-Mannila and Rannik, 1989). This makes it understandable that in the town of Orel, Russia, according to a study conducted by Maja Pankratova in 1983, people other than the wife or the husband participated in household work significantly more than in Finland, the Netherlands, Norway, Poland and Italy. In Orel, some other person besides either of the spouses (typically the grand-mother) cleaned up or washed the dishes in every third family, washed the laundry in every fourth and prepared the food in 18 per cent of the families; the corresponding shares were much smaller in the countries of comparison (Haavio-Mannila, 1989).

Through the official policy of the USSR attempts were made to relieve the load of housework. This was done, among other things, by estab-lishing children's day-care centres. Contrary to the general practice in the Western countries, there were also day-care centres where children could stay for five successive days and nights or even longer at a span. Especially mothers with unusual or irregular working hours took their children to these care centres. In Orel, one fifth of the mothers took advantage of this form of child care and 15 per cent of the mothers considered this system the best possible one (Jallinoja and Pankratova, 1989).

Many researchers point out that Russian men do not participate in household work. As stated above, the share of household work done by women was, at the end of the 1980's, equally large — that is, two thirds — in the USA as in the former USSR. At the beginning of the 1980's, when studies were done to find out to whom children turned to find support and consolation, 40 per cent of the parents interviewed in Orel — but only 20 per cent of those surveyed in the Finnish towns — reported that children turned to their father. The children of Orel also turned to their father for advice and guidance more generally than in Finland. The mother was, however, the main listener and helper in both countries. (Jallinoja and Pankratova, 1989.)

Attitudes to women's participation in working life

Attitudes of Russian women to paid employment have changed during recent years. Before perestroika, from 60 to 80 per cent of women were of the opinion that women were supposed to work outside the home under any circumstances. Newer attitude surveys show that the share of the people who think so has fallen to less than a third. (Pankratova, 1989.)

To what extent the high participation in paid work has led to women's 'overemancipation' is a question under discussion in Russia. It is assumed that women are too masculine or aggressive and lack feminine sensitivity and softness. Being labelled overemancipated hinders women's competition with men in the employment market. Labelling of this kind occurs also in Western countries: when women have been successful in their work, they have been observed to have to take risks in their social life.

When Russian women choose their work they value the pleasantness of the working conditions more than the qualitative aspects of its content (Lapidus, 1993). Traditional views emerge in strong support for men in superior positions. According to an attitude survey, 72 per cent of men and 68 per cent of women preferred men to women in superior positions. One fifth of men and 28 per cent of women considered the gender of the superior irrelevant. Only a small percentage preferred women instead of men as their potential superiors. (Posadskaya and Zakharova, 1990.) In Finland, one fifth of female workers and one fourth of male workers preferred to have a man as a superior. To the majority of Finnish people the gender of the superior was of no importance. However, in the same way as in the USSR, few people in Finland placed the woman ahead of the man in their preferences for a superior (Suomalainen nainen, 1989; Suomalainen mies, 1990).

The stereotypical attitudes to women at work have hindered the full utilization of women's educational resources. Women are not, according to Lapidus (1993), considered as creative as men in research work. It is thought that the feminization of the research profession would stop risk taking in research work, which is necessary in producing new inventions.

In the USSR women were regarded as having different mental and physical qualities than men have. This has been seen, for instance, in surveys conducted in Estonia and Finland. In 1978 the Estonian working age population was asked in a survey what women's opportunities for promotion at work and in society were compared to men's. Only six per cent considered women's chances to be better than those of men, 56 per cent thought they were equal and 38 per cent thought women's chances for advancement were worse. Women regarded, more generally than men, women's opportunities as worse. At the same time attitudes in Finland regarding women's opportunities were slightly more pessimistic: 43 per cent of the Finns surveyed considered women's chances to be worse than men's (Haavio-Mannila and Rannik, 1985; 1987).

In both the countries family responsibilities were regarded as the factor of greatest importance restricting women's chances of promotion in working life. In Estonia, 'women's nature' was mentioned as the second most important obstacle, and women's specific physiological qualities were also brought out as an explanation. In Finland more often than in Estonia men's negative attitudes were considered to be the cause of women's problems in working life. The lower and different professional training of women was regarded as an important obstacle to women's success by a third of the Estonians and by a quarter of the Finns. (Haavio-Mannila and Rannik, 1985.) In both countries, the family was the most obvious scapegoat, but the Estonians regarded the innate gender differences, the Finns the prevailing attitudes in society as the major explanations to women's lesser professional advancement.

Similar results emerged in surveys of young families in 1984. In Tallinn 42 per cent of the women reported that they could make no progress in their careers, because they had so much responsibility for their homes. Only five per cent of the women in Helsinki were of this opinion. Of the Estonians surveyed, 80 per cent thought of their family issues at work; of the Finns, only 40 per cent. The greater importance of the home compared to work was shown by the fact that in Tallinn 70 per cent — but in Helsinki only 38 per cent — of the young married people completely stopped thinking about their work when they came home. Men's and women's responses were quite consistent in both countries. (Haavio-Mannila and Kelam, 1990.)

As stated above, the special protection of women in working life may obstruct the achievement of equality between the genders. Natalia Rimashevskaya (1993) strongly criticized women's special protection, which has caused them to be placed in the role of 'social invalids'. She characterizes this protective and patronizing view of women with the following three arguments:

— because motherhood is an important part of femininity, women represent a specific work force category;

— because of the specific quality of the female work force society must develop measures to help the woman to combine work and motherhood;

— overemancipation is to be blamed for social problems such as divorces, men's drinking, juvenile delinquency, the decline in morality, etc.

During perestroika, it was demanded that women should diminish their participation in paid work and pay more attention to their tasks in the home. Labelling women overemancipated not only meant calling them masculine, but it was also a way of explaining the origin of social problems (Rimashevskaya, 1993). According to Posadskaya (1993a, 1993b), women often were treated instrumentally, as means to achieve some societal goals: they were seen as instruments of solving demographic and ethical questions. Women's active participation in working life was thought to have a negative influence on child rearing and the moral atmosphere of the home; it was said to increase crime, alcoholism, etc. Even these attitudes reflect the duality which has been typical of the attitudes towards women. On one hand, paid work was seen as a duty and a criterion for the 'good woman'; on the other hand, it was supposed to have demoralizing effects.

Glasnost, the freedom of expression, opened people's eyes to the actual situation of women in Soviet society. As evidence of a freer atmosphere two studies can be cited which were conducted in six republics in 1989 by the All-Union Public Opinion Research Centre, namely *The Woman in the Family* (N=1,516) and *The Woman in Working Life* (N=2,604). Urban and rural people over 16 years of age served as the population (Bodrova, 1993). The aim of these studies was to find out if women were overemployed and to what extent the issues surrounding their role in society could be resolved by women returning home and being freed from the chains of production work. At the time of the study there was a lot of discussion on these matters. One of the questions of the survey took this matter up frankly: 'How do you evaluate the fact that the majority of women work outside the home?' One out of three chose the extreme items of the response options: 15 per cent of the respondents were of the opinion that every able woman was to work outside the home, whereas 18 per cent said that women who had a family and children were not to work outside the home. It emerges from the responses that the traditional Soviet view is changing to give women the opportunity to choose for themselves between the home and their participation in working life and to create circumstances in which this choice is really possible. (Bodrova, 1993.)

Also the question 'Which is more important to women, family or work?' was answered in this survey. Thirty-six per cent of the female respondents said that only the family was important, 18 per cent considered the family more important than work, 37 per cent found family and work to be equally important, 3 per cent thought that work was more important than the family, and 6 per cent found the question difficult to answer. The younger women emphasized women's family roles more strongly than did the older women. The mothers of women aged from 25 to 29 years had always been engaged in paid work, and they did not want to work again in two shifts, both in the home and in paid work, especially since there was no infrastructure to facilitate combining work with the family and to lighten household work. (Bodrova, 1993.)

In the study *The Woman in Working Life* subjects were asked to respond to the statement 'Now it is the time to make women go back home to the family'. This idea was supported by 37 per cent of the respondents. Another statement on the questionnaire was 'The woman must work outside the home like the man'. This statement was agreed by only seven per cent. Fifty per cent agreed with the statement 'The woman should work outside the home when she wants'. The idea that women should go back home was supported by 31 per cent of the women and by 42 per cent of the men. A greater share of the women (55 per cent) than of the men (45 per cent) hoped that the woman could choose for herself if and when she would work outside the home. The freedom of choice was supported above all by the well-educated. (Bodrova, 1993.)

Politics

There were hardly any women in the political elite of Soviet society. For instance, the share of women members in the Central Committee of the Communist Party has never exceeded the level of five per cent reached in 1918. Only two women have been members of the Politburo (Lapidus, 1993).

During the period of Soviet power, there was a quota of one third for women in the Supreme Soviet. In the Congress of the USSR People's Deputies, 75 seats had been reserved for women. The system was criticized by arguing that the women in the quota did not represent ordinary women, but were instruments of a political machinery, mere marionettes. Women's displacement from politics increased during perestroika. When the quota system was abolished, women's share in the Supreme Soviet fell from 33 per cent to 16 per cent, and in the republics and the local soviets it fell to less than 5 per cent.

Stereotypical views of the genders as well as the notion that women are treated as a special group needing privileges hindered women's participation in politics at the higher levels. The quota system was demoralizing to women and it diminished women's interest in politics. The women who had been appointed to fill the quota had been selected by the Party and had by no means been elected by or from among the people. Women got used to this sham, and as a consequence they have no experience with independent political activity. Keeping politics dirty and unsuitable for women also inactivated women politically (Rimashevskaya, 1993).

In the attitude surveys concerning the qualities the deputies should possess, the respondents reported that the typically feminine features tended to diminish women's qualifications in politics. Women's passivity in politics and the heavy load of household work were seen to diminish their chances of being elected (Pankratova, 1989). As women do not engage in politics, they do not make their own demands heard, but instead entrust the power to men.

Well-being

Subjectively experienced satisfaction and lack of somatic and psychic symptoms have often been used as indicators of personal well-being. The problems of the double work load, which have stood in the way of Russian women's well-being, emerge in several Russian surveys. In one survey, women were asked how pressed they were at work, and the typical response was: 'It is good that my work is mechanical and simple. As I spend so much time queuing and in housework, it is good that I need not think of anything, at least at work.' (Rimashevskaya, 1993). Similar opinions came forth when the question was asked about women's willingness to change work. Provided that in the new employment the working hours would be more flexible, there were better pay, it were closer to home, its working conditions were better, and the work were more creative and independent, 40 per cent wanted to change work. Only few women paid attention to items that were related to better opportunities to have a career and to participate in the development or management of production (Rimashevskaya, 1993). The evaluation of work was related to the amount of inconvenience it caused to the hard life outside work.

The dissatisfaction of Russian women with their life is reflected in the opinions of physicians. In 1991, 62 per cent of female physicians in Moscow said that they received satisfaction from their work. Nevertheless, their general satisfaction with life was low: only 30 per cent were satisfied and 70 per cent were dissatisfied (Kauppinen-Toropainen, 1993). The dissatisfaction reflects the many social changes which are taking place in former Soviet society. It is difficult for people to control their lives in the midst of these changes. Lack of command over one's life may lead to illnesses and stress.

The young couples interviewed in Tallinn in 1984 were more dissatisfied with their work, relations with their fellow workers, marriages, emotional and sexual relationships with their spouses and the way they spent their leisure time — indeed, their whole life — than their counterparts in Helsinki. There was not much difference in the dissatisfaction between men and women. (Haavio-Mannila and Kelam, 1990.)

A study of some occupational groups (engineers, teachers, technicians and workers) showed that men and women in Tallinn and Moscow had many more symptoms of stress than their counterparts in the Nordic countries (Denmark, Finland and Sweden) and in Michigan, USA, in 1988. Especially women teachers reported suffering from pains, difficulties with sleeping, fatigue, stomachache, anxiety and depression (Haavio-Mannila, 1992; 1993; Kandolin et al., 1991a).

Neither was there much to praise in women's satisfaction with work in the Soviet Union: engineers, teachers and workers in Tallinn and Moscow and technicians at the Kamaz car factory were dissatisfied with their work, wanted to change it, did not get any satisfaction from it, did not enjoy it, did it mainly for money or would not recommend it to their children more generally than members of the Western comparison groups (Kandolin, Pietarila and Kauppinen-Toropainen, 1991b; Haavio-Mannila, 1992; 1993).

When factors affecting the occurrence of stress symptoms were being studied in Estonia and Finland, it was observed that Estonian women often reported suffering from stress symptoms. These symptoms also were connected with time pressure and, contrary to Finland, with white-collar employment. Satisfaction with work was explained in Estonia by being a man, autonomy of work, and low time pressure, as well as good workplace climate. In Finland, satisfaction with work was related to autonomy of work, white-collar position and young age. (Kandolin et al., 1991a.) Especially women and white-collar workers thus felt worse in Estonia than in Finland.

Self-esteem or self-respect is one of the indicators of well-being. Good self-esteem means that the person is satisfied with herself or himself and can cope with changes in pressure. Self-esteem is not a finished product but it continues to develop by stages during one's lifetime. It reflects the atmosphere of the childhood environment, that is to say, how the person has been supported in his or her growth in developing an understanding of himself or herself as a functioning individual. The self-esteem of an adult can also be developed or weakened. Responsibility, varied work and a supportive working climate strengthen self-esteem and increase motivation to work. (Kauppinen-Toropainen and Kandolin, 1992.)

A comparison of 137 Finnish women architects and 65 Swedish, 76 Estonian, and 81 US women engineers in 1986-88 showed that the self-esteem of the US women was the highest and that of the Estonian women the lowest, with the Nordic women in between. In the United States, aggressive personality traits were connected with self-esteem. Neither in Scandinavia nor in Estonia were women with high self-esteem aggressive. In Estonia, self-esteem did not correlate with masculinity or femininity, variables that were measured by four-item scales based on the Bem Sex-Role Inventory. (Kauppinen-Toropainen and Kandolin, 1992; Bem, 1981; cf. Kandolin et al., 1991b).

Before drawing conclusions, it is to be considered how culture-bound our indicators are. The high self-esteem of American women may be related to their culture, that is, the beliefs, values and expressive creations of people bound by the social arrangements of American society. Americans tend to see things positively; they are not shy to express recognition and happiness. In Europe, people are less open about showing positive feelings toward themselves and others. Self-praise, especially, is considered egoistic and self-centred. One tries to avoid the biblical judgment, 'He who exalteth himself shall be humbled.' (Haavio-Mannila, 1993.)

The lower self-esteem of Estonian and Russian women may reflect the collectivistic life style which people had become accustomed to in the Soviet Union. People were brought up to believe that individuality was not a quality worth emphasizing. So, it is likely that Soviet culture has supported a self-image which is more collectively anchored and liable to appeal to social relations than American culture.

Conclusion: women's inconsistent status in changing society

In the articles and studies of Russian women the difficulty of combining work and family life is emphasized, and family responsibilities are blamed for women's low social status. There has been but little theoretically valid research in the USSR and Russia, for instance, on how women's living conditions, personality and careers are linked together. Articles present either broad, general statistics of an entire society or figures that have been picked up from individual studies.

Under Soviet rule, women participated in working life in large numbers due to the ideology of equality and to compensate for the losses caused by the wars. Work was seen as a social duty both of men and of women. All able women of working age either participated in working life or studied full time. The rate of women's participation in work was the highest in the world. To maintain a family, both spouses had to be employed: the system was based on two economic providers in the family. However, after World War II, a great part of the families had to manage with the woman's pay only; the share of one-parent families was as large as 30 per cent of all families.

Women's position in Soviet and Russian working life has been very strong. Half of the work force were women, and women have established themselves in fields and professions which have been perceived as masculine in the Western countries. In the medical profession, 67 per cent of the professionals are women, and there have been many women performing tasks which demand technical expertise. Now along with the emergence of the market economy and tightening competition, the status of women may be threatened, and their participation in paid labour may no longer be self-evident.

Contradictory aspects of the image of the woman in the Soviet Union and, since 1991, in the independent republics of Russia and Estonia, appear in many studies. On one hand, women are pictured as representatives of the weaker gender, who demand special protection and support; on the other hand, women are blamed for being overemancipated and for having lost their femininity.

Also the undeveloped household technology has been a cause of the excessive work load of women; women have had to consume a lot of their energies in daily domestic routines. Also the scarcity of consumer goods, the general insecurity and the queuing of everyday shopping have consumed both time and energy, which is seen in women's fatigue and overburdening. Researchers have observed that men experience standing in queues as demeaning, and so this task has fallen on the wives or other female members of the family.

Women's excessive fatigue and stress are brought forth in many studies. Women's dual role has been referred to when their absence from the political elite has been explained: either women are too exhausted to participate in political life, or politics is seen as dirty and unsuitable for women, which makes them avoid it.

Earlier women participated in politics within a quota system. After its abolition, women's share in the decision making collapsed. The women who had been elected to the representative bodies of the USSR were not considered to represent women's real opinion; these quota representatives were regarded as an output of the state machinery. There is no returning back to the old system — and women do not even desire it. In the post-Soviet period it has, however, been difficult for women to get a footing in the new political practices.

From the point of view of the Western industrial countries, the discussion about women's desire to become housewives may seem strange. This desire may reflect women's aim to develop new and alternative life styles, because earlier the way of life was dictated from above, and participation in paid work was highly prevalent. The desire to remain at home may also be a protest against the former system, which did not allow individual choices. This desire may derive from the idealization of the Western culture and a yearning for a family pattern which was forbidden under Soviet rule and was labelled as bourgeois. Nevertheless, only very few women in Russia or Estonia have voluntarily become housewives because this decision brings with it not only a loss of independent status, but also insecurity concerning the future. In the few instances when women have remained at home, this has happened out of necessity, either because of unemployment or some other external cause. Also the low level of pay has meant that few families are able to live on the husband's income only. At the same time, women are more worried than before about not being wanted in the work force.

Under Soviet rule, before perestroika, there was no question regarding the status of women in society. However, freedom of expression is now permitting the status of women in Russian and Estonian society to be openly discussed, and problems can be brought to the open: the bothersomeness of women's dual role, their unhealthy working conditions, their difficulties in progressing in their careers and in finding self-fulfilment in working life no matter how high their level of education is, their insignificant share of participation in political decision making, as well as the stereotyped and partly conflicting concepts of gender.

According to researchers, the changes during perestroika have favoured men instead of women, for whom life has become more and more difficult in circumstances of economic insecurity. The fall in the standard of living came as a surprise to many people, and the gap between Russia and the rich industrial countries keeps growing (Virtanen, 1992).

The atmosphere has changed from the earlier days of optimism to greater pessimism. For example, the percentage of those who believe that freedom and independence can solve material problems declined in St. Petersburg during the year 1992. Women placed less trust in the market economy than men did. In November 1992, when people in St. Petersburg were asked which they considered more important, freedom or future security, 16 per cent of the women and 26 per cent of the men chose freedom. In another survey carried out in February 1993, only 33 per cent of the women in St. Petersburg, but 55 per cent of the men reported that they could solve their material problems independently, without any help from the state. (EVA, 1993; Protasenko, 1993.)

Difficulties related to the economic transition are reflected in the everyday life and moods of women: they do not believe in miracles performed by the market any more. Women feel that they must themselves try to define how they should participate in the social development. By taking part in political and social activities women can introduce new substance and emphasis into the process of social change.

This chapter has described the change in women's status as a consequence of the social transition in Russia and Estonia. Women's status in the public life was strong in the former Soviet Union compared to many Western countries. Further studies should attempt to determine whether the breaking down of the official ideology of equality after the fall of communism has increased the tension between the genders. Will the abolition of the official policy of equality have a backlash effect on the status of women in public life? Or will a totally new social contract emerge between men and women?

References

Bem, Sandra L. (1981), *Bem Sex-Role Inventory Professional Manual*. Consulting Psychologists Press Inc., Palo Alto, California.

Bodrova, Valentina V. (1993), 'Glasnost and "the Woman Question" in the Mirror of Public Opionion: Attitudes Towards Women, Work, and the Family' in Moghadam, Valentine M. (ed.), *Democratic Reform and the Position of Women in Transitional Economies*, Clarendon Press, Oxford, pp. 180-196.

Dahlström, Edmund (1989), 'Theories and Ideologies of Family Functions, Gender Relations and Human Reproduction' in Katja Both, Maren Bak, Cristine Clason, Maja Pankratova, Jens Qvortrup, Giovanni B. Sgritta and Kari Waerness (eds.), *Changing Patterns of European Family Life*, Routledge, London, pp. 31-51.

Elinkeinoelämän valtuuskunta EVA (1993), *Suomi Pietarissa, Pietari Suomessa. EVA-raportti taloudellisten kulttuurien eroista* (Finland in St. Petersburg, St. Petersburg in Finland. An EVA-report on the differences in economic cultures), Elinkeinoelämän valtuuskunta (Centre for Finnish Business and Policy Studies), Helsinki.

Garnik, Sergei (1993), *Polozhenia detei v Rossii*, a paper presented at the Seminar of East European Research, 4 November 1993, University of Helsinki, Department of Social Policy.

Geiger, K. (1968), *The Family in the Soviet Union*, Harvard University Press, Cambridge, Mass.

Haavio-Mannila, Elina (1989), 'Gender Segregation in Paid and Unpaid Work' in Katja Both, et al. (eds.), *Changing Patterns of European Family Life*, Routledge, London.

Haavio-Mannila, Elina (1992), *Work, Family, and Well-being in Five North- and East-European Capitals*, Suomalainen Tiedeakatemia (The Finnish Academy of Science and Letters) B/255, Helsinki.

Haavio-Mannila, Elina (1993), *Women in the Workplace in Three Types of Societies*, CEW Research Reports, The University of Michigan, Center for the Education of Women, Ann Arbor.

Haavio-Mannila, Elina (1994), 'Erotic Relations at Work' in Matti Alestalo, Erik Allardt, Andrzej Rychard & Wlodzimierz Wesolowski (eds.), *The Transformation of Europe: Social Conditions and Consequences.*, IPis Publishers, Warsaw (forthcoming).

Haavio-Mannila, Elina & Kari, Kyllikki (1980), 'Changes in the Life Patterns of Families in the Nordic Countries', *Väestöntutkimuksen Vuosikirja* XVIII, Väestöntutkimuslaitos, Helsinki.

Haavio-Mannila, Elina & Kelam, Aili (1990), *Socio-Economic Differences of Estonian and Finnish Young Families*, Estonian Finnish Demographical Conference, Tallinn, February 6-8, 1990.

Haavio-Mannila, Elina & Rannik, Erkki (1987), 'Family Life in Estonia and Finland', *Acta Sociologica* 1987 (30), 3/4, pp 355-369.

Haavio-Mannila, Elina & Rannik, Erkki (1985), *Vertaileva tutkimus Viron ja Suomen perheestä, työstä ja vapaa-ajasta* (A comparative study of the family, work, and leisure in Estonia and Finland). Suomen ja Neuvostoliiton välinen tieteellis-teknillinen yhteistoimintakomitea (Finnish-Soviet Commission on Scientific and Technical Cooperation), Helsinki.

Haavio-Mannila, Elina & Rannik, Erkki (1989), 'Family Life, Work, and Leisure in Estonia and Finland' in Kharchev, A. G. & Roos, J. P. (eds.), *Sociology and Society in Finland and the Soviet Union*, Suomen ja Neuvostoliiton välinen tieteellis-teknillinen yhteistyötoimintakomitea (Finnish-Soviet Commission on Scientific and Technical Cooperation), Helsinki, pp. 27-45.

Holmila, M., M. S. Matskovsky & Rannik, E. (1989), 'Young Families and Alcohol Use in Finland and the Soviet Union' in Kharchev, A. G. & Roos, J. P. (eds.), *Sociology and Society in Finland and the Soviet Union*, Suomen ja Neuvostoliiton välinen tieteellis-teknillinen yhteistoimintakomitea (Finnish-Soviet Commission on Scientific and Technical Cooperation) Helsinki, pp. 58-71.

Huida, Outi, Smeds, Riitta, Haavio-Mannila, Elina & Kauppinen-Toropainen, Kaisa (1993), *Perinteiden pölyt ja uudistusten tuulet* (The dust of heritage and the winds of reforms), Teknillinen Korkeakoulu. Teollisuustalous ja työnpsykologia, Raportti 144, Helsinki.

Jallinoja, R. & Pankratova, M. (1989), 'The Employment of Mothers' in Kharchev, A. G. and Roos, J. P. (eds.), *Sociology and Society in Finland and the Soviet Union*, Suomen ja Neuvostoliiton välinen tieteellis-teknillinen yhteistyökomitea, Helsinki, pp. 46-57.

Kandolin, Irja, Rannik, Erkki & Haavio-Mannila, Elina (1991), 'Työ ja hyvinvointi eräissä toimihenkilö- ja työntekijäammateissa Virossa ja Suomessa' (Work and well-being in some white-collar and blue-collar occupations in Estonia and Finland), *Sosiologia* 28, pp. 15-24.

Kandolin, Irja, Pietarila, Päivi & Kauppinen-Toropainen, Kaisa (1991), *Naisten työ ja henkinen hyvinvointi teknisissä ammateissa Suomessa, Tanskassa, Virossa ja Kamaz-tehtaalla Venäjällä* (Women's work and mental well-being in some technical occupations in Finland, Denmark, Estonia and the Kamaz factories in Russia). Työterveyslaitos, Vantaa (manuscript).

Kauppinen-Toropainen, Kaisa (1991), 'Neuvostonaiset havahtuneet kohentamaan asemiaan' (Russian women awaken to better their social standing), *Helsingin Sanomat*, opinion, May 28, 1991.

Kauppinen-Toropainen, Kaisa (1993), 'Comparative Study of Women's Work Satisfaction and Work Commitment: Research Findings from Estonia, Moscow, and Scandinavia' in Valentine M. Moghadam (ed.), *Democratic Reform and the Position of Women in Transitional Economies*, Clarendon Press, Oxford, pp. 197-215.

Kauppinen-Toropainen, Kaisa & Kandolin, Irja (1991), 'Perhevalta: puolisoiden palkkaero ja vuorovaikutuksen laatu' (Power in the family: the difference in pay between the spouses and the quality of interdependency), *Työ ja ihminen*, Työympäristötutkimuksen aikakauskirja 3/1991, Helsinki, pp. 295-312.

Kauppinen-Toropainen, Kaisa & Kandolin, Irja (1992), *Teknillisillä aloilla toimivien naisten itsetunto ja hyvinvointi* (The self-esteem and well-being of women functioning in technical fields), Suomalais-virolainen seminaari naisten asemasta työelämässä ja yhteiskunnassa (A Finnish-Estonian seminar on women's status in working life and society), Tallinn, May 14-15, 1992.

Kauppinen-Toropainen, Kaisa & Gruber, James E. (1993), 'Antecedents and Outcomes of Woman-Unfriendly Experiences: A Study of Scandinavian, Former Soviet, and American Women', *Psychology of Women Quarterly* 17, pp. 431-456.

Kivinen, Markku (1993), *Yhteiskuntaluokat Venäjällä — Alustavia huomautuksia* (The social classes in Russia — Preliminary remarks). A paper in a seminar of Comparative Sociology, University of Helsinki, February 16, 1993.

Kobzeva, Helen V. (1992), *Social Protection and Employment Security of Women Under Conditions of a Monoindustrial City in the Period of Transition to the Market*, Sociologic Research Center, Naberezhnye Chelney.

Konecki, Krzystof (1990), 'Dependency and Worker Flirting' in Turner, Barry A. (ed.), *Organizational Symbolism*, Walter de Gruyter, Berlin/New York, pp. 55-66.

Koval, Vitalina (1989a), *Soviet Women in Science*, Institute of Labour Problems and Political Sciences, USSR Academy of Sciences, Moscow (Manuscript).

Koval, Vitalina (1989b), 'Working Women: Common Problems', *Soviet Life*, March 1989.

Lapidus, Gail (1993), 'Gender and Restructuring: The Impact of Perestroika on Soviet Women' in Moghadam, Valentine M. (ed.), *Democratic Reform and the Position of Women in Transitional Economies*, Clarendon Press, Oxford, pp. 137-161.

Narusk, Anu (1991), 'Parenthood, Partnership, and Family in Estonia', in Björnberg, Ulla (ed.), *European Parents in the 1990's: Contradictions and Comparisons*, European Coordination Centre for Research and Documentation in Social Sciences, Transaction Publishers, London.

Narusk, Anu & Kandolin, Irja, Unpublished data on Work, Family, and Stress in Finland, 1990, and Estonia, 1993.

Niemi, Iiris, Eglite, Parsla, Mitrikas, Algimantas, Patrushev, V.D. & Pääkkönen, Hannu (1991), *Time Use in Finland, Latvia, Lithuania, and Russia*, Tilastokeskus, Tutkimuksia 182, Helsinki.

Pankratova, N.G. (1989), *Women and Perestroika in the USSR*, Institute of Sociological Research, USSR Academy of Sciences, Moscow (Manuscript).

Posadskaya, Anastasia (1992), *Restructuring the Former USSR: The New Uses of Women*. Article edited from a paper, Changes in the employment of Women in the Context of Restructuring in the Former USSR, presented in March, 1992, at a special conference of the Center for Social Theory and Comparative History at UCLA, 'Against the Current', July/August, 1992, 30-35.

Posadskaya, Anastasia (1993a), 'The Role and the Task of National Machinery for the Advancement of Women in the Period of Social and Economic Reform in the Countries of Eastern Europe and the USSR' in Rantalaiho, Liisa (ed.), *Social Changes and the Status of Women: The Experience of Finland and the USSR*, University of Tampere, Research Institute for Social Sciences, Centre for Women's Studies and Gender Relations, Working Papers 3/1993, pp. 75-97.

Posadskaya, Anastasia (1993b), 'Changes in Gender Discourses and Policies in the Former Soviet Union' in Moghadam, Valentine M. (ed.), *Democratic Reform and the Position of Women in Transitional Economies*, Clarendon Press, Oxford, pp. 162-179.

Posadskaya, Anastasia & Zakharova, Natalia (1990), *To Be a Manager: Changes for Women in the USSR*, Discussion Paper No. 65, edited by the Training Policies Branch of ILO, Geneva.

Protasenko, Tatiana (1993), *Tietoja pietarilaisten miesten ja naisten asenteista vapauteen ja aineellisten ongelmien itsenäiseen ratkaisukykyyn EVA:n tutkimusta varten* (Data of men's and women's attitudes to freedom and independent ability to solve material problems in St. Petersburg for a study conducted by EVA/Centre for Finnish Business and Policy Studies), Institute of Sociology, Russian Academy of Science, St. Petersburg (Manuscript).

Raitis, Riikka & Haavio-Mannila, Elina (eds.) (1993), *Naisten aseet* (The Weapons of Women), WSOY, Helsinki.

Rimashevskaya, Natalia (1993), 'Socio-Economic Changes and the Position of Women in the Union of Soviet Socialist Republics' in Liisa Rantalaiho (ed.), *Social Changes and the Status of Women: the Experience of Finland and the USSR.*, University of Tampere, Research Institute for Social Sciences, Centre for Women's Studies and Gender Relations, Working Papers 3/1993, Tampere, pp. 42-74.

Robinson, John (1988), Who is Doing the Housework? *American Demographics* 10:12, pp. 24-28.

Sacks, Michael (1988), 'Women, Work, and Family in the Soviet Union' in Sacks, Michael P. & Pankhurst, Jerry G. (eds.), *Understanding Soviet Society*, Unwin Hyman, Boston, Massachusetts, pp. 71-96.

Shulman, Colette (1977), 'The Individual and the Collective' in Atkinson, Dorothy Dallin, Alexander and Lapidus, Gail W. (eds.), *Women in Russia*, Stanford University Press, Stanford, California.

Suomalainen mies. Hänen työnsä, naisensa ja elämänsä (1990) (The Finnish man. His work, woman and life), A-lehdet Oy:n tutkimus Suomalainen mies 1989, Kerava.

Suomalainen nainen työssä, kotona ja omillaan (1989) (The Finnish woman at work, at home and on her own), A-lehdet Oy:n tutkimus Suomalainen nainen 1989, Helsinki.

Tiit, Ene & Haavio-Mannila, Elina (1981), 'Opiskelijoiden avioliittoihanteista Tartossa ja Helsingissä' (On students' ideals concerning marriage in Tartu and Helsinki). *Sosiologia* 18, pp. 187-193.

Treiman, Donald J. (1977), *Occupational Prestige in Comparative Perspective*, Academic Press, New York.

Virtanen, M. (1992), 'Kolmen kerroksen eurooppalaisia' (Europeans in three stories). *Helsingin Sanomat*, November 22, 1992, C1-C2.

Yasnaya, Ludmila, Kandolin, Irja & Kauppinen-Toropainen, Kaisa (1993), *Gender Differences in Work and Family Roles: A Case of Medical Doctors in Russia and Finland*, Abstract, Third European Congress of Psychology, 4-9 July 1993 Tampere, Finland.

10 The Russian City Today — Changes in St. Petersburg

Igor Travin

Rapid urbanization and its effects on social structure

As in all other European countries, the share of urban population has continuously been increasing in Russia throughout the 20th century. The pace of growth has, however, been exceptional. Between the years 1926 and 1990 the urban population in Russia grew from 16.5 million people to 110 million, and its share rose correspondingly from 18 per cent to 70 per cent of the total population. The 50 per cent limit, i.e. the point at which the urban population outnumbered the rural population, was not reached until the post-war period, in the middle of the 1950's. In the population census of 1959 the share of the urban population was 52 per cent; the highly industrialized countries of western Europe had reached this limit already in the 1920's or 1930's.

Urbanization in Russia can thus be characterized to have proceeded at a tempestuous velocity. After the Second World War the urbanization process was accelerated rapidly and the urban population has doubled. As a consequence, in practically every Russian city the number of native or long-time inhabitants is smaller than the number of those who have arrived later. In St. Petersburg the share of the native population is currently 48 per cent and the share of those who have moved to the city from elsewhere is 52 per cent.

It is quite usual that for this latter population the feeling of enduring attachment to the city has either weakened or has disappeared. Identification with all those aspects of community life that has traditionally been included in the notion 'home town' has weakened. The concepts 'Muscovite', 'St. Petersburgian' or 'Kievan' refer nowadays usually only to a place of residence and not to membership in a community with some characteristic and unique features.

The changes in the interpretation of urban space and the shifting social meanings attributed to it have resulted in a severing of the traditional bonds between the city and its inhabitants. In the traditional Russian urban community the immediate environment — the courtyard, the street, and the block of houses — was crucially important. In the Russia of today this traditional urban community, formed around the courtyard, is to a great extent dispersed, and it is evident that this development is irreversible. The primary socialization, the acquisition of the norms regulating life in the city, traditionally took place in the urban courtyard — and this was the case for the native inhabitants as well as for those who came later. The courtyard was a special 'locus of control', where all members of an urban neighbourhood knew each other. The common courtyards in the old districts within the Russian cities, inhabited mostly by the elderly, symbolize nowadays, however, rather the decay of the traditional inner city. The intense construction that began in the mid-1960's caused a rapid expansion of urban space. The new residential areas had open blocks of houses — a principle followed by Russian architects ever since — and high-rise housing; as a consequence, the courtyard in the traditional meaning of the word as a closed and protected space ceased to be an essential element structuring the social life of the city. The social relations between neighbours in the Russian cities have been continuously diminishing.

The changes in the social structure that have been taking place in the Russian cities have been explored with a large survey research undertaken in 1990 in St. Petersburg — at that time still Leningrad. This research was done by the Institute of Sociology of the Russian Academy of Sciences, St. Petersburg branch.[1]

The respondents were asked, among other aspects of city life, about the quantity and nature of communication in the immediate neighbourhood. With regard to the frequency of contacts with neighbours the survey revealed that 32 per cent of the respondents had contacts with neighbours every day, 44 per cent had contacts sometimes, and 24 per cent of the respondents answered that they never had any contacts in the neighbourhood. Four per cent said that they did not know any of their neighbours, and 37 per cent knew their neighbours only by sight without actively maintaining any contact with them. Moreover, 29 per cent of the respondents did not feel any need for this kind of contact in the neighbourhood and 48 per cent thought that merely casual contacts were sufficient. 15 per cent had the desire to maintain continuous friendships in the immediate neighbourhood, and only 8 per cent thought that it was necessary to create such circumstances that would foster personal contacts, such as clubs or public libraries or the tenants' self-management of residential houses.

It is possible that particularly the lack of continuous contacts with neighbours is responsible for the fact that only 16 per cent of the respondents in St. Petersburg thought their life contained interesting events. 50 per cent considered their life to be monotonous and lacking any memorable events. The respondents were asked a supplementary question: 'Have there been any especially memorable incidents during the most recent two or three months of your life?' 71 per cent of the respondents answered that there had not been any such incidents.

The conclusion may be somewhat exaggerated, but a person whose life is devoid of memorable events is a person without biography. Indirect support for this conclusion is included in some other results of the survey. For example, the respondents were asked about their familiarity with their ancestors. 49 per cent knew the biography of their grandparents and 24 per cent were familiar with the biography of their great-grandparents. Only three per cent of the respondents knew about their ancestors further than two generations back. 23 per cent of the respondents gave an affirmative answer to the question of whether they were familiar with traditions of any kind that had been passed down for generations in the family. The respondents who had some family traditions and the ones who knew their ancestors were to a large extent the same people. The aim of the research was here to measure the depth of the 'social memory' of the respondents, and in the case of two-thirds of the St. Petersburg households this depth amounted two generations, i.e. 30-40 years.

This phenomenon becomes easier to comprehend if we consider the fact that as much as 43 per cent of the respondents were born in the countryside. The children in the families that have come to the city from rural areas hardly maintain any family traditions typical to rural life or know their ancestors several generations back. One-third (35 per cent) had moved to the city because of studies — 16 per cent of these respondents had studied at university level, 8 per cent at a technical college, and 11 per cent at a professional school — and this move to the city had taken place at a young age, when the process of adaptation is faster and easier and the disappearance of the things and events connected to the former life is not experienced as painfully as at a later age. Of the remaining new inhabitants, 15 per cent had moved to the city because of work, 17 per cent in connection with marriage, and 15 per cent in childhood with their parents; hence, the majority of these respondents had also moved to the city at a relatively young age.

The majority of these new inhabitants had lost most of the characteristics of their earlier life in connection with their relocation, and possibly also the recollection of them. For many of these people city life has meant a completely new beginning. To a person coming from a rural background the city does not appear as an entity that has existed for a long continuum of time, as a totality that is structured by urban norms and traditions, but rather as an empty page, on which the new city-dweller rewrites the lines of his or her biography.

The norms that regulate urban conduct are at first unknown, and urban social reality is incomprehensible. Destructive forms of behaviour are thus among the most important symptoms of the 'immigrant syndrome' caused by the rupture of traditional patterns of conduct. Criminologists have observed that the indicators designed to measure deviant behaviour receive substantially higher values with those who have moved to the city from elsewhere than with native city-dwellers. The 'immigrant syndrome' does not, of course, consist of deviant behaviour that can be characterized as 'criminal' — the disruption can have many outcomes of a completely different kind; it can, for example, become manifest in the area of commodity consumption.

Problems and tensions

The significance of consumption is one of the basic characteristics of urban life. In the survey made in St. Petersburg the respondents were asked to identify the five aspects of daily life that were perceived to be in the most critical state. Among the numerous alternatives listed in the questionnaire, the following five were perceived to cause the most trouble in the daily life of the households (the percentage of the respondents choosing the item in question is given in parenthesis):

— The distribution of consumer goods (68 %)

— The distribution of foodstuffs and other daily necessities (47 %)

— Public services (42 %)

— Inadequacies in housing conditions (42 %)

— Personal safety (37 %)

Discontent with the distribution of goods was most widespread. Especially during the last couple of years of the Soviet Union the possibilities of the citizens to act as consumers were extremely limited. The answers received during autumn 1990 reflect the inadequacies of the commodity distribution system in the Soviet Union. The liberation of prices in 1992 has filled the previously empty shop counters with commodities, but because of the high price levels the consumption opportunities of average city-dwellers have hardly increased, even though commodities are now available.

It is, on the other hand, surprising that the activities of cultural institutions rank first among the aspects evaluated positively in the survey: 49 per cent of the respondents were satisfied with the cultural institutions of St. Petersburg. The result may appear surprising, particularly in the present situation when the cultural decline of the society is a topic of discussion virtually everywhere: in parliament meetings, in the media, and in private conversations. The positive evaluation is, undoubtedly, caused by the abundant supply of cultural events in the metropolis, and the situation of the entire country remains to a great extent unobserved by an ordinary city-dweller.

The health services were also evaluated relatively positively. Forty-eight per cent of the respondents described these services in positive terms. This positive estimate was somewhat surprising in light of the fact that only 22 per cent of the respondents evaluated their own health to be good, and only 4 per cent as excellent. The majority of respondents regarded their health as merely satisfactory (59 per cent) and as much as 60 per cent reported suffering a chronic illness of some kind.

The causes of discontent discussed above were related primarily to the functioning of those institutions and structures that affect the everyday life of the respondents. The most serious concerns of a more general nature are nowadays, however, connected with ecological problems. The people of St. Petersburg were alarmed about the condition of the natural environment, as well as about the condition of the historically precious architectural environment.

As late as the year 1986 the housing problem was considered to be the most serious social problem, but at the moment the housing question occupies the second position. Several explanations can be given for this development. One possible explanation is that ecological problems are increasingly often perceived as irreversible and irreparable, whereas the housing problem is seen as solvable, at least in principle or later in the future. The shortage of housing in Russian cities continues to be severe, but at the moment in St. Petersburg it is not quite as acute as it used to be. Nowadays two-thirds of the inhabitants of St. Petersburg live in their own separate apartments, i.e. not in communal apartments in which two or more households share the kitchen and bathroom.

When the inhabitants of St. Petersburg were asked about the new opportunities brought to them by the transformation of the society, the chronic housing shortage is reflected in the answers; but the possible relief of the housing problem was not seen as the most important promise made possible by the change. As the most significant improvements ameliorating the life of future generations were regarded the freedom of expression (51 per cent of the respondents chose this alternative among the five most significant), the general democratization of life (43 per cent), the opportunity to acquire more personal property and wealth (38 per cent), and after these three, the opportunity to improve one's housing conditions (25 per cent).

The respondents were also asked to identify the five most serious issues which, according to their opinion, ought to be the very first ones to be addressed. The following were regarded as the most urgent:

— Environmental protection, preventing the further deterioration of the natural environment (54 %)

— Construction of a new economic order (46 %)

— Transition towards a constitutional state (42 %)

— Relieving the housing shortage (35 %)

— Strengthening the public order, combatting criminality (25 %)

The statistical data presented above indicates that the increase in crime is among the important concerns of the inhabitants of St. Petersburg. This increase in violent crime and aggressive behaviour can be explained in part by referring to the rapid urbanization. The constant migratory pressure directed towards St. Petersburg causes tension between the native residents and the more recent arrivals. The tension is observable in the mutual relations of the city-dwellers on the streets, in the public transportation system, and in the lines, exploding from time to time in seemingly unprovoked aggression.

The increased aggression may, on the other hand, be interpreted to be a consequence of the growing anxiety and insecurity concerning the future. A special scale measuring this anxiety was included in the questionnaire. The results showed that the degree of anxiety was found to be low only with 3 per cent of the respondents, at the medium level with 33 per cent, and high with as many as 61 per cent of the respondents. Male respondents were on average more optimistic than females, and the young were less anxious than the older respondents. The high degree of anxiety observed in the oldest group of respondents gives the impression that the old generation does not believe in any improvements whatsoever in the future. Moreover, a high degree of anxiety was prevalent in all sub-groups.

The city and the evolving civil society

In the Soviet Union the administration, the leading state enterprises, and especially the units of the so-called military-industrial complex (*voenno-promyshlennyi kompleks*) occupied a considerable part of the historically precious building stock in all major Russian cities. In St. Petersburg, where the military industries are especially important — military production has amounted to approximately 70-80 per cent of the total production in the city — the cultural heritage of the city has to a great extent been utilized to satisfy the needs of these industries. The question of the reallocation of this building stock to some other purposes has been taken up with the social transformation; the historical legacy of St. Petersburg should now serve the evolving civil society and the new commercial and industrial life of the city.

The enterprises and administrative organizations created during the Soviet era were, and still are, the most influential economic powers in St. Petersburg. The problems connected with the reallocation of the historically valuable housing stock most likely cannot be solved through merely administrative measures. The task requires a profound basic transformation and redevelopment of the entire cultural infrastructure. For St. Petersburg the preservation of cultural and architectural monuments requires not only the organising of a large-scale restoration and reparation programme, but more profoundly also to some extent the revival of those social and cultural interests that could maintain the cultural heritage.

A good illustration of this point is the development of the opinions concerning the restoration of the Nevsky Prospect, the main street of St. Petersburg. Before the Revolution the Nevsky Prospect was, among its other functions, the centre of religious life of the city. Along the Nevsky Prospect or in its immediate vicinity there were more than ten churches. The Kazan Cathedral, which represented the dominant creed, Orhodox Christianity, was naturally situated at the most central location, but in proximity were also churches belonging to several other religious communities: the German-Lutheran, the Anglican, the Finnish, the French, and the Armenian-Gregorian churches. During the Soviet regime all these churches were closed one by one; one of them was transformed into an indoor swimming pool. The problem of town planners in St. Petersburg has for a long time been what do to with these formerly religious buildings. The churches were regarded as a unique cultural resource, and during the last years of the Soviet era there were plans to transform the religious buildings into concert halls. The Finnish church was changed to an exhibition hall. During recent years the problem of the utilization of church buildings has, however, been solved as the reviving religious communities have begun to reclaim the buildings that once belonged to them. At the same time, the task of maintaining the cultural heritage has shifted from the state to the institutions of civil society.

In this changing situation the social life of the city is receiving a new, ethno-cultural element. Before the Revolution in 1917 the churches were essentially important for the multitude of ethnic communities in

St. Petersburg, for example the German, Polish, Jewish, Finnish and Tatar communities. The churches provided for the cohesion of these communities. The revival of the religious communities will, to some extent, also bring about the revival of the traditional multi-cultural character of St. Petersburg, which disappeared during the 1930's as the schools, cultural centres, and periodicals of minority nationalities were abolished.

The appearance of new social forces and subjects — political, economic and ethno-cultural — is, in addition, likely to cause pressure towards the decentralization of the city administration. Up to this day the structure of the administration in St. Petersburg has consisted of two levels: of the city and district (*raion*) levels. Both levels have their own representative organs, the city soviet and the district soviets, and executive organs, the mayor and city administration and the district administration. The size of the twelve districts of St. Petersburg ranges from 80,000 to half a million inhabitants. As the administrative units are very large, the needs and interests of the citizens cannot always be taken into consideration. Today decentralized administrative structures at the local and neighbourhood levels are as yet non-existent, but it seems evident that such structures are going to evolve in the future, as the majority of the tenants become owners of their apartments and the privatization of housing stock leads to an increased concern about the state of the built environment, about the quality of the services and the infrastructure, and about the personal safety of the residents. Until now the residents have resorted to collective action only on a few occasions, either in connection with electoral campaigns or, quite seldom, with social movements that have usually had only very limited objectives.

The social reality in the Russian city is changing very rapidly today: novel political, economic and cultural institutions are being born and a new kind of social stratification is replacing the old one. The social differentation is proceeding in an accelerating tempo. This flux of a society in transition creates also an unique opportunity for the urban sociologist: the opportunity to observe the crystallization of new social structures and styles of life in urban space, situated in the no man's land between communism and the market economy.

Notes

1. The research was carried out in September 1990 in three different areas of St. Petersburg: in the historical centre, i.e. in the part of the city built before the First World War, in a district with both housing and industry (built during the first half of the 20th century), and in a new high-rise suburban area (built during the 1970's and 1980's). In each of these areas the sample size was 300.

11 Three Scenarios for the Future of Eastern Europe

Timo Piirainen

Introduction

It is impossible to foresee the future — and that is why constructing scenarios of the future is especially important. Activity in the world of uncertainty that has followed the era of the Cold War and antagonism of competing political orders necessitates an ever greater capacity to formulate various alternative visions of the future. We need visions of the possible order of things in the future — even though what eventually will happen is most likely going to be something very different than what was envisioned.

The scenarios presented in this book — for example the alternatives for political development in Russia conceived in Chapter 3 — thus by no means claim to have the status of exact forecasts. Instead of making predictions, the aim has been to formulate a number of the most likely development trends and possible worlds. In addition to envisioning future states of affairs that are more likely than others, thought experiments concerning the future may also concentrate on drafting various possible worlds that are considered especially desirable or undesirable. Visions of the future should thus be regarded literally as manuscripts — the notion 'scenario' traces its origin to the theatre — that may help our imagination to better grasp the perils and promises lying open in the future. (Cf. Jantsch, 1967; Kahn and Wiener, 1967; Mannermaa, 1991, pp. 142-176; Riihinen 1992, pp. 21-24.)

This concluding chapter presents three such scenarios concerning the socio-political future of the countries around the Baltic Sea. The value of these simple scenarios is, in the first place, merely heuristical. The alternative future developments are constructed exclusively on the basis of the very few factors that are assumed to be the most decisive. The scenarios are formulated on the basis of the material presented earlier in this book, covering a time span of approximately 10-20 years.

General trends

The analysis is limited to an area that includes the nation states situated around the Baltic Sea: Russia, the Baltic countries, Poland, Finland and Sweden; for the sake of simplicity, Germany and Denmark are excluded from this examination. The system is extremely heterogenous; it includes countries of very different natures and sizes. Finland and Sweden form a pair that is distinctly different from the rest of the countries in the system: both of them can be described as highly industrialized small states that follow the Scandinavian welfare state model. Another group of countries that can easily be distinguished from these others are the Baltic states Estonia, Latvia, and Lithuania. All three are small transition economy countries that have recently gained independence through the dissolution of the Soviet Union. Poland is to some extent comparable to these three; it is, however much bigger with its population of almost forty million, and it was never annexed to the Soviet empire as were the three Baltic states. Russia, in turn, belongs to a category of its own: its territory is the largest in the world, its population is approximately two and a half times bigger than that of the rest of the system, and in spite of the collapse of the Soviet Union it remains a military superpower. The smaller countries in the system are 'transparent': it is far easier — if not easy — to make an unambiguous estimate of their situation and development prospects. Russia, on the contrary, is a complex and contradictory entity, and making a distinct evaluation of its situation is an overwhelming task.

The Nordic countries Finland and Sweden can be characterized as stable parts of the system and their conduct is to a high degree foreseeable. The Baltic countries and Poland can, for their part, be viewed as having a constant, if not quite linear, trend towards greater stability. Russia, however, is unstable and definite assumptions about its development cannot yet be made. As Russia is overwhelmingly the largest component in the system, instability and uncertainty are going to be the dominant features of the entire system.

The following factors are assumed to be the most decisive in determining the development of the system:

1. regionalization/integration,

2. the poverty gap,

3. ethnic tensions,

4. the strengthening of the social order characteristic to western industrialized countries in the Nordic countries, the Baltic states and Poland,

5. the dominant position of Russia in determining the character of the entire system.

Regionalization/integration. Two antagonistic developments seem to be reshaping Europe. In the west the nation states are integrated to a greater degree of collaboration, and national boundaries are increasingly losing their significance as the locus of power is gradually shifting from the national level to the multinational level on the one hand and to the regional level on the other hand. In the east multinational structures are, however, dissolving, and they are being replaced by new nation states. Europe is thus simultaneously experiencing the dissolution of nation states and the formation of new nation states, as was described in Chapter 2. The traditional concept of the nation state is being both reaffirmed and challenged at the same time.

The development is, however, not necessarily contradictory. The power shift from the old national structures both at the multinational level and the regional level is a development trend throughout Europe. The formation of nation states in the place of such supranational structures as the Soviet Union or Yugoslavia can be seen as tendencies towards the decentralization of power similar for example to the increased separatist aspirations of Wales and Scotland in the United Kingdom. The centripetal forces — integration — and the centrifugal forces — regionalization — can rather be seen as components of the one and same development than simply as antagonistic forces.

In Europe this development can be outlined as a process that is advancing from west to east. The centripetal forces are integrating the Western European industrial nations with each other, while the centrifugal forces are tearing away elements from the old structures in Eastern Europe. These former components of the old structures reassemble to form novel kinds of autonomous actors — to nation states — and thereafter seek to integrate themselves into the supranational structures extending from the west. The components of the dissolved structures are, after gaining the status of autonomous actors, aspiring to become parts of the new structures: the former members of the COMECON, the Warsaw Pact and the Soviet Union attempt to achieve closer collaboration with the European Union and NATO. The westernmost components of the dissolving old structures are the first ones to be integrated into the new structures: the former German Democratic Republic is already a part of the unified Germany and thus a member of NATO and the EU, and Poland, the Czech Republic and Hungary are likely to be the next ones to become integrated into a closer collaboration with the EU. During the following phase of integration, among others the small Baltic republics are likely to enter into a relationship with the European Union.

This process of integration is likely to require a considerably longer period of time for the CIS states. The internal disintegration process of Russia has not even yet come to an end. Because of its internal contradictions, Russia does not have the character of a consequential and autonomous actor in the same sense as the other nation states in the system, and it is thus not able to function in the integration processes in an organized manner. The integration of Russia into the economic community in Europe is very likely to happen later than the integration of the other countries under examination. It is also possible that Russia in its entirety is not going to succeed at all in integrating with the new European structures, but only that some of its regions striving towards greater independence from the central power will collaborate spontaneously with the highly industrialized countries. St. Petersburg, for example, may attempt to shift closer to its Baltic neighbours independently from the central power in Moscow.

Significant differences in standards of living are very likely to remain for the next 10-20 years; this 'poverty curtain' can be assumed to be one of the major characteristics of the area under study. It is not very plausible that the transition economy countries could catch up with the highly industrialized market economy countries on the Baltic Sea (see Chapter 4). Poland and the Baltic countries have, however, better chances to do so: a relatively articulate consensus about the direction of the economic reforms prevails in these countries, and they have also succeeded in taking decisive steps on the route towards a market economy. The rise of the standard of living is likely to be more rapid in these transition economy countries than in Russia, where many of these steps remain to be taken. The Baltic states and especially Poland have also started from a higher level than Russia.

The industries of Western Europe seek to profit from the low wages and production costs in the transition economy countries. The European Union might even attempt to delay the full membership of these countries in order to fully exploit this potential, as is suggested in Chapter 2. In Poland and in the Baltic countries the essential legislative preconditions for foreign investments have already been created; in Russia this legislative basis has not to a great extent been established yet (in 1993) because of the internal conflict. For example the Finnish labour intensive industries, e.g. the textile and clothing industries, have moved large parts of their manufacturing to Estonia. The reserve of inexpensive, well-educated, and culturally familiar labour force situated there is undoubtedly an advantage for the Finnish textile industries in the competition for international markets. At the same time, this sudden explosion of labour supply speeds up the structural change in the old market economies, for example in Finland and Sweden, causing problems of adaptation; the unemployment rate is soaring to unprecedented figures.

Helsinki, the capital of Finland, and Tallinn, the capital of Estonia, are separated from each other only by a narrow sea passage. Vienna and Bratislava, the capital of Slovakia, are the only European capitals situated within an equally short distance from each other. The great difference in labour costs is a factor that is likely to lead to a close affiliation between the two neighbouring cities, resulting in a sort of a twin city. Tallinn is increasing its role in the labour-intensive activities in the area, and this division of labour is speeding up its economic growth. The immediate vicinity of Helsinki boosts the market demand for commodities in Estonia; Tallinn with its cheap prices is already a popular destination for weekend shopping for families in Helsinki.

The greatest difference in standard of living between two neighbouring countries in Europe prevails between Finland and Russia. A comparable difference can be found at the border of the United States and Mexico. The poverty curtain is likely to become visible in Finland, as well as in the other highly industrialized countries of Europe, in the form of increasing social problems. Even under the most favourable conditions the transition economy countries are not going to have the resources to completely alleviate the social problems inherited from the Soviet regime and intensified by the economic and social transformation (see Chapter 8). The poverty of large segments of the population in the transition economy countries is also likely to be a burden for the welfare states of Europe. Especially the two Nordic welfare states in the system under study, Finland and Sweden, are encountering a migrational pressure from the transition economy countries, especially from Russia. The vast differences in wealth are also attracting criminal activity to Finland and Sweden. Even though this criminality may not be as widespread as the yellow press presents, it still is a fact that, given the opportunity, organized crime in St. Petersburg, a city with five million inhabitants, would like to expand its activities to the neighbouring countries.

Tensions between nationalities were pointed out as one of the decisive factors influencing future developments. The most important destination countries for immigrants, for example Germany, France and Sweden, are obviously seeming to approach a 'saturation point', after which their societies will not be able without tension to assimilate more immigrants. Violent outbursts of xenophobia and the recent successes of nationalist ultra-right-wing parties in various countries are symptoms of this saturation. Mass migration across the poverty curtain increases the risk of conflict between nationalities.

Possibly a more serious nationality problem exists, however, in the Baltic countries, especially in Estonia and Latvia. The dispute over the Russian-speaking population which immigrated to these countries during the Sovet regime is a veritable touchstone for the relations between Russia and the Baltic states. The intensity of the tensions between these states depends not only on the extent to which the Russian-speaking population is granted equal rights in the Baltic countries, but also on the political climate in Russia. To calm the nationalist-minded opposition, Yeltsin's government, too, has had to resort to sharp-worded rhetoric directed toward the Baltic countries.

The solidification of the parliamentary democracy characteristic to Western European nations in the Baltic countries and Poland, as well as the unquestioned status of this political order in the Nordic countries was selected as the fourth major feature of the region. The Baltic countries and Poland are taking conscious steps to move away from the Soviet system, and the only main alternative is a political order similar to that in the highly industrialized nations of Western Europe. In Russia this kind of more or less straightforward aspiration toward the social and political ideals of Western Europe cannot be anticipated to the same extent.

The dominant position of Russia was mentioned as the fifth major factor. The population of Russia is almost two and half times larger than the population of the rest of the area. Russia is still a superpower — albeit not on a global scale, as was the Soviet Union, and even though it is torn by internal conflict, it will still always remain a major military power in the European context. Because of its size Russia can give the system more significant development impulses — both positive and negative — than any of the other countries situated in the area under study here.

The above-mentioned four factors — integration/regionalization, differences in standard of living, tension between nationalities and the generally accepted status of parliamentary democracy in all the other countries except Russia — are assumed to be relatively permanent and stable trends or states of affairs during the time period chosen for these scenarios, as long as no other factors exert significant influence on the system. The internal development of Russia is, however, a source of uncertainty. In the scenarios presented here the internal development of Russia is given the status of an independent variable: when the value of this source variable is altered, the state of the entire system also changes. The internal development of Russia determines to a great extent the condition of the whole system in the future.

The three following sections of this chapter are devoted to an examination of the internal development of Russia.

The starting points of Russia

When we examine Russia in the year 1993 as the point of departure, the following factors may be assumed to be the most problematic for the future development:

— geographical magnitude, large population, multinational and multicultural character,

— low level of economic development,

— problems connected to the performance of the political system,

— the weakness of the institutions of the civil society, and

— the ideological vacuum.

The enormous size of the country and the heterogenous composition of its population make the Russian development more difficult to oversee and predict than is the case with the other countries in the system. The disintegration that began with the dissolution of the socialist bloc in Eastern Central Europe continued with the collapse of the Soviet Union; the third phase of this disintegration, the decentralization of power inside the territorial boundaries of Russia (see Chapter 3), is going on at this moment. If the countries included in the system are examined as autonomous actors, quite good predictions can be made concerning the character of Poland, the Nordic countries and the Baltic states: territorially they are quite likely to remain very similar to what they are at the moment, and sudden fragmentation inside these national units does not seem to be a very likely possibility. Decision-making power is merely likely to gradually shift from the nation-state level both to regional and international levels, and this power shift is likely to be a relatively peaceful and controlled process. It is not yet easily foreseeable, however, how Russia will conduct itself as an actor in the international community. The power may shift from Moscow to the regional *(oblast)* level, but this development can either be controlled or uncontrolled. The degree to which the decentralization can be controlled depends greatly on how soon an efficient executive power can be restored in Moscow. Yeltsin's victory in the confrontation with the parliament in October 1993 put an end to the stalemate between the executive and legislative powers, but the relations between the central government and the regional powers remain far from clear.

The problems of the political system can basically be divided into three categories. These are the friction between old and new structures, the legitimacy crisis, and the unclarity of the party system.

In Chapter 3 it was argued that the dissolution of the Soviet Union has not yet brought a very significant qualitative change to the political system of Russia. The structures created during the Soviet regime still regulate political life and they have obstructed the implementation of economic and legislatory reforms. Unlike in the other transition economy countries, the basic constitution essential to the new political and economic order has not yet, as of November 1993, been established in Russia. The conflict between the old and new structures is hindering the recovery of the Russian economy. The most visible antagonism, the struggle between President Yeltsin and the Congress of People's Deputies, was extinguished by force in October 1993, but much of the inertia of the old system still remains, for example, at the level of regional administration, in the military forces and in the management of the traditional heavy industries. The antagonism that prevailed between the parliament and the president can be regarded as merely the tip of the iceberg.

A prevalent distrust and lack of legitimacy is the second main problem of the political system in Russia. Uncertainty about the future and difficulties in daily life have reduced people's trust and interest in politics and parliamentary decision making in nearly all transition economy countries (cf. e.g. Economic and Political Reforms, 1991). In Russia this legitimacy crisis appears to be especially serious. When the Russians were asked in an opinion poll (Byzov and Lvov, 1993) about their confidence towards the major political institutions in the country, the answers were divided in the manner shown in Table 11.1.

The level of popular confidence in the Russian Congress of People's Deputies and the Supreme Soviet — the old parliamentary institutions dissolved by Yeltsin in October 1993 — has turned out to be catastrophically low. In Moscow the distrust was found to be even greater on average than in the country in general. Especially the Congress of People's Deputies and the Supreme Soviet have during the last two years been presented in a very negative light in the Russian mass media. Television and the majority of the newspapers can be defined

Table 11.1. The trust shown by Russians in the most important political institutions in February 1993. Figures in percentages, the shares of those having no opinion omitted. N = 1650. *Source:* Byzov & Lvov, 1993.

Trust	Congress of People's Deputies	Supreme Soviet	President	Government
Yes	6	5	15	6
Rather yes than no	9	10	23	19
Rather no than yes	16	19	13	19
No	51	44	30	29

as 'progressive' and pro-Yeltsin; these media have eagerly portrayed the old parliamentary institutions as the first and foremost enemies of the people. The popularity of Yeltsin and his cabinet was not, however, very high, even though it was naturally higher than that of the old parliament.

The question is not, however, only of the confidence in the existing political institutions, such as the parliament, the cabinet, or the president. None of the foremost political figures seems to evoke confidence, and there are no alternative political choices that are popular among the citizens. The results of the opinion poll referred to above showed that, with the exception of Yeltsin and of the now imprisoned leader of the parliament uprising, Aleksandr Rutskoi, all leading politicians are more distrusted than trusted by the people. The lack of confidence does not seem to depend on the political orientation: the liberals, the centrists and the national-patriots were equally unpopular.

The obscurity of the party structure is a third factor that makes it more difficult in Russia to adopt a political system resembling the ones in western democracies. There exists an abundance of political parties and movements of different kinds. Most of these parties are very small, and locating their position on the political map is often difficult. It is, for example, impossible to visualize the Russian political parties on a distinct right/left axis. The diagonal in Figure 11.1 makes ideological distribution of the political parties in Russia more intelligible. The two axes describing the political field are the dichotomies paternalism/liberalism and egalitarianism/differentiation. At one extreme of the vertical paternalism/liberalism-axis prevails the faith in a strong and authoritarian state, at the other extreme the liberalist idea of the state as a 'night watchman' taking care only of the most necessary tasks is dominant. The one extreme of the horizontal axis is the traditional Russian radical egalitarianism (cf. Pipes, 1974, pp. 153-162), a notion which the Soviet socialism also attempted to accomplish in its own way. Another extreme of this horizontal dimension is the idea of the social usefulness of the differences in wealth and income. Some of the most significant political parties in Russia are placed in this field in Figure 11.1.

The results of the opinion poll show that ordinary Russians have quite a vague conception of the composition of the party structure in Russia and, in general, of the function of political parties in the parliamentary system. When asked in February 1993 what party they should vote for in a parliamentary election, as many as 48 per cent of the respondents did not mention any party (Byzov and Lvov, 1993). In addition, splintering of political sympathies was great among those who were able to identify a party: in February 1993 no party would

Figure 11.1. A description of the political field in Russia. The figure should be regarded as an illustration; it does not attempt to give an accurate picture of the situation. Only some of the numerous political parties and movements are mentioned.

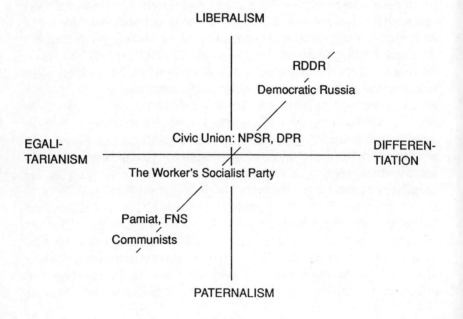

Table 11.2. Support for the six most popular Russian political parties in February 1993. (%) N = 1650. *Source:* Byzov and Lvov, 1993.

The People's Party of Free Russia (NPSR)	10
The Russian Movement for Democratic Reform (RDDR)	8
The Democratic Party of Russia (DPR)	8
The Communist Party of Russia	8
Democratic Russia	5
The Front for National Salvation (FNS)	3

have gained more than ten per cent of the total votes, as Table 11.2 shows.

The Russians also do not yet have a clear understanding of what parliamentary election procedures should be like. 39 per cent of the respondents could not say at all how the procedure should be. Only five per cent preferred an electoral system in which the candidates were nominated by the political parties, i.e. the system applied in western democracies. The most popular choice was an electoral system on a regional basis; this practice applied in the Soviet Union was preferred by 38 per cent of the respondents.

As the parliamentary power and the executive power at the level of the central government are weak and disorganized, it is likely that a considerable part of the decision-making and executive power will shift to the political and administrative elites at the local and regional levels. Besides local actors, many other interest groups, especially the representatives of the mighty military-industrial complex, are also likely to make decisions over the heads of the central government and parliamentary institutions. Corporatism as a political order has often been applied when the governments have been weak. Corporative agreements and the continuation of the fragmentation of Russia are thus the two directions of development assumed in Chapter 3 to be the most likely ones.

The missing tradition of the civil society was mentioned above as one of the major obstacles on the road to political democracy in Russia. The Soviet regime abolished all organized political opposition. All activity that did not acknowledge the objectives of the system prevailing under the Soviet rule was bound to be 'private' and 'informal' by nature, i.e. it was carefully banished from the public and political domain (cf. Alapuro, 1993). There were no opportunities for the development of alternatives to the prevailing political elite. When the monolitical power system suddenly collapsed there were no political forces or movements that could have filled the vacuum left behind by the old regime. Following a strong and authoritarian leader is the most natural alternative in such a situation, and in 1991 Yeltsin was this kind of political leader. Yeltsin's popularity has, however, constantly been decreasing ever since. In spite of his diminishing popularity Yeltsin received a vote of confidence from the people in the April 1993 referendum. The majority of Russians see Yeltsin as the only alternative, if not the best possible one, and no political movement or politician has been able to challenge him successfully. The lack of political alternatives with roots in a civil society is even more apparent after the dissolution of the parliament and its last violent attempt to retain its power in October 1993.

The foundation of the democratic order characteristic to western industrialized countries has gradually been laid in the course of decades and even centuries. In Russia this foundation is still rather precarious. The institutions of a civil society never had time to develop to their full bloom in imperial Russia, and 75 years of Soviet power was a long enough period of time to uproot the sprouts of civil society that had managed to develop. The practices of the dissolved Russian Congress of People's Deputies, as well as the almost total indifference of the people towards the parties, are sad evidence of the detachment of the political parties from civil society, i.e. the lack of any social or political movements that would be popular and widespread among the people.

Besides the political vacuum the Soviet regime left behind also *a moral and ideological vacuum* which was described in Chapter 5. Along with the Soviet regime disappeared also the foundations of the world view and identity of the Soviet citizen, the belief in the future of socialism and pride in the socialist fatherland. According to the opinion polls, nothing has come to replace these old values and ideals; religion, for example, has not managed to fill the ideological vacuum to a significant extent. *Homo sovieticus* had an optimistic character, whereas in today's Russia the prevalent mood is pessimism. Uncertainty concerning the basics of daily life, the sudden explosion of income differences and social inequality, and the rapid growth of crime nourish among the people a feeling of moral abasement. A quotation from an interview in St. Petersburg during 1993 illustrates the everyday sentiments:

> Nowadays it is not difficult only materially but also in a moral sense. I'm afraid to let my child stay outdoors for any more than is necessary, or to leave her alone, even in the staircase of the house. All this has suddenly emerged to the surface, all this scum and filth is lifting up its head. And it is that's why everything has become worse materially, too, because somehow... the wicked qualities of all the people have come forth. Formerly they were somehow under control, there was some order present. You could go somewhere and visit places, and it was completely safe. Nowadays there is no safety. It is as though the powers of satan were on the loose. (Piirainen, 1994.)

Authoritarianism was mentioned as a major characteristic of the Russian mentality. If the feeling of moral abasement grows deeper, the longing for a strong authority that could restore the honour of Russia can become widespread. The ground is favourable for all kinds of populist demagogues.

* * *

The legacy of the Soviet regime is the most burdensome in Russia. The problems there are more difficult than in the Baltic countries or in the transition economy countries in Central Europe, in which a certain consensus prevails concerning the aims of the reform policies — a basic agreement, transcending political boundaries, that the development should lead away from the Soviet system as rapidly as possible, and that this development cannot be accomplished without toil and hardships. Among the points of departure in Russia are, on the contrary, political confusion, moral and ideological crisis, missing traditions of a civil society, and low level of economic performance. These four factors can reinforce each other, creating a vicious circle that may drag Russia into a long period of social and economic stagnation.

The class structure in Russia

In this analysis class structure is chosen as the most significant factor determining future development in Russia. The formation of a class structure in Russia, the relative proportions of the population groups with different life chances, is to a considerable extent likely to determine also the make up of the political arena. Political processes are to a large extent class-based processes, and this is especially true for societies where inequalities and class differences are sharp. It seems likely that the inequalities of income and standard of living are going to be rather drastic in Russia; the construction of a social policy that would even out these differences is not in sight at least for the following few years.

The class structure is significantly affecting Russia's ability to emerge from the problematic conditions of departure described in the previous section. These conditions for their part also have an effect on the further development of the class structure; these mechanisms were discussed in Chapters 6 and 7.

For the purposes of this analysis social classes are defined in as simple terms as possible. They are regarded as determined by — as the Soviet sociologists put it — both 'objective' and 'subjective' conditions. Among the former are the resources and life chances possessed by the members of a social stratum: e.g. economic resources, security, positions in production and in the labour market, and access to culture and education. A 'subjective factor' is the class habitus characteristic to each social class: the totality of the patterns of behaviour, attitudes and social activity considered typical of the members of a certain stratum of population.

Large middle classes are usually considered to be a stabilizing element in society. In Russia, too, the growth of the middle classes is regarded as an extremely important factor contributing to the solidification of the civil society and democratic order (cf. e.g. Bystrova and Yeremicheva, 1992). The middle classes — in the sense they are known in the industrialized countries of the west — do not, however, yet exist in Russia. The outlines of the developing middle classes are at the moment only vaguely being formed. A multitude of most dissimilar political parties and movements in Russia are addressing their messages to this imaginary middle class (cf. Lvov, 1993); their insignificant support among the people may be interpreted as evidence of the fact that such a class basis for political activity is still largely missing.

The official self-image of the Soviet Union was that of a 'society without classes'. Russia, on the contrary, is a class society, a society marked by inequality and conflict. Russia has already received its bourgeoisie: the new rich can already be distinguished from the vast majority of the population as a privileged stratum. In Chapter 6 of this book two further strata are distinguished in addition to this thin layer of the new elite; they are named 'the survivors' and 'the proletariat'. These two are proto-classes, embryonic states of social classes. The class boundaries are, however, gradually becoming more distinct, the life chances of the strata are developing in different directions, and thus also their class habitus are divergent. For the 'survivors' the market economy means a promise for the expansion of life chances and for a better middle-class tomorrow. For the proletariat the transition towards the market economy means ever-deepening poverty.

The relative proportions of these two social strata are of extreme significance for the future development of the Russian society. It is not yet clearly predictable how their proportions are going to develop during the time period chosen for the scenarios. In the following thought experiment the sizes of these strata are altered in order to then consider what the Russian society would be like in each of the cases. The proportion of the 'survivors', the stratum reaching out for a western middle-class lifestyle, is given the status of an independent variable. This source variable is given three different values: two-thirds, one-half, and one-third.

The first and the most optimistic alternative is, consequently, the classic two-thirds society. Most of the people gain from the economic development in this alternative while one-third becomes impoverished and marginalized. This variant can be titled 'the USA variant'. As in the United States, a class division of this kind produces a relatively stable social order. The ruling ideology is liberalism, and the parties supporting market economy and parliamentary democracy dominate the political arena. Such a social policy that would even out the differences in income and standard of living does not enjoy widespread support, and any ambitious programmes against poverty are not yet even affordable. The situation of the impoverished minority is visible in social problems and recurring unrest; the latter, however, is usually relatively easily extinguished by the majority.

After take-off, economic growth is fast. As a consequence of the large size of the social strata possessing purchasing power, domestic market demand expands rapidly. The decentralization of political and administrative power proceeds in a controlled manner, and the result is a federation resembling the United States. The division of power between the president and the parliamentary institutions is accomplished with an arrangement resembling that in the United States.

The second alternative in the thought experiment is the 50/50 society. On the ruins of Soviet socialism a society is built in which half of the population experiences an expansion of its life chances while the other half is impoverished and pauperized. In the absence of foreign examples, this variant can be called 'the Russia variant'. The 50/50 division produces a different political structure than the two-thirds alternative. In this alternative also the proletariat is politically influential and the political arena is divided into two sectors. The 'survivors' support liberalistic parties, such as Democratic Russia (*Demokraticheskaia Rossiia*), whereas the proletariat feels attraction towards the political parties placed in the lower-left corner of the diagonal in Figure 11.1, i.e. towards the nationalist and neocommunist movements, which in the traditional Russian spirit emphasize strong egalitarianism and the importance of the authoritarian state. To a certain extent this division would recall the familiar division between the slavophiles and the western-minded, the *zapadniks*. This split into collectivist lower classes and upper classes striving to accomplish the ideals of western European individualism has sometimes been regarded as the prime mover of Russian history and also as the source of devastating tensions (cf. e.g. Pastukhov, 1992). During the Soviet regime this division disappeared from sight; in this future scenario the traditional cleavage has been revived in a novel form.

The intensity of the conflict may vary, and various intermediate forces are likely to be formed between the liberalist and nationalist-neocommunist blocs. The existence of two major classes equal in their size and conflicting in their interests will, however, maintain the bipolarity of the political arena. In a situation of extreme conflict the military may interfere in political life. Because of its bipolarity the Russian political life is inconsistent, and abrupt alterations of policies may be possible.

Economic development is slowed down as two contradictory forces pull Russia in opposite directions. The purchasing power of the 'survivors' is, however, high enough to stimulate domestic production and commerce. Two different and separate cultural patterns are formed: on the one hand an individualistic middle-class life style founded on money-based consumption, and on the other hand a pattern of living based on the traditional network economy.

The one-third alternative — which may be called 'the Argentina alternative' — means the proletarization of the vast majority of the people. The purchasing power of the population and the domestic market demand are low and, as a consequence, economic development continues to wallow. The population is to a considerable extent living in a non-monetary network economy characteristic of developing countries.

The political system is unstable in this alternative. The governments are weak and their message does not reach the large masses of the people. Political life is largely based on corporative mechanisms and agreements between various interest groups. The actual decision-making power shifts to a large extent also to regional economic and political elites. Parliamentary politics does not interest the poor majority of the people very much; representative democracy does not seem to offer any solutions to the most urgent problems of daily life. As the political mobilization characteristic of modern societies is missing, populist and messianist movements are the ones that gain mass support easiest. In the programmes of the populist leaders two central themes usually appear: imperialist chauvinism and authoritarian leadership. In arguing on the basis of these simple and traditional notions they present easy solutions to the complex problems of the Russian society. A good example is Vladimir Zhirinovsky who has promised to solve the economic problems of Russia in 72 hours. In the following quotation (Janov 1992, pp. 9-10) he tells how this could be possible:

Zhirinovsky: Very simple. We'll send a military force to the territory of the former German Democratic Republic, say, one and a half million men, carrying among other things nuclear weapons — and everything will be arranged. (...)

Interviewer: It is very easy to give people such promises. There is, of course, a vast mass of proletarized people who will swallow the bait.

Zh.: They sure will!

I.: But the entire population of the country is not, however, proletarized. There are also those who have managed to preserve their common sense.

Zh.: Yes, there are. They are going to vote against me, but they are going to be a minority.

I.: But now they are a significant majority. Are you counting on such massive degradation?

Zh.: Yes, yes, yes!

I.: So this is your creed? That the whole county becomes pauperized?

Zh.: Yes, yes, yes!

I.: Oh, then you are going to receive such a terrible country that it is going to swallow you, too. You promised to change everything in 72 hours, but in the 73rd hour it is going to eat you. Because you are not going to be able to do that, not in 72 hours, not in 72 days, and not in 72 weeks.

Zh.: History will tell.

Zhirinovsky — who was in the article called 'the nuclear Robin Hood' — confesses in the above quotation that a widespread impoverishment of the people is the precondition for the success of his populist campaign. It is not very likely that precisely Zhirinovsky could manage to gain widespread support among the Russians — but in any case, populist policy-making may have also internationally dangerous consequences in a military power where the powers of the president are large.

In the 'Argentina scenario' the army may intervene in domestic politics in order to stabilize the situation. A cycle is possible in which weak parliamentary governments, populist leaders and military governments alternate.

The modernization of Russia and the future of Eastern Europe

It is tempting to reduce the discussion about the size of the middle classes to a larger historical question concerning the special features of the Russian modternization. The events related to modernization in Russia have, as is known, had a very significant influence in international affairs, too. The influence of the Russian internal development has, of course, been the most important with regard to the future of its neighbouring countries in Eastern Europe.

A simple way of viewing modernization in Russia is to divide this development into a series of separate 'projects'. If we follow this simple scheme, the first project of modernization would then be the attempt to Europeanize Russia. This project can be regarded to have begun with the founding of the new capital, St. Petersburg, at the outlet of the river Neva in the westernmost corner of the Russian Empire in the beginning of the 18th century. The modern capital was built at record speed to become the window of Russia to Europe: in just two decades its population had reached one hundred thousand (e.g. Berman, 1988, pp. 173-285). To Russia's neighbours in the west, this Europeanization was bound to mean conquest and annexation to its empire.

The second grand project of modernization was socialism, the attempt to create a communist society — the most advanced stage of human development. This project has just recently come to an end and the nations that were situated in the domain of the collapsed Soviet empire are now building new societies on the ruins of socialism.

Is this the eve of a third grand project? Are we witnessing the beginning of Russia's 'great leap' towards the market economy? If it is so, are the consequences of this third great project going to be as upsetting as was the case with the two preceding projects?

Each one of these three modernization projects has its principal actor, a force whose role is to carry out the task of modernization. The *primus motor* of the first project was in principle, according to the Western European model, the enlightened autocrat. Peter the Great does not, however, conform to the image of an enlightened sovereign; he can rather be regarded as a cruel, capricious, and in his manners a barbaric eastern despot. St. Petersburg, the new capital and cradle of Russian enlightenment, was built by slave labour in a similar manner to that used to erect the pyramids. The amount of human suffering caused by the construction work was terrible: during the first three years alone 150,000 labourers perished (Pipes, 1974, pp. 126-127; Berman, 1988, p. 178). The successors of Peter the Great in the Romanov dynasty were not especially enlightened, either; the majority of them can with good reason be characterized as narrow-minded mediocrities.

The leading role in the second project was supposed to be played by the revolutionary working class. The working class was, however, far too small in the beginning of the 20th century to be able to function as the prime mover of a splendid modernization project. The overwhelming majority of the Russian population was scattered around the vast countryside; the forcible industrialization of Russia began under the rule of Stalin. As the political mobilization of the great majority of the Russian people was extremely difficult, it was possible for the most unscrupulous political group, the Bolsheviks, to rapidly invade the power vacuum left by the dissolving imperial rule and annihilate the competing political movements. The Bolshevik rule was strongly elitist; this elitism was legitimated with their alleged position as the avant garde of the working class and of progress.

This elitism culminated in a period of despotism. The human costs of Stalin's tyranny were even more terrible than those inflicted by Peter the Great — if the number of those perished in the construction of pyramids is used as a measure. If Stalin was a despot and a grand modernizer, the Peter the Great of the socialist project, his successors in the dynasty, for example Leonid Brezhnev or Konstantin Chernenko, can for their giftedness and accomplishments be ranked in the same category with such statesmen produced by the Romanov dynasty as Paul I or Nicholas I.

The leading role in the third project of modernization that just has begun in Russia is reserved to the middle class. It is, however, doubtful whether this kind of middle class yet exists in Russia. In Chapter 7 it was argued that the social structure of Russia is in many ways similar to that in the advanced capitalist countries, if the examination is focused on the organization of work and production. Russians are highly educated and their work tasks also resemble those typical in Western Europe. But if we examine consumption and life styles, as was done in Chapter 6, the picture is entirely different: the share of the middle classes of the total Russian population (in the sense the notion 'middle class' is used in the western industrial countries) is in the uncertain situation of the year 1994 no larger than the share of the working class was in 1917, the year of the October Revolution.

The very tragedy of the Russian modernization is related to the fact that the idea of modernization has always been brought to Russia from abroad, but a social force capable of genuinely carrying out this modernization has been missing in the country. In the absence of a strong guarantor of modernization, the idea has in practice been transformed to its opposite. Modernization in Russia has not been generated from below, it has not been fostered by an unfolding civil society, but instead a ready-made model of a modern society has been brutally forced from above on a society that has been quite unprepared for it (cf. Yanov, 1987). The consequence of all this violence and human suffering has been a bizarre — and colossal — travesty of a modern society. Imperial Russia did not bring forth a capitalist society with flourishing commerce and industry, but a backward police state. The socialist Soviet Union did not create the realm of wealth and freedom it promised; its dissolution left behind millions of people having only a ragged suit of clothes and a pair of worn-out shoes.

The third project of Russian modernization, the transition to an advanced market economy, has, however, better chances of success than its predecessors. The project is evidently less utopian than the preceding one: the end state of the socialist project, communism, existed only as a distant vision, whereas there exist many relatively well-functioning examples of a market economy and parliamentary democracy in the present empirical reality. The preconditions for the development of the prime mover of the modernization, the middle class, are also far more favourable than was the case with the previous projects. The vast majority of the Russian people consisted in 1917 of illiterate peasants; the Russia of today is, on the contrary, a highly industrialized and urbanized — if not necessarily modern (cf. Srubar, 1991) — country, where the people are highly educated. The freely operating and predominantly liberal public media are preparing the ground for the growth of a civil society and the fortification of a democratic order. It is worth emphasizing that never before in Russian history has freedom of speech prevailed to the same extent as now. The connections to the rest of the industrialized world are more numerous than ever before and the patterns of thought characteristic to advanced capitalist countries may quickly take root in the Russian society through these links. It seems quite impossible that the Russian society could ever again be sealed as tightly from outside influence as it was during the Soviet regime.

Spain and Portugal adopted the political order characteristic of advanced capitalist countries after a long totalitarian period. The starting points of Russia are more problematic than was the case with those countries, but a genuine modernization in Russia is still not an improbable development. The tragedy of Russian history — and at the same time of the history of its Eastern European neighbours — lies in the dialectic of its modernization: the impulse for modernization has come from the outside, but since a genuine carrier of modernization has been non-existent, this modernization has turned into its destructive opposite and progress has reverted to sinister reaction. Russia is, however, by no means doomed forever to this unfortunate dialectic. The preconditions of a democratic development are not yet ready, but nevertheless there has never been as favourable a situation for the growth of democracy as the present one.

Three scenarios concerning the future of Eastern Europe

The class structure in Russia, i.e. the relative size of the social class that is capable of carrying out the modernization in Russia, was set as the explanatory variable for the scenario concerning the future of the entire system of Eastern European countries. As this explanatory variable was given different values, three development alternatives for Russia were received as a result; these scenarios were named the 'USA alternative', the 'Russia alternative', and the 'Argentina alternative'. We can now view these alternatives within the systematic context of Eastern and Northern European countries that was provided at the beginning of this chapter and describe briefly how the system would behave in the case of each of these alternatives.

The 'USA-alternative' is the most agreeable of these three possible worlds. Because of the political stability of Russia the integrative processes advance rapidly from the west towards the east. Russia is a consistent and predictable political actor, and from the point of view of the member countries of the European Union, no major risks are connected to the closer integration of Russia to it. Russia avoids, however, contrary to the Baltic countries, full integration into the European Union; it cannot yet fulfill its requirements concerning for example social security or environmental protection.

Russia is an attractive goal for foreign industrial investment due to its relatively low level of wages and to its liberalist legislation. The Russian economy grows rapidly and purchasing power increases, which means new markets and new opportunities for economic cooperation with the neighbouring countries. These increasing markets also provide a strong impulse for economic development in Russia's western neighbours. The economic activity in the Baltic Sea region becomes very intense as Russia is able to make large investments to reconstruct its infrastructure. Poland and the Baltic countries are catching up with the Western European standard of living and the distance between Russia and the industrialized countries of Western Europe is diminishing, too.

The conflicts between nationalities are becoming less severe in the Baltic countries. This is due in part to the diminishing share of the Russian-speaking population in the Baltic countries: a part of this population migrates to Russia as living conditions there improve. The Russian government also strives to avoid nationalistic positions that could unnecessarily provoke friction between different ethnic groups. As relations between Russia and the Baltic republics become normal, the ethnically original population of the Baltic republics no longer regard the Russian-speaking minority as a threat to their national cultures, as was the case during the Soviet regime, and the old tensions are vanishing. The large number of the impoverished in Russia is, however, a constant source of social problems; these problems are reflected especially in the Nordic welfare states Finland and Sweden.

If the 'Russia-alternative' comes true, the result is a world characterized by conflict and contradiction. Because of the ambiguity of Russian politics, it has largely remained outside the integrative development in Europe. Western-minded and nationalist governments are alternating in Russia; sometimes various small centre groups or populist parties assume a decisive role in a political life that is characterized by a power struggle between two opposite blocs of almost equal size. Foreign policy is sometimes openly positive to integration, sometimes outspokenly nationalist and isolationist.

Similar abrupt changes are typical of Russia's economic policy, too. The governments that are in favour of a free market economy strive to stabilize the economy and stimulate new entrepreneurship and foreign investment. Nationalist governments, however, nullify these attempts whenever they rise to power; they favour subsidizing the old industries from the Soviet era, investing in the military and defence, and putting up large-scale egalitarian social welfare programmes. From the point of view of the European Union, Russia without an unambiguous economic policy is a risk factor, and it remains outside European integration. Because of the capricious nature of the national politics, local and regional actors in Russia strive to attain as much autonomy as possible in order to independently arrange their relations with the rest of the world.

As a result of the ambiguity of its economic policy, economic growth in Russia remains relatively slow, and demand in the Russian market does not grow to be a decisive impulse for the development of industry and commerce in the neighbouring countries. The most interesting markets continue to exist elsewhere. The risks connected to long-term investments in production in Russia remain relatively high, and investments of this kind are increasingly being channelled to Poland and the Baltic countries, which are able to provide a more stable environment.

The conflicts between nationalities are sharpened in the Baltic republics. The rhetoric of the nationalist political parties heightens the conflict between ethnic Russians and the native population of the Baltic republics; populist election campaigns refer to the alleged suppression of Russians in the neighbouring countries. Because of the internal pressures, the liberalist political parties in Russia are also forced to resort to chauvinist tones in their statements concerning the Baltic countries. In this oppressive situation the Baltic republics seek shelter within the organizations of the Western European nations. From the point of view of the west, the friction between the native and Russian populations makes these republics awkward companions; the question concerning the position of the Russians in the Baltic countries is one of the main questions of dispute between the Western European countries and Russia.

The differences in the standard of living between Russia and the industrialized countries of Western Europe remain constant. The widespread poverty in Russia causes strong migrational tendencies to the west, especially to the neighbouring countries. Partly due to the loud nationalism and chauvinism in Russia, the attitudes towards the migrants in the neighbouring countries are not the friendliest possible; open conflicts between native populations and migrants are quite frequent.

The 'Argentina-scenario' means an existence at the base of a volcano. Russia is not a developed market economy; it is rather a developing country with a population living to a great extent outside the money economy. The shift of power from the central government to the regional level has taken place chaotically; in practice, the corrupt regional elites hold the power, and the central government has only very limited means to control these elites. Russia does not have the prerequisites for an organized integration into the community formed by the industrialized nations. Mainly only the economic and political elites are integrated to the western life style. The behaviour of these elites resembles the conduct of colonial rulers: the profit from economic activity in Russia is spent on luxury articles or invested abroad; large-scale investments in Russia are far too insecure, and domestic entrepreneurs strive in the first place to secure quick profit with a minimum of investment.

The situation in Russia is also internationally recognized as one fraught with the utmost hazards. Development aid is given to Russia in order to help lift it on its feet. The financial aid disappears, however, like water in the sand: the corrupt administration, the rickety infrastructure and production system, and the apathy of the large masses of impoverished population form a vicious circle that is hardly to be broken only with an injection of help from outside. The poverty of Russia hinders the development of the neighbouring countries and of the global economy, too. The neighbouring countries try with all available means to protect themselves from the migrational pressures from Russia as well as from the mounting social problems.

The tension between nationalities makes the situation in Eastern Europe explosive. The Argentinian government resorted to a military venture, an effort to capture the Falkland Islands by war, in order to unite the dissipating nation and to ensure the support of the impoverished people. As their popular support crumbles, the weak governments of Russia, too, appeal to threats from outside enemies. The situation of the Russian minorities in the neighbouring countries is a far more convincing argument for the existence of foreign aggression than a territorial dispute over a couple of distant and barren islands. Imperialistic arguments, in addition, find a more sympathetic response in Russia than in the real Argentina; appealing to authoritarianism, to the traditional mistrust towards the west that was further cultivated during the Soviet regime, and to the widespread sentiment of Russia's lost honour quickly attracts popular support. The technically superior British navy made an end of Argentina's expansionist policies. In the case of a military power like Russia a similar intervention would obviously not be a realistic solution.

Afterword

In the opening chapter of this book a utopian scheme was presented in which an old 'Clausewitzian' world was succeeded by a new, 'post-Clausewitzian' world. The post-Clausewitzian world was characterized as a world of intelligent production and intensive economic growth, in which the use of military policy exerted by nation states has become antiquated and inappropriate. This utopia is based on the idea of modernization: the Clausewitzian world consisted of pre-modern or only partially modern societies, whereas the post-Clausewitzian world is a community of 'thoroughly modern' (cf. Beck, 1986), 'post-industrial' or 'post-modern' societies.

Most of today's societies are not, however, 'thoroughly modern' societies of this kind. The logic of these 'pre-modern' societies is different from that of the societies that have been modernized to a greater degree. This different rationality of action is apparent also in their relations to other nations. Such societies as Argentina or Iraq may exercise aggressive expansionist policies, and rational arguments can also be presented to justify this aggression, whereas military aggression exerted by, say, Sweden or Germany is rather difficult to imagine today and it would be very difficult to find any rational grounds for undertakings of this kind.

A European superpower that in its essence is a pre-modern society, is undoubtedly an anchronism. We assume that European nations behave according to the rationality of modern societies, following the logic of the post-Clausewitzian world. Russia, however, still is an anachronism of this kind. The Soviet regime conserved pre-modern social forms for decades; now the tin, or the iron curtain, has been opened and Eastern Europe is heading towards a new project of modernization. Maybe a genuine modernization is possible this time and the perilous anachronism will disappear. In such a case we will have come far closer to the utopia.

How about the west — that is, the nations that during the era of the Cold War were referred to as 'the West'? Should we just acquiesce in reacting to the developments in Eastern Europe or might it be possible that we too could in some way contribute in helping the prime mover of modernization on its feet in that part of the world that once was the Soviet Union? What can Western Europe do?

Manoeuvring solely on the level of diplomacy or the transfer of financial aid and expertise to the transforming economy countries is hardly sufficient. If we seriously wish to foster the development of democratic institutions in Eastern Europe we should create contacts between the east and the west at the level of ordinary citizens and the institutions of everyday life. The most effective contribution, evidently, would be the building of bridges between the civil societies in the nations in the former west and former east. The 'ice cream diplomacy' mentioned in Chapter 2 is a beautiful example of this kind of activity, economic cooperation that increases the life chances of the people and, at the same time, brings societies closer together.

References

Alapuro, Risto (1993), 'Civil Society in Russia?' in Iivonen, Jyrki (ed.), *The Future of the Nation State in Europe*, Edward Elgar, Aldershot.

Beck, Ulrich (1986), *Risikogesellschaft. Auf dem Weg in eine andere Moderne*, Suhrkamp Verlag, Frankfurt am Main.

Berman, Marshall (1988), *All That Is Solid Melts into Air. The Experience of Modernity*, 2nd edition, Penguin Books, Harmondsworth.

Bystrova, A.S. & Yeremicheva, G.V. (1992), 'Demokratizatsiia v zerkale sotsiologii', *Filosoficheskaia y sotsiologicheskaia mysl*, no. 2/1992.

Byzov, L. & Lvov, N. (1993), *Referendum: byt ili ne byt?* Obzor resultatov issledovaniia, provedennego 18-23 febralia v raslichnih regionah Rossii, Rossiskii fond konstitutsionnih reform, Moskva.

'Economic and Political Reforms in Central Europe' (1991), *Journal für Sozialforschung*, vol. 41, no. 3/1991.

Elinkeinoelämän valtuuskunta EVA (1993), *Suomi Pietarissa, Pietari Suomessa. EVA-raportti taloudellisten kulttuurien eroista*, EVA, Helsinki.

Jantsch, Erich (1967), *Technological Forecasting in Perspective*, OECD, Paris.

Kahn, Herman & Wiener, Anthony (1967), *The Year 2000*, Macmillan, New York.

Käkönen, Jyrki (1991), *Realismista utopiaan. Kohti kansalaisyhteiskuntien yhteisöä?*, Ateena-kustannus, Jyväskylä.

Lvov, Nikolai (1993), *Konseptsiia 'srednego klassa' v Rossii perioda modernisatsii sotsialnoi strukturi*, Institut sotsialno-ekonomicheskih problem narodonaseleniia RAN, Moskva.

Mannermaa, Mika (1991), *Evolutionaarinen tulevaisuudentutkimus*, VAPK-kustannus, Helsinki.

Pastukhov, Vladimir (1992), 'Novogodnie razmyshleniia o sudbe Rossii', *Obshchestvo*, 1 January 1992.

Piirainen, Timo (1994), *Structural Change and Survival Strategies: Adaptation to the Market Economy in Russia*, manuscript.

Pribylovsky, Vladimir (1992), *Dictionary of Political Parties and Organizations in Russia*, PostFactum/Interlegal, Moscow.

Riihinen, Olavi (1992), 'Näkökulmia tulevaisuuteen' in Riihinen, Olavi (ed.), *Sosiaalipolitiikka 2017*, WSOY, Helsinki.

Srubar, Ilja (1991), 'War der reale Sozialismus modern? Versuch einer strukturellen Bestimmung', *Kölner Zeitschrift für Soziologie und Sozialpsychologie*, vol. 43, 3/1991.

Yanov, Aleksandr (1987), *The Russian Challenge and the Year 2000*, Columbia University Press, New York.

Yanov, Aleksandr (1992), 'Fenomen Zhirinovskogo', *Novoe vremia*, no. 41/1992.